R83647

F

Edmonton
Library
Fore Street N9
807 3618
-2. AUG. 1978

25. SEP. 1978

11. JUL. 1979

30. APR. 1980

**LONDON BOROUGH OF ENFIELD
LIBRARY SERVICES**

This book to be RETURNED on or before the latest date stamped unless a renewal has been obtained by personal call, post or telephone, quoting the above number and the date due for return.

The Lea-Francis Story

Barrie Price

B T Batsford Ltd   London

© A B Price 1978

First published 1978

All rights reserved. No part of
this publication may be reproduced,
in any form or by any means, without
permission from the Publishers.

ISBN 0 7134 0785 9

Filmset in 9 on 10 pt. Monophoto Times by
Servis Filmsetting Ltd, Manchester
Printed in Great Britain by
Cox & Wyman Ltd, Fakenham
for the Publishers B T Batsford Ltd
4 Fitzhardinge Street, London W1H 0AH

Contents

ACKNOWLEDGMENT 6

FOREWORD 7

AUTHOR'S NOTE 8

CHAPTER ONE Cycles 10

CHAPTER TWO The First Motor Cars 18

CHAPTER THREE Motor Cycles 23

CHAPTER FOUR Post-Armistice Motor Cars 32

CHAPTER FIVE Light Car Development 36

CHAPTER SIX Supercharged 55

CHAPTER SEVEN Decline 84

CHAPTER EIGHT Reconstruction 105

INDEX 141

Acknowledgment

The author would like to thank the following for their assistance during the many years of preparation of this work:

Alan Lea
The late Norman Lea MIEE MIMechE
The late Gordon Ingleby Francis MIMechE
Charles van Eugen MBE FIMechE
Colin van Eugen
Mrs G H Leek
The late Hugh Rose MIMechE
Kenneth Rose
Peter W Pringle
C T Delaney
Gr Capt R B Wardman
G H Percival
The National Motor Museum, Beaulieu
IPC Press Ltd
The late S H Newsome JP
A K Haworth MIMechE
Peter Ingall
Peter Mitchell
The Herbert Museum, Coventry

Col R B Leech
J H Hewitson
The late G T Andrews
Kaye Don
The late Eric Bellamy
Jack Lea
Geoffrey Smith
Mrs R M V Sutton
Michael Sedgwick
G N Georgano
Albert Ludgate
E S Meredith
F R W England
T Helm
H Pendleton
The late T G Moore
R H Derrick
A Ramsay
Jack Ridley

Foreword

The city of Coventry, traditionally the home of the lace and ribbon trade, underwent a period of great change and expansion in the last quarter of the nineteenth century, becoming the centre of the youthful cycle industry.

The companies founded by the cycle pioneers were soon to interest themselves in the development of the internal combustion engine and its adoption for use in road vehicles. The formation of the industry was to accelerate further the development of Coventry into one of Britain's leading manufacturing cities.

The engineering facilities and expertise were quickly transformed to munitions manufacture with the commencement of the First World War and just as quickly switched back to car and motor cycle production with the return of peace and the short-lived but meteoric trade boom that followed.

Approximately 25 Coventry-based manufacturers of motor cars exhibited their wares at the Olympia show of 1922 and a similar number of motor cycle firms were in existence.

The depressions of the 1920s and 1930s were to wither these numbers to a mere handful although the majority of the survivors were to emerge as giant industrial concerns. The 'City of Cars' had become so vital to the British economy that it was singled out by the German High Command for the mightiest onslaught that the Luftwaffe was to mount against England in the second great conflict. The year 1945 was again to see a return from war production to the needs of peace and while the leading companies were to be expanded still further, the few surviving independents were gradually forced to amalgamate or close their doors.

The quality manufacturers were particularly vulnerable to economic blizzards, and of the totally independent firms engaged upon private car manufacture as the mainstay of their business, Lea-Francis was the last to disappear. It is only fair to add, however, that the company underwent one major reconstruction in 1937 and prolonged its life by 10 years with general engineering sub-contract work.

It will be seen that the fortunes of the Lea-Francis company ran parallel with the state of the British economy and business continued despite financial problems of staggering magnitude. Fortunately, perhaps, the majority of employees were totally unaware of these difficulties and went keenly about their business of making good machines. The comparatively large output during the boom years was undoubtedly a great industrial feat, for both the Lower Ford Street and Much Park Street works were distinctly cramped and badly designed for motor car production.

It says much for the engineers and employees concerned that now, some 50 years after the firm had reached its zenith, Lea-Francis cars should be sought after, restored and held in high esteem the world over.

A B Price   WIXFORD

Author's Note

The history of Lea-Francis can best be considered as three separate eras. Each of these timespans were to see the manufacture of quality vehicles and it is refreshing to note in these present times, with companies governed by accountants, and design by committee, that the success and public acclaim of Lea-Francis products was largely due to the work of three men: they were straightforward mechanical engineers of no mean ability, and their mark was clearly seen on the products of the day.

The first era (1895–1922) saw concentration upon cycles and motor cycles under the aegis of R H Lea. The second stage (1923–35) was to witness considerable success in the field of expensive light and medium-sized cars of high efficiency, from the

Mr and Mrs G I Francis. A photograph taken about 1930

R H Lea photographed in about 1890

Herbert Tatlow and Clifford Ingall in the works 'H'-type 12/40

drawing board of C M Van Eugen. The final reconstructed company (1936–62) again concentrated upon high-efficiency medium-sized cars for which R H Rose was responsible. Production was now aided by a high proportion of bought-out units from the greatly expanded motor components industry, but the economic climate and diminishing coachbuilding trade caused the virtual abandonment of car production in 1952. A further ten years were spent on general engineering sub-contract work, while service facilities for all car repair work have been maintained to the present day. Development work on a new car project began in 1977 and the 'Lea-Francis' name will emerge once more.

Charles Marie van Eugen

Tom Delaney at Brooklands in No. 14053

George Leek

Mr and Mrs Hugh Rose

R M V Sutton in the practice car for the 1928 TT

CHAPTER ONE

Cycles

Richard Henry Lea and Graham Inglesby Francis entered into partnership in August 1895 for the purpose of manufacturing high-grade cycles. They were particularly well fitted for this venture, both being well known in the cycle industry.

Lea was born on 23 February 1858, the son of a cabinet maker. His childhood was spent with his two brothers and three sisters in the family home at Lutterworth, Leicestershire. He was educated at Manchester Grammar School and joined Messrs Singer & Co. in 1878, remaining with them until commencing business with Francis. He spent a considerable period abroad in pursuit of sales, travelling to India, the Far East and the USA, returning in 1885, and was appointed works manager of the Singer 'New Works' in 1888.

He was a great innovator and filed 42 patents, mostly connected with cycles, prior to the First World War, the first in conjunction with George Singer being dated 1881. While in Calcutta in 1884, he designed a two-speed cycle gear, although even at this early date he had been anticipated, for a three-speed cycle gear by Jay was on the market in 1883.

Upon Lea's appointment as works manager, he applied considerable thought to improvements in machinery and plant, and was responsible for several noteworthy developments in the production of wheel spokes. In addition a patent was taken out for a rapid thread-tapping machine, and his interest in the internal combustion engine can be seen in several patents relating to gas engines and their ignition, these machines supplying factory power during this period.

The career of Graham Inglesby Francis ran parallel with that of Lea. Although basically an engineer, he had a wide commercial experience, and like his partner had spent a considerable time abroad.

He was first employed by the woodworking machinery firm Messrs Ludw, Loewe & Co. of Berlin, following which he travelled to the United States of America, taking a post with Brown and Sharpe and then Pratt and Witney, internationally known companies in the field of machine tools.

After returning to England, he was appointed general manager of the 'Auto Machinery Co.' of Coventry in 1891. This firm was formed in 1886 by Hillman and Sumner. Hillman was a director of the Premier Cycle Co. and later became a well-known motor car manufacturer. The 'Auto Machinery Co.' was a pioneer in the ballbearing industry, and exists to this day, although now famous for nut and bolt manufacture.

The commencement of business saw the occupation of small premises in Days Lane, Coventry, and a private partnership between Lea and Francis. The intention from the outset was to achieve the highest standards of design and manufacture of gentlemen's bicycles, and the machines were, therefore, directly competitive with the wares of Sunbeam, Beeston-Humber and Dursley-Pedersen. The cycle at this date was a fine example of light mechanical engineering and rapidly approaching its zenith. The reason for this state of affairs was the stimulus given to the industry by the upper classes and indeed the aristocracy who were taking a great interest in the new and healthy pastime of cycling. If a census of the owners of cycles found in Hyde Park at the turn of the century had been taken, it would have read like a passage from Debrett. Catering for this market was, therefore, a lucrative business, and of great appeal to perfectionist-minded persons like Lea and Francis.

The design of the first machines was the work of Lea, and in fact the cycles were sold under his name in the early years. The remaining months of 1895 were spent in purchasing plant and new and expensive machine tools. G I Francis was responsible for this aspect of the business, and it is significant that the majority of the machinery purchased was American, Francis being impressed with the Americans' prowess in this field which he had studied at first hand.

> REGISTERED "LEA" NULLI SECUNDUS TRADE MARK.
> LEA & FRANCIS.
> COVENTRY.
>
> # Lea
> ## AND
> # Francis
>
> DAY'S LANE,
> Coventry, Aug., 1895.
>
> R. H. LEA, M.I.M.E., FOR NEARLY 17 YEARS WITH SINGER AND CO., AND, FOR THE LAST SEVEN YEARS, MANAGER OF THEIR NEW WORKS.
>
> G. I. FRANCIS, FORMERLY WITH BROWN AND SHARPE, AND PRATT AND WHITNEY, OF AMERICA, AND LUDW. LOEWE AND CO., OF BERLIN (THREE OF THE LARGEST AND MOST CELEBRATED MACHINE-TOOL MAKERS OF THE WORLD), AND, FOR THE LAST FOUR YEARS, MANAGER FOR THE AUTO MACHINERY CO., LTD., OF COVENTRY.
>
> **Beg to inform you** that they have entered into partnership, and are now completing arrangements for the manufacture of highest grade cycles. These will be known as the "LEA" Cycles, and no effort or expense will be spared to make them, in every respect, of the highest possible quality. The accumulated knowledge resulting from seventeen years' experience and experiment will be brought to bear on every detail of Design and Construction.
>
> LEA & FRANCIS will exhibit at the coming NATIONAL SHOW, and, in the meantime, beg to invite correspondence from AGENTS of repute.

It is doubtful if any 'Lea' cycles reached the hands of the public in 1895, although four machines were exhibited at the Stanley Cycle Show held at the Crystal Palace in December. In addition to complete cycles, Lea and Francis exhibited several separate components, the frame lugs displayed – all stampings and machined practically all over – excited favourable comment from the Press, as did the totally enclosing and neat chain case, while the 'steering lock' was said to be the best yet seen. The cycle frames utilized round tubes for compression and oval for tension members.

The first advertisements for Lea machines appeared in November 1895 in time for the National Show, and they were, as in subsequent years, very simple, merely stating the name and stand number, although in this first instance, the makers saw fit to add the silhouette of a fairy pointing skywards, not altogether appropriate since Lea & Francis cycles were amongst the heaviest machines in production.

Immediately after the commencement of business, the partners entered into negotiations to purchase a works in Lower Ford Street, the property of Lord Leigh. The transaction was completed in the spring of 1896. The site was bounded on the north side by the houses in Lower Ford Street and the River Sherborne to the south, and occupied an area of approxi-

The original notice of intent to trade by Messrs Lea and Francis, August 1895

mately two acres with access at the western end of Lower Ford Street. The original buildings consisted of one private house converted to offices, and one two-storey workshop. It was typical of the tightly knit industrial community of Coventry at that time that they had as neighbours Singer & Co., R H Lea's former employers and Bayliss-Thomas & Co., competitors in the cycle days and again in the early twenties with a light car.

In view of the considerable capital investment now made, the decision to convert to a limited liability company was taken and Lea & Francis Ltd was formed on 21 May 1896 with a nominal capital of £20,000 made up of £1 units. Eleven thousand five hundred and one shares were taken up by October 1896. The original directors were Lea, Francis and F S Matthews. The latter was formerly general manager of the Sparkbrook Manufacturing Co. of Birmingham, well-known cycle makers in the early years. He then held a post with the Premier Cycle Co. and in fact managed their German depot for eight years before joining Lea & Francis. He was made responsible for sales and opened the London office and showroom late in 1896.

A considerable interest in the new firm was taken by H J Hampson from Cheshire, well known in the early cycle and motor industry. It was he who many years later introduced Lea-Francis to the Vulcan Motor & Engineering Co. Ltd of Southport, a move which ultimately had unfortunate results and is discussed in vintage circles to the present day.

The first works manager was James Stone, and the first company secretary John Rudd; the latter soon left to become secretary to the local hospital. F A Griffin also joined the firm in the capacity of general manager and although an engineer by profession, he took over the mantle of company secretary on Rudd's departure.

Production got under way in 1896 and several agents were appointed, including the well-known firm of Benetfink & Co. who were given sales rights for London and the home counties, presumably with the exception of sales made direct to the public from the company's new London showrooms. These premises were situated at the corner of Dover Street and Piccadilly, strategically placed to catch the eye of West End society. Lord Burleigh was among the earliest customers.

The firm put on a fine display at the 1896 Cycle Show with a stand in a prominent position, liberally stocked with potted palms and as many as five ladies' and five gentlemen's machines. All were finished in black with red wheel rims, which gave them a striking appearance and was to become the standard colour scheme for many years. Incidentally, the red rim tradition was carried on until the firm's demise with the same colour used as a circular perimeter for the car radiator badges.

Several improvements were introduced during 1897 including a new disc hub and a very neat installation of the repair kit in the end of one handlebar and an oil can in the other. An improved gearcase embodying celluloid covers, together with a simple but effective tyre pump spring clip were included; both the latter were patented. The range was also extended to include both 'Cob' and '28 in' machines – 'Improvements of Sterling Merit' wrote R H Lea in his advertising for the '98 season.

No radical improvements were made in 1898 apart from the addition of foot rests and an improved steering lock. The marque was by now firmly established, and regarded by many as the finest on the market. Proof of this fact is to be seen in *Cycling* dated 1 October 1898, which contained the first recorded advertisement of a used Lea cycle for sale. At £14 this was easily the highest-priced machine in the used cycle columns.

The most expensive machine then produced was listed at £25, a considerable sum in 1898. Demand was now fully taking up production and virtually no advertising was found to be necessary. Lea cycles were built individually, and in a painstaking manner with much extensive component testing, with the result that maximum output seldom exceeded 20 per week.

The Crystal Palace Show in December 1899 was to witness another impressive display of 10 machines, now known as 'Lea-Francis' cycles. An ornate wrought-iron signpost structure was devised as a centre piece for the stand by Lea, a piece of furniture which was to remain in use until the old company's final appearance at Olympia in 1930.

R H Lea planned a new extension to the factory during the first year of the twentieth century, working from his home. The Lea family had recently moved into a large residence known as 'The Elms' in Cox Street, a short distance from the works. The house was previously occupied by G I Francis, who had elected to move into the countryside at Tile Hill.

The year 1900 proved a successful season for Lea & Francis cycles and further refinements were implemented. The freewheel was given a great deal of thought and a new pattern of outstandingly good design was ready for the following season. The new unit was carried on a ball race of its own, thus releasing the rear wheel bearings from the chain load. The frictional losses in the new freewheel are believed to be the lowest ever achieved.

Rear brakes were now either of the band type

"Lea-Francis" Light Roadster.

This machine is what it professes to be—viz., a Roadster, but it is built in a somewhat lighter form than our Full Roadster type, which, of course, is fitted with gear-case.

Its distinguishing features are: Frames—22, 23, 24, 25, or 26 in.; 26in. wheels; 1¼in. roadster tyres; narrow tread; no gear-case; aluminium rims; Brooks B10 saddle; new front brake; Sturmey-Archer or B.S.A. three-speed gear.

Other details are in accordance with specification given on page 11.

Please also note remarks on page 6 with reference to this machine.

NET CASH PRICES:

SINGLE GEAR.	TWO-SPEED GEAR.	STURMEY-ARCHER OR B.S.A. THREE-SPEED GEAR.
£14 18 6	£16 0 0	£16 6 0

Coventry Chain Co.'s "Chainette," 7s. 6d. extra.

Average weight of 23in. machine, with three-speed and complete with Trip-Motion; does not exceed 29lbs. With single gear, 23in. machine averages 27½lbs.

Ladies' Light Roadster.

The Ladies' Model cannot be made quite so light as above on account of the necessity for fitting a gear-case, but it is appreciably lighter than the Full Roadster type. See remarks on page 7.

Price is same as page 9.

The Lea-Francis 'Light Roadster', as advertized in the 1911 catalogue

Variable Gears.

"LEA-FRANCIS" THREE-SPEED GEAR.

THE above illustration will give an idea of the simplicity of the mechanism, and the small number of component parts as compared with other gears.

It is an exceptionally free-running gear—this valuable feature being specially noticeable when the gear is having power transmitted through it.

This additional freedom is largely due to our patent free wheel; the effect of which—owing to its special design—is not only to make the machine "coast" freely, but—what is of far more importance ensures ease of propulsion.

We give our clients the option of either the Sturmey-Archer or B.S.A. Three-Speed Gears, both of which are so well-known that it is scarcely necessary to illustrate them here.

or an improved rim design incorporating operation by Bowden Cable. The famous 'trip motion' for easy mounting and dismounting was also introduced in 1900. This device held the pedal rigid for ease of mounting.

Four differing designs of cycle were offered for 1901, ranging in price between £22-10*s* and £25-10*s* and weighing between 32 and 34lbs, a little lighter than in previous years. The range was carried through until late 1902 without change apart from the addition of a coupled brake layout of neat design.

The National Cycle Show of November 1902 was to witness Lea-Francis bicycles embodying another new braking system. This design was the work of Francis and employed rods and levers concealed within the handlebars; the new scheme was even more efficient than before and was praised by the cycle Press for its modern and extremely tidy appearance.

Sales were still good and the firm's success prompted the directors to investigate motor car manufacture. The new extension to the factory was now complete and thus space was available for new projects.

During 1903 Alexander Craig, a close associate of Lea and Francis, was commissioned to design and produce a car of unorthodox design. The venture was unsuccessful and severely tested the firm's finances (see Chapter Two).

Cycle production continued without change during 1904 and the most expensive model, at £25-10*s* was the highest-priced machine exhibited at the Crystal Palace in November 1903. Sales were now falling and the clientèle catered for by Lea and Francis were beginning to tire of cycling. The motor cycle was fast developing to a point of reasonable reliability and constituted a further threat to the high-grade bicycle trade.

No alterations were made for 1905 but 'Fagan' two-speed hub gears or 'Sturmey-Archer' three-speed gears were offered as additional equipment. In an effort to improve sales and no doubt raise some much-needed finance, all models were reduced to £20. An innovation at the Cycle Show for 1905 comprised an antique spinning wheel adapted to show the frictionless freewheel to advantage.

The following season was to witness the introduction of a patent Lea-Francis two-speed gear. This was the work of F A Griffin and arrangements were made for both Griffin and Stone to operate a separate company for the production of cycle gears for sale to other manufacturers. Their first customers were the Sparkbrook Co. Ltd of Birmingham.

The new gear was of the epicyclic type with direct drive on high with a reduction of approximately 24 per cent for low. The unit was fitted in conjunction with the standard Lea-Francis freewheel. It was, of course, a very finely made mechanism and was exhaustively tested for some months before introduction.

Lea and Francis remained firmly wedded to the manufacture of top-grade machines only, despite the contracting market, and prices were again reviewed, the single-gear type being offered at £18-4*s* while £22-10*s* was the price tag of the most expensive three-speed machine.

The Lower Ford Street bicycle was now approaching the pinnacle of its development and the Press were positively eulogistic in their appreciation. *Cycling*, in November 1905, found that Lea-Francis had a 'fineness of detail and finish and an excellence of construction which cannot fail to attract the keenest critic'.

The makers saw fit to take a full page for advertizing in the leading trade papers for the duration of the National Show in November 1905. It is interesting to note that the term 'Leaf' was first used by the makers in this publicity, although it was coined in 1900 for their telegraphic address.

The 1906 season was a difficult one and the market for expensive bicycles had contracted seriously. Sales from the West End showrooms were virtually at a standstill, resulting in their closure in September of that year. F S Matthews had emigrated to Canada and the London depot had been managed latterly by W H Francis (brother of G I Francis) who had been appointed a director of the company.

The nominal capital of Lea & Francis Ltd was increased to £40,040, of which £17,510 was now paid up. Shareholders were composed entirely of local people, all close associates of the founders. Colonel Cuthbert Dawson, a keen motoring and sailing enthusiast was also appointed a director. He was, a little later, to become the first British owner of a Bugatti car.

R H Lea was now busy experimenting with lighting devices for the rear of cycles and motor vehicles. In this venture he was greatly assisted by his son, Norman, and the Lea-Francis machines for 1907 were to be fitted with an early form of reflector. The firm's two-speed gear was also refined with particular attention to the smoothness of change between gears.

Sales continued at a low level and the company elected not to exhibit at the November 1907 National Show. The directors, however, refused to deviate from the policy of manufacturing only one grade of machine – the finest. Fortunately, business improved during 1908.

Marcus Nash, a retired Army Major, RA, joined the firm in 1908 and was elected to the Board. He invested £10,000 in Lea & Francis shares, a large sum for those days, and stayed until receivership in 1931. He undoubtedly enjoyed his time at Lea & Francis and was a

OPPOSITE
The Lea-Francis three-speed gear, as advertized in the 1911 catalogue

15

Christopher Hefford with his Light Roadster cycle; regularly used for almost 50 years

great supporter of the motor cycle project, encouraging his colleagues with enthusiasm. Nash began by looking after the commercial aspects of the company under G I Francis, who was, once more, beginning to take an interest in the ballbearing industry. He concentrated on sales at a later date and covered large mileages in his 12/40 saloon during the twenties. He was, apparently, incapable of much feeling for machinery and when his car was left unattended at the works, a rare occurrence, it was borne off to the service department by George Andrews for a rapid rebuild. Invariably, the brake pedal would be almost on the floor, steering seized through lack of grease and dents to be found on all wings – a state of affairs to which Marcus Nash was quite oblivious. Nevertheless, Nash worked hard for Lea-Francis and was a very valuable member of the Board with qualities of fair mindedness, and, like the founders, absolute integrity. It is sad to recall that he eventually lost his entire investment after so many years' service.

During 1908, R H Lea perfected his 'reflex' rearlight and a patent was granted. The device was well received, and sold in considerable quantities, used by all classes of vehicles, while civil undertakings bought them for use in road repair and warning signs. A company was formed to handle the patent known as the Reflex Road Light Co., of Holborn, London E.C. Manufacture was later taken over by Components Ltd, of Bournbrook, Birmingham. It is interesting to record that when the Much Park Street factory stores were transferred in 1963, a quantity of these reflectors, made 55 years beforehand, were found to be still in stock.

The company returned to the Cycle Show held in November 1908, with the same range of cycles, still further refined and once more the most expensive exhibited. The Lea-Francis gear was now offered with a three-speed option, while a considerable amount of phosphor bronze was now in evidence, utilized for the brake mechanism in the form of shrouds for all sliding surfaces, while the gearchange knob and handlebar end plugs were now of ivory. G I Francis designed new pedals which were the subject of a patent. They were of aluminium into which rubber studs were inserted; a little trouble was experienced in service because the inserts eventually worked loose. They sold well nonetheless, and in addition to being fitted to Lea-Francis cycles, were also used by other manufacturers.

Production was increased by 20 per cent during 1909, and the cycles were continued for 1910 with minor changes. The gearchange lever was now fitted on the handlebars, and some thought was given to weight reduction. Aluminium wheel rims were fitted and neat aluminium carriers for front and rear were offered. Prices ranged from £17 for the single gear machine, up to £18-18s for the three-speed type.

Business recovered completely in 1910, and a record number of cycles were sold that year. An additional model was offered for 1911, known as the 'Light Roadster' single-gear, small-wheeled versions of which weighed $27\frac{1}{2}$lbs.

The Lea-Francis two-speed gear was now only supplied to special order, while three-speed Sturmey-Archer or BSA gears were offered as a cheaper alternative to the Lower Ford Street triple-ratio unit.

Increased production enabled a reduction to be made in prices and in November 1910 the new 'Light Roadster' could be bought for £14-18s-6s, while the three-speed standard cycles now cost 16 guineas.

The firm's policy of refusal to alter design for the sake of change is explained by Lea in 1911 – 'The cycle should not be reduced to the level of a Matinee hat – a mere cork on the ocean of fashion', while Lea-Francis brakes, now acknowledged to be the finest and most expensive in the world were said to be – 'Like Caesar's wife – above suspicion'.

The reflex lamp was explained to the public as follows: 'Its construction is so unique that it burns – nothing! and requires no attention. The wick cannot be turned too high or too low, for the simple reason that there is no wick. You cannot run short of oil, because none at all is required. The Reflector is always bright because the Lamp is a "non-smoker" and you may rely upon it coming brilliantly into action even when an over-taking motor car is still a long way off, thus securing your perfect safety. Moreover, you have the satisfaction of knowing that the motor man pays for the Carbide which lights it up, and that is as it should be because it is only fast motor traffic which has rendered a rear light essential to one's safety – It's a Moon in a Nutshell.'

Lea was fond of citing three qualities to head advertisements, and we read that Lea-Francis brakes were renowned for 'Reliability, Efficiency and Smart Appearance', while the cars of the twenties rejoiced as models of 'Elegance, Efficiency and Economy'.

The 1911 season was a successful one, cycle sales were satisfactory and 'reflex' lights were selling in very large numbers. The company, however, suffered from a crop of imitators in this field and the products of some were of dubious quality. Lea was forced to reduce the price of his lamp to 2s-6d and later to 2s in order to remain competitive.

A German company was foolish enough to market a 'Chinese Copy' of the Lea-Reflex and a law suit was enacted by Lea-Francis in March 1910 to protect their patent. The case dragged on until October 1911 when the German court found for the Coventry firm and the infringers were mulcted in heavy costs. Two further cases were fought and won in France.

Coventry Corporation were now using 'Lea-Reflex' lamps in quantity to 'stud' all the road signs in the city.

The Lea cycle pedal was now made under licence by Bramptons Ltd, makers of the famous cycle forks, and henceforth were known as 'Brampton-Leaf' pedals.

During 1912, serious development work was proceeding on a twin-cylinder motor cycle which was placed on the market in August of that year and was to be the principal occupation of Lea & Francis until the outbreak of war.

Cycles continued without change apart from detail refinements such as the fitting of improved aluminium carriers and leather mudguard flaps. A 'Winter' model was introduced for the 1912 season, finished in black and priced at £15-8s-6d while the lowest-priced machine was now offered at £14-8s-6d.

The final appearance of Lea-Francis at the annual Cycle Show, now held at Olympia, was in November 1912 for the 1913 season. Four machines were exhibited, both ladies' and gentlemen's 'Tourist' and 'Light Roadster' models. Once again prices were altered, all four being listed at 16 guineas, although the 'Winter' model could be purchased for £15-10s. At these prices they were to remain until the end of production.

No further alterations were made to cycle design and manufacture continued through 1913 and 1914 with the last machines being assembled during the First World War.

The Lea-Francis pedal cycle had, from its introduction in 1895, been designed and produced with a very high proportion of factory-built components and was never an 'assembly' job. The handlebars, brazed-up frame, brakes and chain sprockets were all produced at Lower Ford Street. The wheel spokes were threaded on a machine designed by R H Lea and were fitted in Lea-Francis-built hubs, although the rims were supplied by the 'Roman' company. Saddles were supplied by Brooks, chains by Hans Renold and tyres largely by Dunlop.

The company never produced a tandem or tricycle, concentrating solely on ladies' and gentlemen's safety bicycles of the highest grade and built with little regard to cost. They were undoubtedly unsurpassed in their sphere and the reputation thus secured was of immense help to the sales of the motor cycles and cars which followed in later years.

CHAPTER TWO

The First Motor Cars

The year 1903 witnessed the first faltering steps of Lea & Francis into the realm of motor cars with the engagement of consulting engineer Alex Craig for the purpose of designing a medium-sized 3-cylinder car.

Alexander Craig, OBE, MIMechE, was born in 1870, educated at Masons College, Birmingham, and served an apprenticeship at the Crewe locomotive works. He joined the shipbuilding firm of Dennys of Dumbarton as electrical engineer before entering the motor industry as under works manager of Humber Ltd in 1896, where he planned and built the original motor cycle and car shops.

Craig then became an independent consulting engineer with offices in Hertford Street, Coventry and built up a reputation in this field. His first commission seems to have been the design of a 3-cylinder Maudslay car in addition to planning their Parkside factory for its production.

The Maudslay engine was interesting as an early example of overhead camshaft design. The vertical valves were operated via rollers from the camshaft, which was driven by a universally jointed vertical shaft and skew gearing. The whole cam assembly was pivoted and could be thrown back by undoing two fly-nuts to give easy access to the valves. Porting was extremely good by the standards of the day and 25hp was claimed from this unit of some $4\frac{1}{2}$ litres at approximately 1400rpm. The dimensions were square, 127mm bore and stroke.

This unit appears to have been successful and was undoubtedly advanced for 1901. An 18hp version of similar design was also provided and the Maudslay Company continued to build engines of this basic type for private cars until 1914 and commercial vehicles into the thirties. They were also in the vanguard of 6-cylinder development announcing 40hp and 60hp cars so fitted in December 1903, thus rivalling Napier and Sunbeam.

Craig retained his interest in the Maudslay firm and served as managing director and ultimately chairman from 1910 until his death. Small and of quiet disposition, this academic man was also an able administrator, although one suspects he was happier when at the drawing board. He also interested himself in motor cycle development and read a paper before the Cycle Engineers' Institute (forerunners of the IAE) on this subject in 1902. His services were also enlisted for design work by the Standard Motor Co. Ltd in 1903, who were commencing business in Much Park Street. This plant was occupied by Lea-Francis Cars 35 years later.

The car Craig designed for Lea & Francis was a most unorthodox machine, and, unfortunately, a certain failure from its inception. Successful manufacturers had, by 1903, with the principal exception of Lanchester, settled down to a conventional mechanical layout which was to remain largely unchanged for many years. The underfloor engine of enormous length and weird transmission of the Lower Ford Street product was bound to meet with the stiffest sales resistance, even if it could have been developed to a point of all-round performance the equal of its competitors.

The chassis and suspension was conventional but a horizontal 3-cylinder engine of 4in bore by 6in stroke (3680cc) based on the Maudslay pattern was fitted in an underfloor position. With a view to providing easy access to the valve, carburation and ignition arrangements, the head of the engine was located well forward and could be reached from the front of the car by lifting up the hinged scuttle assembly.

In order to dispense with the need for a countershaft or excessively long driving chains, the engine was elongated to a point where the connecting rods measured 2ft 9in between centres. This arrangement was claimed to reduce piston sidethrust due to the reduction of the angle of con-rod obliquity and also to promote 'sweetness of running'. How excessive length assisted the latter was not made clear, but the immense flywheels at each end of the crankshaft no doubt made the greatest contri-

The first test run with the 1903 car

bution in this direction. Pressure lubrication was used for all crankshaft bearings and the small ends via drillings in the connecting rods.

The valves were situated at the side of the combustion chamber, thus being on top of the engine, no doubt for reasons of accessibility. In other respects the unit closely resembled the Maudslay, but the increase in dimensions, combined with the fitting of two flywheels resulted in a power plant of great weight; 15bhp was claimed at 700rpm with a maximum speed of 2000rpm.

Clutches were fitted in each flywheel and driving chains were positioned at each side with differing sprockets in order to obtain two gear ratios. A further ultra low and reverse gear was fitted in the nearside hub. The offside rear wheel was fixed to a spindle running the full width of the car upon which the nearside wheel was free to rotate independently. Cooling was provided by a flexibly mounted low-slung radiator and an eccentric water pump.

The whole vehicle was certainly well finished, the connecting rods being machined all over and the front axle and steering gear appeared to be machined on most faces. Chassis weight was quoted as 16cwt and the car was considerably over-priced, initially at £787-10*s* and later at £850.

Lea and Francis realized that the car was of an experimental nature and in order to protect the cycle business, a new company known as the Lea & Francis Motor Syndicate Ltd was incorporated on 29 June 1903 for motor car development purposes only. A capital of £10,000 was authorized, but only £3942 was issued and fully paid up. It was agreed that if two cars were not built, properly tested and made ready for exhibition within 12 months, all assets were to be transferred to Lea & Francis Ltd. The conditions were fulfilled and the first public appearance of the vehicle was in chassis

form at the Crystal Palace in February 1904.

Two cars were fitted with 'Roi de Belge' bodies by Mulliner of Northampton, one with totally enclosed driving chains and the other with open chains and some brake linkage modifications. A total of three cars were built but operations were suspended in 1905 and efforts were made to realize as much material as possible.

One car was sold to Hans Renold, the famous chain manufacturer and a personal friend of R H Lea. The second car stood in the Lower Ford Street works for several years, eventually going to a buyer in Daventry while the third was destroyed in a fire in the experimental department.

Lea & Francis succeeded in selling a manufacturing licence for the Craig-type engine to the Singer Co., and they built a limited number of 2-cylinder cars of similar layout but with a conventional gearbox bolted directly to the engine. Singer also tried to sell a 3-cylinder version but it is doubtful if any were produced. It is recorded that the 2-cylinder model was rough and suffered from considerable vibration when compared with the larger type.

Clifford Hateley Ingall was in charge of Alexander Craig's design office at this period and spent much of his time at the Lea-Francis works. It fell his lot to deliver the number one car to Renold in Manchester and then spend a week instructing the family chauffeur in the matter of driving and maintenance, common practice in those days. It is recorded that Ingall was invited to a series of hectic parties at the Renold's residence and had to return home in haste to collect his dinner jacket.

He was released by Craig in order to join the Singer Co. for two years to take charge of experimental motor car work. He worked with A Alderson, Singer's chief draughtsman who, like Ingall, was to join Lea-Francis in later years.

In May 1908 a decision was taken to wind up the Lea & Francis Motor Syndicate Ltd and this was duly effected in July 1909. The venture ended with a deficiency of £3375 and the loss was subsidized by the cycle company. It is thought that the actual amount lost was considerably above the figure stated and was met from the directors' own pockets. Alex Craig felt no benefit either, since his remuneration was to have been in the form of share allotment. Ingall returned to Craig's design office in February 1906 as leading draughtsman and a great deal of consulting work was carried out during the next four years. Craig received commissions for the design of motor cycles, cars, lorries, motor rail coaches and boat installations of Maudslay engines. In these ventures, they were assisted by R H Lea's two sons, Alan

OPPOSITE
Chassis view of the 1903 vehicle showing the hinged camshaft

Front view of the 1903 car

and Norman as apprentice draughtsmen.

Upon Craig's appointment as Maudslay's managing director in March 1910, the independent design office was closed and Ingall also transferred to Maudslay as assistant works manager.

Craig was responsible for many patents, nor were they all connected with the motor industry and among his applications to the Patent Office are listed, *inter alia*, a device for treating rheumatism, improvements to railway carriages, infants' feeding-bottle teats and gas producers.

He was also appointed a director of the Rover Co. in 1926 and became chairman in 1931. He died in 1935 at the age of 65.

CHAPTER THREE

Motor Cycles

A decision to join the ranks of motor cycle manufacturers was taken in 1911. An experimental lightweight machine had been made some nine years beforehand. This was fitted with a 1½hp Clement-Garrard power unit but the project was shelved. The Clement-Garrard Company was a Birmingham firm with premises in Ryland Street. They specialized in producing small engines and adapting them to fit pedal cycles.

The initial plans for the new motor cycle were formulated by R H Lea, assisted part time by C H Ingall and Norman Lea with encouragement from Marcus Nash. Ingall joined Lea-Francis full time in March 1912 and was made responsible for the final design adopted. The main objects were to produce a high-grade, medium-powered touring machine featuring silence, comfort and as much protection for the rider from oil, dirt and inclement weather as possible. The resulting cycle was ready for production in August 1912, after much hard work and long hours by those responsible. It was immediately well received by press and public alike.

In order to save development time and cost, a decision was taken to utilize a proprietary engine and the well-tried 3¼hp JAP power plant was chosen. This unit was a 50° side valve V-twin of 60 × 76mm bore and stroke (430cc). Carburation was by Amac, although experiments were made with a seven-jet device of Maudslay manufacture designed by Everest, the latter firm's head tester. It gave good results but was rejected, probably on grounds of cost.

The transmission was outstandingly well designed. Chain drive was used throughout and Ingall conceived a very neat two-speed dog engagement gearbox. The gear teeth were of a very fine pitch in the interest of silence. The circular casing was eccentric in relation to the mainshaft and was rotated in the frame bottom bracket to secure primary chain adjustment.

A substantial four-spring 'Cush' drive was incorporated together with multi-plate clutch and all the chains were totally enclosed with rigid chain cases not unlike the pedal cycles.

The rear wheel was made quickly detachable by interposing a dog engagement between the wheel and sprocket. The chain thereby remained undisturbed when the wheel was removed. The whole operation merely requiring the removal and replacement of a single screwed spindle. The sprocket ran on an independent bearing – again the family resemblance with the pedal cycle and freewheel can be detected. This feature was the subject of a patent filed jointly between Lea and Ingall and was a boon to owners who were often beset with tyre trouble in the early years. Both front and rear wheels were interchangeable and were shod with 26 × 2¾in tyres.

Long footboards were fitted and early on in production a cast-aluminium silencer was located across the front of the frame which acted as an additional shield from mud and water. After much deliberation, the magneto was neatly housed between engine and gearbox, well protected from bad weather, while the high-tension leads were carried in conduits.

Mudguarding was ample with deep valances and the whole machine bristled with careful attention to detail and was exceedingly well finished. The complete motor cycle turned the scales at 220lb. It possessed excellent road manners and handled well with effective 'V'-rim brakes. Hill-climbing abilities were notably good with a maximum speed of 45–50mph. The price, full equipped, was £68-5s.

One of the first buyers of the new machine was George Bernard Shaw, who in his middle fifties took up the healthy pastime of motor cycling. He arrived at the Lower Ford Street works in his chauffeur-driven Lanchester car in mid-winter and promptly waved this luxurious outfit away; after a briefing on the driving and maintenance of his new toy by Ingall, he set off for London. Shaw was watched until out of sight by anxious Lea-Francis men who reported that he was steering none-too-straight a course.

Production was in full swing by 1913 and C H Ingall was made works manager and was later appointed a director. He remained with the firm until June 1919.

The second generation were now taking an active part in Lower Ford Street affairs. Norman Lea spent all his spare time on the motor cycle development programme, often working late into, and occasionally straight through, the night on modifications to trial machines. Alan Lea was employed in the machine shop as chargehand over the milling section where the cutting of the fine-tooth gears together with the slotting of motor cycle and pedal cycle sprockets was carried out.

Gordon I Francis, popularly known as Don, son of the joint founder, assisted with the production and testing. He rode practically all the motor cycles produced in pre-war days and soon became a very skilful and well-known trials competitor. He commenced his apprenticeship in 1906 in the Griffin and Stone gear division at Lower Ford Street.

When the motor cycle was in full production, the company decided on a policy of competing in reliability trials as a means of gaining useful publicity. These events, being well reported in the Press, had captured the imagination of the

TOP LEFT
The first motor cycle

FAR LEFT
Same machine; note the exhaust pipes are not yet fitted

ABOVE
A Lea-Francis test party at the bottom of Saintbury Hill near Broadway. R H Lea is driving his brother-in-law's Rover, Alderson is in the rear seat and C H Ingall on the far left

LEFT
The 'quickly detachable' rear wheel

public and the fortunes of the competing makes were keenly followed.

The first sporting event in which the name of Lea-Francis appeared was the 1913 Colmore Cup trial organized by the Sutton Coldfield and North Birmingham Automobile Club and held in February. Norman Lea and Gordon Francis, although failing to achieve awards, impressed everybody with the silence and excellent hill-climbing powers of the Lea-Francis bikes. The clean condition of the machines at the finish, due to the ample mudguarding, was in marked contrast to their competitors.

D W Popplewell entered the MCC Land's End event at Easter and gained a silver medal. Three machines took part in the Scottish Six-Day Trial; C H Ingall retired on the second day and N W Downie, the Lea-Francis Edinburgh agent, had to give up on the following day, both experiencing valve stem distortion due to overheating on the climbs. The side-valve JAP engine was rather prone to this complaint if extended for long periods. G I Francis ran the full course with no difficulty, however, and gained a gold medal.

The ACU six-day event which followed closely upon the Scottish trial was supported by Norman Lea and Gordon Francis. Lea failed on Kirkstone Pass but still achieved a silver medal while the skilful Francis rode well and was awarded a gold, his mount was also one of the fastest in the speed test recording 53·26mph.

The intrepid works riders were not satisfied with the gruelling conditions faced in the trial and, upon its completion, went on to climb successfully the Honister Pass from the steeper Buttermere side.

Further successes followed in lesser events during 1913. Lea performed with distinction in the SUNBAC reliability trial in October. The flexible machine was impressive in the slow-running and acceleration tests.

The Lea-Francis $3\frac{1}{4}$hp motor cycle had made a great impact in its first season and was continued for the 1914 season virtually without change. An additional oil pump was fitted for emergency use and a front stand which could fold away neatly under the crankcase was added. The company frowned upon the $3\frac{1}{4}$hp machine being used for sidecar work but offered an alternative set of low gears giving $6:1$ and $10\frac{2}{3}:1$ for buyers who used the cycles for this purpose.

An interesting display was staged at the November 1913 Motor Cycle Show with the actual gold-medal-winning machine being exhibited. Working and sectioned models of the salient features of the design were on view, and the rapid rear wheel removal facility was the subject of a demonstration. This feature had already attracted other makers. Clyno, amongst others, had negotiated a licence agreement with Lea-Francis for manufacturing rights.

Six new $3\frac{1}{2}$hp machines were also exhibited. The engine in this model, although similar to the $3\frac{1}{4}$hp in appearance had oversquare dimensions of 70mm bore × $64\frac{1}{2}$mm stroke (494cc).

The motorized cycle was, once more, enjoying a vogue and Lea-Francis made available a pedal cycle with neatly brazed-on lugs for attaching the BSA-built 'Auto Wheel'. A machine so fitted was on show.

Competition successes continued and the London–Exeter trial held on Boxing Day saw the firm's London agent, A J Sproston, taking a gold medal while the Colmore Cup event, held in the Cotswolds in February 1914, was a Lea-Francis benefit with Norman Lea winning the Colmore Cup for best performance in the trial. Don Francis achieved best solo performance for a trade entry.

The Easter London–Land's End event was entered by four Lea-Francis riders. H R Whitmore retired, but A M Rex finished and J Appleyard gained a gold medal, both on $3\frac{1}{4}$hp models, while A J Sproston on a $3\frac{1}{2}$hp also achieved a gold.

The Coventry and Warwickshire Club Open Trial saw Norman Lea a little off form, he failed on one hill due to hanging on to top gear too long, but Don Francis achieved a silver cup. H R Whitmore had better luck in the London–Edinburgh event and won a gold medal as did Sproston on a $3\frac{1}{2}$hp combination. The Scottish Six-Day Event saw Sproston taking another gold, together with Norman Lea on a new three-speed $3\frac{1}{4}$hp machine. W R Davenport on a standard two-speed, $3\frac{1}{4}$hp model managed a silver medal but Don Francis, on the first MAG 6/7hp sidecar model, was forced to retire from this gruelling trial with a fractured down tube.

More trouble was experienced with down tube failure when Francis broke another one later in this fateful year while on active service in France. It was this experience which prompted him to take an interest in the pressed-steel motor cycle frame, resulting in the well-stressed little Francis-Barnett machine of post-war years.

As war clouds were gathering in July 1914, the English Six-Day Trial was held, with Lea and Francis, this time both on $3\frac{1}{4}$hp machines, taking gold medals.

Several new projects were undertaken during 1914. A three-speed gearbox was designed and built within the same circular casing as the two-speed model. The new gearbox was fitted in Norman Lea's trials bike and caused consternation by seizing on its first trial run. An increase in clearance for a large diameter plain bush was found to be necessary. Lea had promised to take Geoffrey Smith, then editor of *Motor Cycle*, on a survey of trial routes in Derbyshire the following day and so the erring box was stripped, rectified and re-assembled, the job being completed at 3 a.m.

The company then decided to tackle the high-powered sidecar market and accordingly designed and built a new machine utilizing the Swiss MAG 742cc V-twin (72mm bore × 91mm stroke) power unit. This engine was ideal for a Lea-Francis machine, being a high-grade production notable for silence, smoothness and long life. The inlet valves were placed above the exhausts and all the operating mechanism was totally enclosed. An Amac single-lever-type carburettor was utilized.

A new frame was designed using straight tubes for all members except the top tube and the engine was sandwiched between flat steel plates which connected the down tube with the saddle tube and rear forks. The engine was thus relieved of all frame stresses.

Another three-speed gearbox was evolved in which the casing was suspended from a single trunnion bolt with a slotted clamp below in order to effect primary chain adjustment. The gears were engaged by dogs operated by two selector forks. A very neat quadrant change bearing the Lea-Francis monogram was produced and the connection to the gearbox was made by twin Bowden cables. Standard ratios were to be 4·7, 6·9 and 14·7:1 but the lower gearing of 5·25, 8 and 16·25:1 was adopted for the prototype with a view to its use in trials. The clutch was a single dry-plate type lined with Ferodo material; 26 × 3in Palmer tyres were interchangeable. A spare was carried attached to the rear of the sidecar. Further thought was given to the design of hubs and the new heavyweight machine was fitted with large diameter ball journal bearings and double thrust races in addition.

A de-luxe 'Gloria' sidecar was specially designed for this motor cycle. It is interesting to record that Lea-Francis were to occupy the premises used for the manufacture of Gloria sidecars in Much Park Street some 25 years later.

The first prototype was completed in June 1914 and was entered in the Scottish Trials by Francis and Ingall. The latter, being passenger, had some anxious moments on the rough terrain encountered for the outfit had a very poor ground clearance. The outbreak of the war caused further development work on this machine to be shelved and DU 5872 was the only example built.

The War Office was busily engaged, during the latter half of 1914, in placing orders for large numbers of motor cycles for the use of despatch riders. Lea-Francis decided to compete for this valuable business and accordingly designed a single-cylinder military model. The first example was completed in October and resembled the twin-cylinder type in most respects having a similar wheelbase and transmission system (three-speed).

This motor cycle, although of excellent design and built to Lea-Francis' exacting standards, did not succeed against the well-entrenched Triumph and Douglas machines and no orders were forthcoming.

Several improvements were incorporated in the twin-cylinder machine for the 1916 season, all were fitted with the three-speed gearbox and the clutch was now a Ferodo-lined disc type while the cush drive was transferred to the engine sprocket. The petrol tank was enlarged to hold 1¾ gallons and handlebars were finished black. The price was £69-10s and the single-cylinder type was also offered to the public, curiously at a mere 25s less. It is doubtful if more than one of the latter type were constructed and in fact production was running down as the factory switched to work of national importance.

The Lea-Francis motor cycle had made a great impact in its first two seasons of production, although output seldom exceeded 10 per week. The great majority were sold on the home market, either direct from the factory or accredited agents, among the latter, Messrs Sproston & Grace of London were particularly successful while a number were exported to Italy. Several commercial firms were using Lea-Francis sidecar machines and perhaps the most interesting belonged to a Nottingham brewery who fitted a body resembling a bottle of 'Bass' for advertizing purposes.

The tragic month of July 1914 caused an upheaval at Lower Ford Street, as it did all over Europe. The immediate consequence was a loss of youthful members of the staff and work force. Alan Lea joined the RASC as a driver – ironically he had never driven anything, but rushed round to the Maudslay works for a fortnight's practice on their lorries, which were used in large numbers by the War Office. He later transferred to tanks and was commissioned. Norman Lea joined the RNAS as a radio engineer and rose to the rank of Lieutenant Commander. Don Francis, as captain in the ASC was soon in charge of the motor cycle repair depot at St Omer, and W A Davenport saw service as a despatch rider, and later ran an army motor cycle instruction school.

The works were left in the overworked but capable hands of R H Lea, G I Francis, Nash and Ingall, and the production of the 3½hp motor cycle continued on a much-reduced scale, some being finished in khaki, while the

Italian Government bought a large number of second-hand machines for the use of their despatch riders.

The company undertook the manufacture of range-finding gear, and sundry instrument manufacture for the Admiralty. These contracts occupied the works until the cessation of hostilities. Motor cycle manufacture was suspended entirely in late 1916.

R H Lea used a 3½hp machine fitted with a box sidecar for his personal transport early in the war and was unfortunate enough to be hit amidships by a car in the centre of Coventry early in 1915. The accident caused a broken leg and effectively ended his motor cycling days. Perhaps this fact caused him to look at the design of light cars, and certainly he was impressed with the success of the GWK friction-driven machine. In what spare time was available to him, he carried out experiments with a pneumatic tyre running on the rim of a cone-shaped flywheel. The result of his findings were encouraging, and a patent for this device was granted in August 1917.

The experiment involved the Coventry Simplex 4-cylinder engine, which, incidentally, Ingall had designed with the aid of Alan Lea as far back as 1910.

The reproduced patent sketch shows the projected light car. It is not made clear where the driver and passenger were expected to sit, possibly this consideration proved insuperable for the project was abandoned, and no such car was built.

C H Ingall had also been busy with improvements to transmissions, and had designed and patented a variable gear in early 1916. The Rudge Multi Motor Cycle had enjoyed a considerable vogue, and was fitted with an expanding crankshaft pulley, which gave a very smooth and infinitely variable transmission, albeit at the cost of short-lived driving belts. Ingall, having in mind a light car application, went one stage further, and coupled an expanding pulley on the crankshaft with a contracting pulley on a counter shaft, thus obtaining a wider range of gearing. Neither of these transmission systems brought any benefits to their patentees, and there is no record of any commercial use having been made of them.

The years 1917 and 1918 passed without any further development or change. The paid-up capital of the company had now risen to £21,000 and Miss Helen Hewitt became secretary for the duration of the war. This stalwart, and rather forbidding lady joined the firm in 1895. The precise and correct commercial system at Lower Ford Street was largely due to her efforts, and the strict rules of conduct that obtained in the general office under Miss Hewitt seem incredible today. Nevertheless, she is remembered with affection by those who served with her.

Colonel Dawson retired from the Board in 1917 and his place was taken by C H Ingall.

Upon the cessation of hostilities in November 1918 much thought was given to the postwar programme, unfortunately the directors were not united on the question of policy. G I Francis, being absorbed by his interest in the ballbearing industry took little part, but R H Lea was determined to manufacture light-

The patent for the Lea-Francis light car, 1917

27TH AUGUST, 1917.   The Light Car and Cyclecar   259

A LEA-FRANCIS LIGHT CAR.
An Extremely Novel Type of Friction Drive from Cones and a Pneumatic Disc.

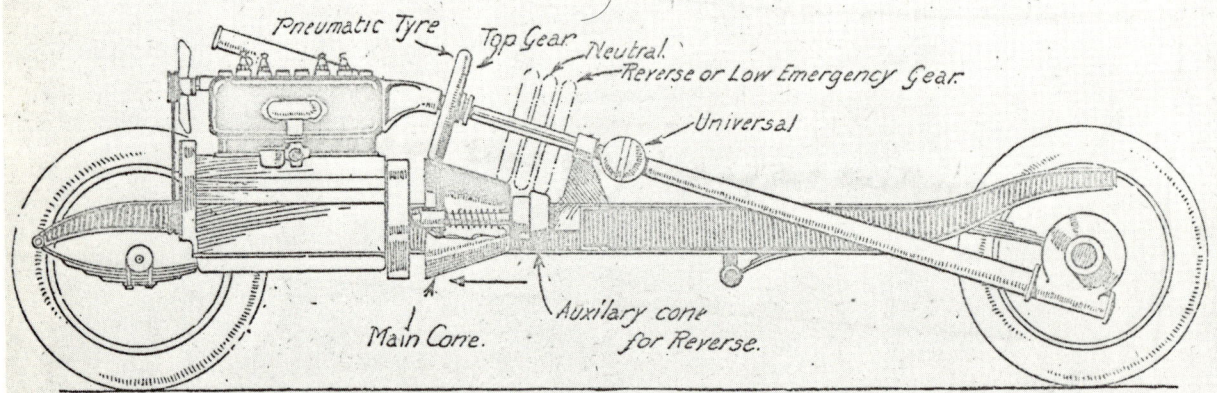

The ingenious friction drive of the Lea-Francis light car, the subject of a recently published patent specification.

and medium-sized motor cars. Marcus Nash felt that the company should adhere to their pre-war policy of cycle and motor cycle production, as he pointed out, the firm's whole reputation had been built upon 'Wire and Wind'. He was supported by Ingall. It was decided to continue motor cycle production, and also embark on the design of several types of cars. The cost of the latter operation, which was initially unsuccessful, was to cause grave problems in 1922 (see Chapter Four).

Alan Lea returned from the services at Christmas 1918 and rejoined Lea-Francis as a draughtsman, working under Alderson on the new car project, and in addition undertook motor cycle development. He also achieved success in reliability trials.

Norman Lea and Don Francis did not return. Lea stayed on in the RNAS to complete the radio equipment installation in the R.34 and eventually joined the Marconi Company. Don Francis designed a pressed-steel-framed motor cycle during the war with Maurice Wilks, who was later to take a prominent part in the successful rise of the Rover Company. Maurice Wilks decided not to proceed with Francis on the motor cycle project, electing instead to join Captain (later Sir John) Black at the Hillman Co. They did in fact marry the Misses Hillman. Family ties were strong in those days, for Francis succeeded in interesting his own brother-in-law, Barnett, in the pressed-steel motor cycle, and the successful Francis-Barnett Co. was thus formed with premises next door to Lea-Francis in Lower Ford Street.

C H Ingall found that he could not agree with the new policies at Lea & Francis and left in June 1919. He returned for a short period in 1926–7 as a sales representative, but did not find fulfilment in this post, and joined the design staff of Morris Motors. He was largely responsible for the 'Oxford-Six', the first Morris car to use hydraulic brakes, and he remained at Oxford for the rest of his working life.

Motor cycle production at Lower Ford Street recommenced early in 1919. The first machines were identical to the pre-war models utilizing the 3½hp JAP engine and two-speed gearbox.

Later in the year, the Swiss-built MAG engine was adopted as an option. This engine was also of 496cc (64 × 77mm) and possessed an inlet-over-exhaust valve layout. AMAC carburettors were used, and ignition was by Thompson-Bennett Magneto. The price of either machine was initially £125, rising to £130-15s early in 1920 – approximately twice the 1915 tag.

The small number of motor cycles built before the war had gained such an enviable reputation that the company took firm orders for the total 1920 production, envisaged at approximately 400 units, even before the Olympia Show opened in November 1919. Research indicates that production was a little slow in gaining momentum, possibly due to shortages of material which would be encountered during the shift of industrial production from military to domestic use. It appears that only about 100 machines were delivered in 1919.

The detachable wheel was still attracting interest, and another licence agreement was sold to Bayliss-Thomas for use on 'Excelsior' motor cycles.

Little competition work was attempted in 1919, although A J Sproston gained a gold medal in the London–Edinburgh event, while his team mate J A W Armstrong was disqualified for arriving too early at a control. The following year was to see a return to normal, and many successes were obtained.

The traditional MCC London–Land's End Trial held at Easter saw two Leafs entered, ridden by Sproston and W Cooper; both achieved silver medals. The London–Edinburgh event at Whitsun was to be a Lea-Francis benefit. Three machines were entered and all received gold medals. Sproston took part in the Scottish Six-Day Marathon and despite breaking a chain four times in one day, he still contrived to win a silver medal.

The Lea-Francis motor cycle was essentially a comfortable and refined touring machine and there was never any accent on performance. Nevertheless, a private owner, J Newall, entered a BMCRC event at Brooklands with a MAG-engined 3½hp model in August 1920 and covered a flying kilometre at 60·13mph. The only modifications from the standard were lengthened exhaust pipes, improved lubrication and TT pattern handlebars – this machine was offered for sale afterwards at £115.

A new and enlarged motor cycle for sidecar work was developed during 1920 and was ready in time for the Olympia Show in November. A long-stroke version of the 3½hp MAG engine was used having dimensions of 64 × 92mm bore and stroke (592cc) and rated nominally at 5hp. A three-speed constant-mesh gearbox was fitted and clamped between the engine side-plates in a conventional manner. This feature necessitated positioning the magneto ahead of the engine; it was, however, shielded from the elements by a neat valance.

The chain cases were aluminium castings on this larger model. Some initial problems with an unpleasant vibration attended the early 5hp cycle, indeed, Lea-Francis tried, unsuccessfully, to persuade the MAG company to take back the first batch of engines.

ABOVE AND OPPOSITE
The 1924 machine owned by H Tarrant of Ross-on-Wye

The smaller machine continued in production, but was now fitted with a revised version of the pre-war three-speed gearbox. The selector mechanism was simplified and the old fine pitch gearing gave way to a coarser pattern in order to withstand the stress of sliding pinion engagement.

Prices for 1921 were fixed at £125 for the 3½hp and £145 for the 5hp in solo form, while the latter cost £185 when fitted with a coach-built sidecar. The large machine was tested by *Motor Cycle* in April 1921, which found the performance excellent but stated that the long wheelbase made for a rather awkward riding position.

A Conville and H R Hancock entered 3½hp cycles in the London–Edinburgh Trial, to gain gold and silver medals respectively, while J Richardson used a 5hp combination in this event to take another gold. He followed up this success by running through the Scottish Six-Day Trial to pocket a bronze medal in the company of A J Sproston, with a solo 3½hp, who netted another gold.

A sports version of the 3½hp cycle was introduced for the 1922 season, which was shorn of the extensive mud guarding, and utilized footrests instead of boards, while TT handlebars were fitted into a lowered steering head.

The clutch on the 5hp model was now moved from the engine shaft to the gearshaft, while a Brampton 'spring link' final drive chain was incorporated to improve 'sweetness of running' at low speeds. Prices were reduced to £110 for the 3½hp, £125 and £157-10s for the 5hp solo and combination respectively.

Occasional entries into competition were still made by private owners. A 5hp machine gained a silver cup in the Land's End–John O'Groats MCC Trial held in June 1923, while G E Wood entered a 3½hp in the Paris–Nice Trial held in the previous February. He was unfortunately penalized for late arrival at Dijon.

The year 1924 then witnessed a further drastic cut in prices, and the machine was to some extent spoilt by the scrapping of the refined Lea-Francis gearbox; a Burman unit was substituted, and the cast-aluminium chain cases were deleted in favour of a simple pressed-steel guard. The appearance of the bike as a whole seemed less attractive, and sales even at the new figures of 66 guineas solo, and 84 to 94 guineas for various combinations, remained at a low level. The 3½hp type had been dropped altogether early in 1923.

R H Lea devised a new sidecar titled 'The Coupette' which incorporated a wooden superstructure hinged in such a way as to swing down out of sight into the body for fine-weather riding.

Production of motor cycles ended early in 1924 and the remaining machines were offered to the staff at discount prices, while C B Wardman Ltd cleared the last machine in their showroom for 50 guineas in October 1924.

Approximately 20 Lea-Francis motor cycles have survived out of a total production of approximately 1500. The most successful agent was A J Sproston through his firm of W H Elce & Co. Ltd. He and his wife were victims of the Croydon air disaster in January 1925.

CHAPTER FOUR

Post-Armistice Motor Cars

Early in 1919, Arthur Alderson was engaged by R H Lea to design and produce a medium-sized motor car. Alderson had been a draughtsman for many years with the Singer Company, and before his departure he had designed the Calcott Car, which had enjoyed a considerable vogue prior to the war. R H Lea felt that Alderson would repeat this success at Lea-Francis, but it was not to be, and the new car, a heavy and ponderous machine, was to prove almost unsaleable. The wartime profits amassed by Lea & Francis were completely dissipated in this venture, and in addition the production arrangements for the new car were ineptly handled.

Herbert Austin who was much better at making and selling this type of vehicle announced his 'Twelve' in 1922, and possibly this car, ironically one of the most successful British cars of all time, together with the post-war economic slump, drove the final nails into the coffin of the Alderson Lea-Francis.

The design was entirely conventional, and extremely robust in construction, attention to detail was excellent, and the general finish commensurate with that expected of Lea-Francis. The long stroke 4-cylinder engine was designed and built entirely at Lower Ford Street, with dimensions of 69×130mm, thus falling into the popular 11·9hp category. The unit was fitted with side valves, and had a non-detachable cylinder head, fitted with duralumin valve caps. The crankshaft ran in three main bearings, and the big ends were splash lubricated. Craig influence could be seen in the aluminium crankcase, which was fitted with large circular covers for the purpose of big end inspection.

Camshaft design was somewhat rudimentary, consisting of a splined shaft, onto which the separate broached cast-iron cams were fitted. No study whatever was made of cam and valve spring design, although no problems seem to have been encountered and the slow-running engine behaved satisfactorily, possibly with a certain amount of clatter. The valves were located on the nearside, while the Zenith carburettor was bolted directly to the offside of the cylinder block, which was 'cored' for the induction passage. Ignition was by Bosch magneto, while the Lucas dynamo fitted snugly into the timing cover, and was gear driven. No water pump was fitted, and the water outlet divided into two pipes, before entering the header tank of the large tapering radiator.

The cooling arrangements were not entirely adequate. Don Francis borrowed the works prototype for a weekend's testing, and with forceful driving proceeded to make it boil before reaching Leamington Spa. He was strongly admonished by R H Lea upon his return, who thought that cars should be tested only in a gentle fashion.

The drive was taken via a steep-angled cone clutch to a separate four-speed gearbox of ample dimensions with right-hand change, while the selector arrangements were the subject of a patent by Alderson. The production of this box was apparently an arduous operation, resulting in a nervous breakdown for its designer, although the result of his labours produced one of the easiest changing mechanisms available, double declutching being scarcely necessary. The engine and gearbox were carried in a subframe, and the 9ft wheelbase chassis carried semi-elliptic springs all round; the track was 4ft 2in. An open prop shaft of 'spidery' appearance transmitted the power to a fully floating rear axle. This unit consisted of an aluminium centre casting to which malleable-iron axle tubes were bolted. Brakes, both hand and foot, operated shoes in 12in drums on the rear hubs by rods. Artillery wheels were fitted, shod with 760×90mm tyres.

R H Lea was responsible for the design of the coachwork, which was originally standardized as a large two-seater with dickey. The bodies were built by Avon Bodies Ltd, and this began a long association with this Warwick-based company.

Ample space was allowed behind the front seats for luggage, etc., and the nearside seat was staggered a little behind the driver's, while the passenger's feet rested upon a toolbox. R H Lea felt that most passengers would be of the 'fair sex' and thus being naturally shorter than their partners, would appreciate this footrest. Lea was granted a patent for this arrangement. Weather protection was well conceived, and the complete body was built to the highest standards. A neat detail feature was the front wing stays, which were forgings embodying radiator supports and headlamp brackets in one piece. The stays were also hollow to take the wiring, which was thus protected from the elements.

The car was apparently pleasant to handle, and gave a very comfortable ride, but the performance of the long-stroke engine was sluggish, even though one report speaks of 50mph being attainable, a figure then considered satisfactory for this type of car.

Alderson was assisted in the drawing office by Alan Lea and A A Sykes. The project was carried through with commendable despatch and the first car (Chassis No. 1) was on the road by early 1920. This machine carried a simplified body with a single pane folding windscreen, and no side curtains. It was retained for six months for testing purposes, and was then sold to Robert Ewbank of Pontefract, who had become a director of Lea-Francis. He was also a motor cycle agent in Pontefract and his firm is in existence to this day. A further six cars were constructed during 1920.

C B Wardman, later to become chairman of Lea-Francis, was appointed London agent, although he failed to sell any cars at this stage, taking Chassis No. 3 in September 1920, but returning it unsold nine weeks later. Chassis No. 7, registered DU 40, was retained by the company until the closure in 1936. Latterly fitted with a truck body, it was used as a works hack for many years, and is said to have towed 5000 new chassis to local coachbuilders during the course of its life. There was obviously merit in its robust construction.

Three cars were sold during 1920, and an enthusiastic report was published in *Motor* in October of that year. Curiously no advertizing or press notices appeared whatsoever during 1921, and only three more cars were disposed of. However, very large quantities of raw materials and finished components for serious production were entering the Lower Ford Street stores.

Yet another three cars provided the total sales for 1922 at a price of £395 per car. They were originally listed at £700. The financial position became very serious early in 1922, and an alliance was formed with the Vulcan Motor Engineering Co. of Southport, who were themselves members of a syndicate known as the British Motor Trading Co., under the chairmanship of Sir Thomas Polson. The Board was reconstructed in November 1922 with C B Wardman as chairman, and L T Delaney as managing director. S T Lea (no relation of R H Lea) was appointed sales director, and Marcus Nash became secretary. The previous directors remained with the exception of H J Hampson and Robert Ewbank who both resigned. H E Tatlow from Ruston-Hornsby was brought in as works manager.

Alderson now joined the Triumph Co. and was responsible for the production of that firm's first motor car, a 10hp machine built on conventional lines. This contract was offered to Alderson in 1921, and he commenced work on the project while still at Lower Ford Street and was assisted by Alan Lea and A A Sykes. The Triumph Co. paid Lea-Francis for the work on a contract design basis. Sykes later became chief designer of Triumph, where he remained for many years.

During the years 1919 to 1922, three further distinctly different prototype light cars were designed and built. The first machine was entirely the work of R H Lea, whose object was to achieve as low a centre of gravity as possible. A horizontally opposed air-cooled twin-cylinder engine was purchased from H W Weaver. This successful unit, known as the Coventry Victor Vibrationless Twin, continued to be produced for many years.

The drive from the power plant was by vertical chain to a three-speed Sturmey-Archer gearbox, placed well below the engine centre line, and thus near the ground. The chassis side members were also 'dropped' amidships, while the final drive was by a bevel gear axle. No differential was fitted. This car was taken to Southport for the completion of the coachwork by Vulcan but the design was abandoned, although the little car gave good service, and was used daily by Alan Lea for some 18 months. It was then sold to Alfred Blundell, a Daimler draughtsman, who continued to run it for a number of years.

The next, and final, 2-cylinder car was designed jointly by R H Lea and Alderson, and consisted of a chassis built on conventional lines with quarter-elliptic springs all round (7ft 6in wheelbase). The power unit was a Bradshaw oil and air cooled horizontal twin – of square dimensions, viz: 76mm bore and stroke (690cc), rated at 7·1hp. Cooling was assisted by a large flywheel cast in the form of a fan, which was fitted on the front of the engine while the long induction pipe passed through the top of the crankcase before branching off to each cylinder, thus forming a 'hot spot'. The clutch was unusual, being a metal-to-metal cone running in oil. Curiously the oil capacity, including the gearbox, was said to be a mere six and a half pints. The unit was bolted directly to the gearbox which had four speeds, an unusual feature for so small a car. The Belsize-Bradshaw car utilized a power plant bearing a family resemblance to the Lea-Francis unit, but having only three speeds, and cylinders arranged in 90° V. The drive was taken to the rear axle which consisted of two aluminium casings bolted together vertically on the axle centre line. This basic conception was to remain a Lea-Francis feature until the end of the old company in 1936. It was fitted with a spur gear differential, and while the whole unit was praised in the Press for its robust build, it did, in fact, suffer from transmission weaknesses which proved to be the Achilles' Heel of all early Lea-Francis cars. The axle on this prototype appeared to be of fully floating design. The handbrake utilized a pair of shoes working inside a drum attached to the nose of the bevel pinion. A torque arm, geometrically imperfect, was attached to the nearside casing, and was anchored to a chassis cross member. The foot brake operated on the rear wheels in a conventional manner. The wheels were of disc type carrying 650×65mm tyres.

The dummy radiator shell design was the work of R H Lea, and was of the distinctive and handsome type used as a basis for all the vintage cars excepting the last prototype 18hp of 1932.

Only one Bradshaw chassis was produced, it was exhibited at Olympia in November 1922 and was listed at £190, complete with a neat two-seater body of typical Lea-Francis appearance (judging by an artist's impression). Specification included side curtains and leather upholstery. It appears that this solitary vehicle was never sold and is thought to have passed over to Vulcan, never to be seen again.

The final prototype car built in 1922 was primarily the work of Alderson, and was to be the basic model decided on for production in 1923, and from which all subsequent Lower Ford Street Lea-Francis cars were developed.

The chassis of this car bore several features common to the Bradshaw machine, including the rear axle, but the front springs were semi-elliptic, although the wheelbase remained at 7ft 6in with a track of 3ft 6in.

The engine selected for this car was a Coventry-Simplex 4-cylinder side valve unit of 60×95mm bore and stroke (1074cc) and rated at 8·9hp. The crankshaft ran in two main bearings, and the unusually large sump carried two gallons of oil. The camshaft was located on the nearside, and was gear-driven, together with the magneto, while the dynamo drive utilized an inverted tooth chain. The cylinder head was detachable and the Zenith carburettor was located on the offside, bolted to a long induction pipe which ran across the top of the engine.

This proprietary unit achieved a certain popularity, and eventually became the well-known Coventry Climax. Interestingly the original Coventry Simplex engine design contract was given by H Pelham-Lee to Alexander Craig in 1910, and the first unit was the work of C H Ingall, assisted by Alan Lea, again demonstrating how closely interconnected the motor industry was in Coventry in those early days.

The Simplex engine fitted to the Lea-Francis used a cone clutch, and a Meadows three-speed gearbox was bolted on directly to form a unit construction, the ratios being 4·79, 9 and 14:1. The original front axle designed for this

Mr and Mrs Don Francis in the Alderson car retained at the works for 16 years

car was tubular with the stub axles on top of the axle beam, and fixed rigidly to their king pins, which swivelled in the axle eyes. The steering arms were clamped directly on to the bottom of the king pins. The king pin lug on the stub axle appeared alarmingly frail, and in fact one broke up on the prototype car when at speed (a serious accident was mercifully avoided). Unfortunately for Alderson, who was driving, the passenger happened to be the managing director, R H Lea, and relations thereafter became a little strained.

The first 8·9hp chassis was exhibited at Olympia in November 1922, and was afterwards fitted with a two-seater body having an additional single dickey seat in the rear. The car was listed at £235 with an additional £15 for a self-starter, if required.

The first completed prototype (Chassis No. 5000), was despatched to the London sales office and was sampled by the Press who praised the appearance and spoke of a very comfortable ride for such a small vehicle.

After the Olympia Show, an appraisal of the situation was made. The 12hp car, although immediately available, was attracting very little interest, while the Bradshaw car was clearly regarded as a freak. Many enquiries had been received for the 8·9hp model and some orders had been placed but it was obviously unfit to give to the public in its existing state. To complete a dismal picture, sales of the excellent, but expensive, motor cycle were falling off.

The new directors appealed to G W Watson of the Royal Automobile Club for advice – a new chief engineer was the result.

CHAPTER FIVE

Light Car Development

The appointment of C M Van Eugen as designer to the company and general manager of the motor car division was to mark a turning point in the history of Lea-Francis. Under his guidance the firm was to attain its zenith, and produce considerable numbers of fine sports cars, much sought after by enthusiasts today.

Charles Marie Van Eugen was born in Holland in 1892 and commenced an engineering apprenticeship with Simplex of Amsterdam in 1907. He came to Coventry in July 1913 and quickly found employment on the design staff of the Daimler Co., serving at the Radford works for some years. Towards the end of the First World War, he joined the ABC firm and was responsible for development of the ABC Dragonfly aero engine. The Armistice was declared while the new engine was undergoing bench tests and Van Eugen left to join Briton Cars of Wolverhampton as works manager. He then took a post with the Royal Ruby Cycle Co., and later joined the Clyno concern as designer before moving to the Swift Co.

Van Eugen obtained release from Swifts, then a part of the British Motor Trade Syndicate and thus connected with Lea & Francis (via Vulcan), and entered the Lower Ford Street works on 27 December 1922.

Any lingering Christmas cheer must have been dispelled that day, for he was to discover enormous stocks of castings, machined parts and raw material for the unsaleable 11·9 together with three or four completed 8·9hp cars, all ordered by dealers but still bristling with technical shortcomings.

Van Eugen hastily made some vital improvements, including the design of a completely new front axle, and the small car was prepared for series production with an initial batch of 50. It was given the official designation of 'C'-type.

The first production drawing (chassis frame) is dated 3 January 1923 and the first production car (Chassis No. 4999) was completed on 14 March and despatched to the London sales depot as a demonstrator.

Four original pattern prototype cars were built (Chassis Nos. 4997–5000). The first three were rebuilt as production machines while it appears that No. 5000 was dismantled. Three prototypes were mustered for the Scottish Show in January, together with an 11·9hp. The latter, running true to form, remained unsold.

Deliveries of 'C'-type cars commenced in April. Larger header tanks and modified axle-shafts were fitted after the first 25 cars.

A longer wheelbase chassis (8ft) was soon adopted, although curiously coachwork dimensions remained unchanged. A further batch of 50 cars were sanctioned fitted with larger petrol tanks, modified rear springs and stiffer axle-shafts but a total of 91 'C'-type cars only were produced, the last being Chassis 5088 delivered on 18 August 1923. Four cars were supplied with coupé bodies while the remainder were fitted with the standard two-seater or 'chummy' styles. The majority were built by Robinsons of Foleshill Road although individual cars had bodies of a similar specification by Ward & Co., Timms & Co., Eley & Son, Coventry Supply Garage and Motor Bodies Ltd. Two cars were exported to Malaya, but the remainder stayed at home.

The little car was priced at £235 in two-seater form and £250 as a 'Chummy', while the well-appointed fixed-head coupé commanded £295, electric starters included.

The first appearance of a Lea-Francis car in competition (Chassis No. 5012) coincided with that of G W Wilkin who ran through the London–Land's End Trial held at Easter in 1923 and gained a bronze medal.

Henry Meadows & Co. of Wolverhampton were becoming prominent as engine and gearbox manufacturers at this time, and had recently introduced a light car engine of 1247cc (63×100mm bore and stroke, 9·8hp RAC rating). It was extremely well made, possessing excellent torque and unfailing reliability, although somewhat heavy. This engine was investigated by Lea-Francis in May 1923 and was immediately accepted for installation in the 'C'-type car.

The new engine was a push-rod, vertical overhead valve unit with an integral crankcase and cylinder block of cast iron and a detachable cylinder head in the same material. It became apparent later that this Wolverhampton-built product possessed a very long life between overhauls if one was prepared to tolerate a certain amount of timing-gear rattle, and, as with all splash-fed engines, avoided over-revving for other than short periods.

The new Lea-Francis car, titled 'D'-type, was in production by July 1923. The first car, a Chummy (Chassis No. 5089), was delivered on the 14th of that month, a mere four weeks after the date of the first sealed production drawing. In addition to the change of power unit, the car was fitted with an enlarged petrol tank, wider springs and stiffer rear spring mounting brackets. Further attention was paid to the transmission and the long battle between increased engine power and weight versus the delicate spur differential was now in progress. This basic rear axle design was eventually scrapped in 1927 after Van Eugen positively refused to struggle with it any longer. Incredibly, the directors constantly refused to allow him to embark upon a complete re-design until long after the stocks of castings and materials he inherited had been used up.

A total of 71 'D'-type cars was delivered in 1923, of which the standard two-seater and Chummy types accounted for all except two d/h coupés, three f/h coupés and one coupé-Cabriolet (Chassis No. 5156). Four cars were exhibited at Olympia including two of the coupés and the solitary coupé-Cabriolet. The rather ponderous coachwork of the latter necessitated a special set of heavy-duty road springs. No further orders for this type were forthcoming but the other body styles were well received and a healthy order book produced an air of optimism for the 1924 season. Prices remained similar to the previous 'C'-type, although the Meadows engine was a substantial improvement allowing speeds of up to 50mph. The lighter body styles made for a total weight of a mere 11½cwt; this figure, allied with the 20bhp engine, made for a lively performance when compared with the majority of its competitors. Fuel consumption averaged 34mpg.

One car (Chassis No. 5131), manufactured in October 1923, is still in existence in New Zealand and is considered the oldest Lea-Francis car in existence, while J H Woodhouse of Nottingham still campaigns Chassis No. 5150 in various events.

Great efforts had been made during 1923 to sell more of the Alderson-type larger cars in order to liquidate some of the stocks of parts and materials, and, in fact, a total of 17 cars were disposed of during the year, two of which were fitted with the enlarged 13·9hp engine. Sixteen vehicles were fitted with the Avon bodies, while one example was despatched to Southport for the fitting of Vulcan-built four-seater coachwork.

The year 1924 saw an acceleration of activity; the 'D'-type was selling well, and its price of £250 was equal to that commanded by the Humber 8/18, one of its principal competitors. The Lea-Francis certainly scored with its distinctive appearance and superior performance, which was substantiated by a growing list of successes gained in competition work.

C B Wardman and family at Southport in an early 'D'-type

'D'-type fixed-head coupé

The total number of 'D'-type cars delivered in 1924 was 243, the last car (Chassis No. 5508) leaving on 22 December. The bulk of production consisted of two-seater and Chummy types, although full four-seater tourers became available towards the end.

Fourteen d/h and eight f/h coupés were delivered. One chassis (No. 5388) was supplied to Scotland Yard and fitted with a van body of quaint appearance, while R S Crump, chief designer to Henry Meadows, purchased a 'Chummy' (Chassis No. 5307).

Mechanical improvements carried out during the year consisted of enlarged petrol tanks and radiators, while rear-spring anchorages and axle casings were again stiffened. Exhaust systems were enlarged in diameter after 200 cars, resulting in a small saving of power.

Considerable success attended these early cars in the field of reliability trials including a first-class award in the Newcastle and District MCC event of December 1923. During the London–Exeter held on Boxing Day, C N Green (on what appeared to be a 'C'-type with 'D'-type engine) gained a gold medal despite ignition bothers. He achieved another gold in the same car in the London–Edinburgh at Whitsuntide.

The Colmore Cup Trial, held in March, was, however, a Lea-Francis débâcle. Works manager H E Tatlow entered the sports 'D'-type mentioned later, and was supported by C N Green and G T Francis on standard models. Tatlow's car broke its torque arm anchorage and this dug into the road and almost tore the rear axle out of the car. Green stripped his differential pinions while Francis rammed a bank and was forced to retire. All these disasters took place at the bottom of Abberley Hill, close to Shelsley Walsh. Furious work commenced at Lower Ford Street on the following Monday morning involving further stiffenings and modifications to the rear axle generally. All these changes were immediately applied to production cars.

The Easter London–Land's End run also saw failure by Wilkin and Tatlow, although Green gained a silver medal.

The adverse comment resulting from failures in competition work was a serious matter and Lea-Francis decided to prepare a new trials car with great care for the forthcoming RAC Small Car Trials to be held in May. A great deal of publicity surrounded this event which was to be of six days' duration – mainly spent storming Welsh hills with a final day of performance testing at Brooklands.

Tatlow's new 'D'-type trials car (Chassis No. 5314), fitted with an enlarged 'E'-type radiator, soon to be adopted as standard, was skilfully driven and performed in an outstanding manner throughout the trial. In company with Palladium and Gwynne 8 cars the Lea-Francis achieved a long lead over all other competitors. The 'Leaf' was the fastest car in seven out of nine hill climbs, fairly rushing up Bwlch-Y-Groes, and changing up immediately after surmounting the steepest section of 1 in 4·5. Tatlow was third in the acceleration tests and tied for second place in the speed test with a Gwynne 8 recording 55·55mph. The Palladium beat them both with a speed of 59·21mph.

The 'D'-type averaged 35·4mpg of Pratts 50/50 mixture and used five pints of Castrol oil during the trials. It was awarded a silver medal and also a special gold medal by the RAC for the most meritorious performance. It is of interest, in view of the passage of 50 years since this event was held, to record that the lively Gwynne 8 averaged 46mpg, despite very hard driving and a low compression ratio – has progress been so great!

Sales of Lea-Francis cars certainly received a boost after the Small Car Trials which was followed with gold medals won by Green in the London–Edinburgh and Coventry–Torquay events, while Tatlow enjoyed a troublefree run from Land's End to John O'Groats to gain a silver cup. Several other successes followed in minor events with 'D'-type cars before the end of 1924. It is sad to recall that Tatlow's car, nicknamed 'Bwlch-Y-Groes Wizard' – a legend it bore upon its bonnet – was eventually destroyed in a fire at the Avon body works while undergoing some coachwork modifications.

However, the 'D'-type car, although finding a steady market, was regarded as a rather austere machine, and it was decided to develop a more sophisticated model utilizing the same engine. Work began on the 'E'-type in the summer of 1923, and it proved to be a larger and more comfortable vehicle. The principal mechanical change concerned the gearbox, which was to be a new four-speed type, designed by Van Eugen, and built entirely at Lower Ford Street. This unit was tackled first, and the initial production drawing is dated 7 August 1923. The new gearbox was an immensely strong and sizeable affair bolted directly on to the engine. The aluminium casing was circular, while all the gears and shafts could be withdrawn from the rear. This unit, with minor changes, and with different ratios to suit the type of car to which it was fitted, remained in production until the introduction of the 'Duo'-type for the 1931 season. It was also taken up by the Vulcan Co. for use in their private cars.

Gear changing was easy, and it was pleasant to handle, while the delightful 'growls' on the indirect ratios are much enjoyed by vintage enthusiasts today. Curiously the contemporary

Press described it as quiet in all gears – possibly the road test cars were hand-picked.

A delightful story, probably apocryphal, concerns the testing of these gearboxes. It was said that the cars were driven down the Binley road, parallel with a tramcar. If the tram could be heard above the gearbox, the car was passed, but if the gears obliterated the noise of the tram, it was rejected.

The first gearbox was mounted in a special 'D'-type sports model (Chassis No. 5161). This particular machine, the very first Lea-Francis sports car ever built, was fitted with a polished-aluminium body by Robinsons. It had long flowing wings, a V windscreen and Dunlop bolt-on wire wheels. The car looked very smart and rakish, possibly marred a little by the bullet-shaped tail. This particular car was fitted with an axle ratio of $4\cdot3:1$ and $28 \times 3\frac{1}{2}$ tyres, while the indirect gear ratios used in this case were $17\cdot4$, $10\cdot21$ and $6\cdot73:1$. Shock absorbers were fitted, the steering column was raked, and instrumentation included a rev-counter.

The little car was said to be capable of over 60mph, and although the engine appeared standard, it was in fact hand-picked for a higher output than normal. The sports 'D'-type was intended for production, but only the one car was actually built.

'E'-type car development continued during the first half of 1924. The rear axle was rebuilt with a stiffer casing which obviated the need for tie rods. The axle-to-spring anchorage now consisted of very large bronze trunnion bearings which swivelled on the axle casing. This re-design allowed the axle to rise and fall without loading the springs with a twisting motion. The previous pattern caused the cars to rise up at the rear when moving off from rest. The radius arm, differential gears, axleshafts and brakes were all enlarged and improved.

The new car possessed a wheelbase of 8ft 9in with a 3ft 8in track, and the chassis now had an additional cross member. The radiator was widened by 2in and many other details were improved or scaled up while low-pressure tyres were now standardized, although sceptical buyers continued to specify the outdated high-pressure type.

Full four-seater coachwork was now available, built by Avon Bodies, although the two-seaters continued to be manufactured by Robinsons, but since the two coachbuilders employed similar hardware and fittings both bodies appeared to come from the same house. Windscreens were now raked, and weather equipment was much improved. Certainly the new cars were among the smartest in their class, and had a road performance to match.

Development of the 'E'-type proceeded at a more leisurely pace than with previous models, and the intention was that it should be ready for the 1925 season. In fact the first car (Chassis No. 5515) was delivered to the sales department on 22 August 1924.

Five cars were exhibited at Olympia in October, including two saloons, one by Avon and the other, titled De Luxe, bodied by Vulcan. Prices ranged from £262-10s to £350. The new cars were acclaimed by press and public alike while their modern appearance called forth special comment although the saloons appeared perpendicular in the extreme. The performance of these very comfortably equipped closed models must have suffered by reason of weight and wind resistance.

Production now leapt forward, aided by the total closure of the motor cycle business which had been running down for 12 months. Ninety-three 'E'-type cars were delivered before the end of the year, all except three being standard two- or four-seater tourers. The odd cars were Chassis Nos. 5553 and 5630, which were the first 'Leafs' to be fitted with Cross & Ellis coachwork, both being yet more ponderous saloon versions. The third car was a specially prepared chassis and engine fitted with a Robinson sports body intended for competition work (Chassis No. 5582).

A three-speed version of the 'E'-type was offered, known as the 'F'-type, all fitted with standard two- or four-seater touring coach-

Norman Norris and Bert Tatlow in the trials 'D'-type Chassis 5314

39

work and priced lower than the four-speed cars by £12-10s. Thirty-three such cars were built during the last three months of 1924.

Work commenced on two further variations of the 'E'-type before the end of the year, one utilized the enlarged 69mm bore 4EC engine, designated type 'I', while the other, type 'H' used the 4ED 'sports' engine which was shortly to be introduced by the Meadows concern and was destined to be their most famous product. While bearing a strong family resemblance to the 4EB and 4EC units, the new model was given a separate aluminium crankcase and a full pressure-fed three-bearing crankshaft. Ports were enlarged, and nos. two and three exhaust ports were 'Siamesed' whereas the 4EB and 4EC engines had separate exhaust ports for each cylinder. The new engine was said to deliver 38bhp in standard form. This figure was a little optimistic, however, and the best of a batch of engines subjected to a bench test at Lower Ford Street gave 36bhp at 4100rpm. Despite these modest figures, the 4ED would propel the early lightweight 12/40 cars at close on 70mph with brisk acceleration and outstanding hill climbing powers.

The touring 4EC unit delivered approximately 28bhp at 2900rpm. Once again, the cars so powered gave a good road performance, albeit with a modest maximum speed, due to the excellent low speed torque available.

The 12hp models were given 12 volt electrics and Solex carburettors while the 12/40 'H'-type boasted a special exhaust system, stiffened springs, heavy-duty propeller shaft and Dunlop bolt-on wire wheels. The first drawing of these larger engined cars is dated 28 July 1924 and one 'H'-type (Chassis No. 5700) was completed in December and fitted with an extremely attractive three-door sports four-seater body by Cross & Ellis. Finished in polished aluminium, this car was retained as a factory development and competition machine for some time. Tatlow took this car through the Boxing Day London–Exeter Trial for its first run out. It performed without a hitch to gain a gold medal, as did the three other 10hp models entered, driven by G W Wilkin, a Lea-Francis salesman, H Woollen and R T Horton, the latter perhaps better known for his racing exploits with MG cars in the thirties.

The increase of activity at Lower Ford Street was beginning to reflect in the financial affairs of the company and although the year ending 31 July 1924 showed a trading loss of £5123, this was a small figure compared with the total deficit of £58,161 which had accumulated in the period between the end of the war and July 1923. It is staggering to find, in view of today's alarming costs of development and tooling, that the total expenditure on jigs and patterns for the 'E'-type chassis came to a mere £359.

The directorate was reduced at this time by the resignation of G I Francis who had taken very little part for some years, being largely concerned with the Swedish Skefco Bearing Co. A change also took place in the representation from Southport. A S Fitch retired, and his place was taken by Thomas Rimmer, the Vulcan works manager.

George Andrews joined Lea-Francis during the year in order to look after spares and service, a position he held, with minor interruptions, until the demise of the firm in 1962. He then looked after Lea-Francis matters at A B Price Ltd until his death in October 1968. GTA, as he was known at the works, was president of the Lea-Francis Owners' Club for many years and his help and advice will be remembered with gratitude by 'Leaf' enthusiasts for many years to come.

H E Tatlow had joined Lea-Francis in 1923. He was previously responsible for private car production at Ruston-Hornsby of Lincoln, and was engaged by C B Wardman as works manager, and eventually transferred to London sales in 1929. Always keen on competition work, he managed the racing teams for several seasons.

The year 1925 saw the firm gaining further momentum with deliveries of 176 10hp 'E'- and 197 12hp 'I'-types. Standard bodies predominated with Cross & Ellis gradually superseding Robinson for the two-seater style. Four saloon, three d/h and two f/h coupé bodies were fitted to the 'E'-type chassis, and a few attractive pointed-tail sports versions were built. One car was fitted with a Clayton front-wheel braked axle. Twenty-eight saloons produced by Vulcan and Avon were used on the higher-powered 'I'-type, together with five d/h, and one f/h coupé. Once again, several sports bodies were built, being low-waisted, two- and four-seaters finished in polished aluminium.

Eighty-six three-speed 'F'-type cars were also sold, all standard tourers, but only four 'H'-type 12/40 sports-cars were assembled, and unfortunately none appear to have survived. One example (Chassis No. 5879) was sold to Avon Bodies to be fitted with special coachwork for use by one of their directors.

Lea-Francis felt that there was a market for a cheaper car, and accordingly produced a short-chassis version of the 'F'-type shorn of all accessories, and fitted with a simple two-seater tourer body of somewhat shapeless appearance. This car was designated type 'G' and retailed at £210, an undoubted bargain, but the profit margin for the manufacturer was somewhat slender. Fifty-five of these vehicles were completed during 1925. The first car (Chassis No. 6650) was fitted with a body built

The first 12/40 type 'H'. Chassis No. 5700

by the Bent Wood Timber Co. Robinson produced the next 47, their last body for Lea & Francis being delivered in September (Chassis No. 6197). Cross & Ellis later took over the manufacture of this type.

One special 'G'-type (Chassis No. 6184) was completed with a Clayton front-wheel brake axle, wire wheels and a 1½-litre Anzani engine, for evaluation of this power unit, which was making a good impression in AC and Frazer-Nash cars. The sports coachwork was by Messrs Cross & Ellis.

Further technical developments were undertaken in 1925, concerned mostly with front-wheel brakes. Van Eugen designed an extremely neat and efficient rod-operated system comprising 12in diameter cast-aluminium shoes, working in well-finned drums, and operated via pushrods passing through the kingpin centres. The brakes were thus unaffected by steering lock, and were also readily accessible for adjustment purposes, fly nuts being provided at the front end of the main fore and aft operating rods. The first drawing is dated 20 January 1925, and the initial set was fitted to Tatlow's trials car (Chassis No. 5700) for development testing.

The company now returned to profitability, and the 13-month period up to 31 August 1925 resulted in a trading surplus of £4154. In addition, considerable investment in new machine tools had been undertaken, and work began on a new shop intended for chassis assembly, as conditions had become distinctly cramped. The ornate wrought-iron gates (still standing) were also erected during this year, to replace the previous dilapidated corrugated-iron structure.

An improved sales force was formed with travelling representatives covering all parts of the country and taking part in various competitions in their demonstration cars. Norman Norris joined the firm in April as full-time competition driver. An extremely skilful and popular figure, he achieved success in practically every event he entered.

The reliability trial successes of the previous season had attracted the interest of sporting motorists, and regular convoys of 'Leafs' were to be seen in the major events of 1925. The Colmore Cup Trial was the first event of note on the calendar and four cars were entered. C E Smith with a new polished-aluminium sports four-seater 12/22 (Chassis No. 5810) failed to finish although placed third in the acceleration test. Tatlow's 12/40 was easily the fastest in this part, while second spot was taken by Lea-Francis agent Harold Goodwin who used a sports model Bean 14, another car for which he held a franchise. The other Lea-Francis competitors in this event were R T Horton, who proved fast in all tests, and C E Turner.

The Victory Cup Trial held in March saw successes by Horton and Smith but Tatlow retired with ignition trouble. The following weekend was the occasion of the Economy Cup Trial held by the Midland CC. The Leafs of Tatlow, Smith and Dallason carried off the team prize in addition to individual bronze, silver and first-class awards. Tatlow's car was fifth fastest up Sudeley Hill, beaten only by super sports machines in the form of Brescia, Bugatti, Special Sports Morgan, 30/98 Vauxhall and Riley Redwing cars.

The London–Land's End event was entered by no less than 14 productions from Lower Ford Street. Twelve cars finished, netting six

41

ABOVE AND OPPOSITE
Products of receivership. Ace of Spades drophead coupé by Carbodies, Chassis 20040; Ace of Spades close-coupled coupé by Cross & Ellis, Chassis 20039

gold and six silver medals. The Dunlop Trophy Trial held in April was to see the first appearance of Norman Norris who gave a good account of himself and was third in the acceleration test using the 'Bwlch-Y-Groes Wizard' 'D'-type car. His team mate, H Taylor, on a similar car, was however the slowest entrant on this occasion. T B Tennant gained a first-class award in a Scottish Two-Day Event and the Surbiton MC Grand Cup Trial with an entry of four Lea-Francis cars resulted in silver medals for Tatlow and C E Smith while the old 'D'-type car of Norris carried off the Sopwith Cup.

Also in this year, the Junior Car Club organized a high-speed trial for lights cars at Brooklands consisting of 34 laps of a special course devised inside the famous circuit. L D Marr and Norris entered the event; the former retired with engine trouble on the eighth lap but Norris gained a gold medal. This was in spite of an incident caused by a Frazer-Nash which ran across his bows with a broken steering gear just as Norris was passing. Fortunately this resulted only in a crumpled wing.

Four cars driven by H Stevens, Tatlow, Norris and Marr, entered the London–Holy-head run, and all gained silver cups. The latter three, being Lea-Francis personnel, carried off the Trade Team Prize. The following weekend saw Norris, Tatlow and Smith competing in the Vesey Cup Trial held by the Sutton Coldfield Club; all gained first-class awards and Tatlow in addition took the Carless Cup.

The traditional MCC London–Edinburgh event of Whitsun, held amidst violent thunder storms, attracted a very large entry including 11 Lea-Francis cars representing most models. Norris still used the old Bwlch-Y-Groes car; the director L T Delaney, accompanied by his daughter, competed in a 12/22 saloon; Tatlow used the prototype 12/40 (fitted with front wheel brakes); C N Green was in his veteran 1923 car; A A Mauleverer, a prominent Lea-Francis agent, drove a 12/22, and several other works personalities took part.

The Coventry cars were accompanied by photographer W J Brunell who drove a distant cousin in the form of a new model 14hp Vulcan saloon. This car was installed with a long-stroke (69 × 120) Meadows engine similar to the 4ED in general design, since Vulcan had decided to build a car with a Meadows engine after its good showing in the Lea-Francis.

Every Lea-Francis and the Vulcan entered in the Edinburgh gained a gold medal and a 10hp car which was used as an official vehicle also gave a good account of itself. It was now apparent that light cars in general had achieved such a state of overall excellence and reliability that these popular and enjoyable long distance events were no longer fully extending the capabilities of cars and their effect on the buying public was beginning to wane.

Wilkins and Saltmarsh had a trouble-free run in the MCC 875-mile marathon from Land's End to John O' Groats, while Norris and Tatlow obtained awards in a Northern Two-Day Trial. The Scottish Six-Day Trial was supported by the factory and further successes were achieved; the Surbiton MC London–Barnstable event saw silver cups going to all six Lea-Francis cars which competed. A host of further trials successes were obtained during 1925; the final event of the season was the London–Exeter Boxing Day run resulting in two gold and five silver medals out of eight cars entered. Norman Norris in the old 'D'-type car and Bert Tatlow in the prototype 12/40 were consistently the most successful throughout, although they were well supported by members of the sales staff and agents, running, in the main, standard 12/22 cars.

The JCC staged a further high-speed trial for production cars at Brooklands in October and 1½-litre cars were required to cover 37 laps of the course (102 miles) inside the 2½ hours. Bert Tatlow's 12/40 (Chassis No. 5700) was easily the fastest car competing, lapping at 62–3mph to finish in 98 minutes and creating a fine impression. He was accompanied by A A Mauleverer, Norman Norris and J P Dingle, who all gained gold medals, but H Steven's car dropped out with magneto trouble.

New models for the 1926 season were ready in good time for the Olympia Show held in the previous October. The main improvement concerned front-wheel brakes which were now standard on all cars except the low-priced 'G'-type which remained unchanged.

Modifications applied to all models concerned a further re-design of the rear spring frame anchorage and a stiffer rear cross member. New type letters were allocated as follows: type 'K' – De Luxe 10hp; type 'J' – Standard 12hp car (also styled for an unexplained reason – 12/22); type 'M' – 12/22 chassis with 12/40 engine; and type 'L' which was reserved for the Super Sports 12/40 chassis with wire wheels, long aluminium wings, celluloid dashboard with rev counter and 'ships funnels' for scuttle ventilation.

One hundred and thirty-three 'J'-type cars were delivered before the end of 1925, the first car being completed in May. Open-touring bodies were still easily the most popular forms of coachwork although seven Vulcan and one Avon saloon types, together with a few coupé styles were sold. One hundred and eleven 'K'-type 10hp cars were despatched before 31 December, all tourers excepting two chassis sold to Wilson Motors of London who built on striking flared wing, boat-decked sports bodies under the trade name of Burghley. Only four 'L'-type sports cars including the pre-production car (Chassis No1 6400) and one 'M' were built in 1925. The 'M'-type (Chassis No. 6649), sold to Temple Press, proprietors of *Motor*, was the first Lea-Francis to be fitted with the twin carburettor 52bhp 'Brooklands' version of the 12/40 engine.

All 4ED engines were now coming through with duralumin con-rods whereas the first units delivered were fitted with a steel rod machined all over, as was the crankshaft, so it is possible that these first carefully balanced and assembled engines may well have given around 40bhp.

The production of Vulcan private cars had slackened considerably – basically the products were stodgy and unappealing. In 1925, only 4-cylinder cars were being built, a side valve 12hp car using a Lea-Francis four-speed gearbox in an otherwise typical Vulcan worm-drive chassis, slung on semi-elliptic springs with rod-operated Rubery front-wheel brakes, artillery wheels and heavy but well-built factory-produced coachwork. This pedestrian machine was hard put to achieve 45mph and an attempt to offer an alternative car with more ginger was made with the Meadows-engined 14hp version previously mentioned. Curiously, this model appears to have been fitted with a gearbox from another maker. Sales of this car, however, did not develop as anticipated and the Southport directors decided to re-enter the medium-sized 6-cylinder market currently enjoying a vogue with offerings by a great number of manufacturers including, *inter alia*, such unlikely challengers as Calcott and Calthorpe.

The outstanding success of the Lea-Francis marque prompted the Lancashire concern to indulge in an early form of the questionable habit of 'badge engineering' and a new car built on typical Vulcan lines with a 6-cylinder engine by Meadows was constructed and advertized as a Lea-Francis Six.

The first and possibly the only example was exhibited at the Scottish Show in November. It certainly appeared to be a smart machine with a sporting five-seater tourer body, wind-up windows in the front doors and a radiator, placed well forward, of Lea-Francis lines but embodying two vertical struts in the centre. It is strange to note that the staff at Lower Ford Street knew nothing whatever of the production of the first 6-cylinder car which was to bear their name until it was presented as a 'fait accompli'.

The continuing increase of orders for Lea-Francis cars was extremely gratifying for the staff at Coventry but the demand for engines, now reaching 80 to 90 per month, was stretching the resources of Henry Meadows to the limit. A decision was made, therefore, to offer an alternative car with the well-tried London-built Anzani engine, primarily as an insurance policy.

This car was designated type 'N' and the initial drawing was dated 11 November 1925 while the first car was completed in March 1926. The Anzani engine appeared to have been hastily redesigned to follow Meadows practice in certain respects and although it possessed side valves and the pressure-fed three-bearing crankshaft of their standard unit, the magneto was placed at right angles to the crank line on the offside front of the crankcase.

The fitting of carburettor, exhaust manifold, dynamo and starter also followed the pattern of the standard Lea-Francis models thus making for few alterations to the basic design. Some 40bhp was developed and the road performance of the Anzani cars was not below the standard 12/40 model. The steering box support was located on the chassis frame on this car and not on a crankcase bearer arm as on the models with the Wolverhampton power plant. The radiator was, curiously $1\frac{1}{4}$in narrower than standard. In all other respects, the chassis was a standard 'J'-type.

In the event Meadows managed to cope with the demand and only 53 'N'-type cars were built during 1926 and nine of these were fitted with Meadows engines at the last moment. The lack of orders was a serious matter for the Anzani firm, who had entertained high hopes of developing a large business with Lea-Francis.

The standard production cars remained unchanged throughout 1926 with few exceptions. A modified radiator with attachment lugs sandwiched between the frame and the neat forged headlamp stalks was adopted. The height of the cooling element was also increased by 1in to $22\frac{3}{4}$in (drawing date 24 August 1926). Differential pins were stiffened yet again in March 1926 and an improved steering box was introduced at the same time.

The 'L'-type sports-car was now fitted with two port, 6 to 1, compression 'Brooklands' engines in most cases, together with Hartford shock absorbers all round and Dewandre Servo assistance for the brakes. In this form, the car was known as the 12/50 and was priced at £375 when first listed. Weight was now 19½cwt and Rudge knock-off wheels laced on the outer rim only were utilized. Standard tyre size was 4.50×19, although some buyers persisted in specifying the old high-pressure 710×90 size.

The works' 12/50 demonstration car, a converted 'N'-type (Chassis No. 11007) was tested in the late summer of 1926 and this handsome car was much admired. It was found capable of exceeding 70mph with close on 60 available in third gear, while the outstandingly good and even brakes were able to stop the machine in 32ft from 30mph with light pedal pressure. The well-equipped three-door, four-seater Cross & Ellis body was praised for its quality, comfort and spaciousness.

Good production figures were attained during 1926 with 632 'J', 163 'K', 87 'M', 86 'L' and 60 'F'-types passing through the factory gate.

Financial results for the year ending 31 August 1926 revealed a profit of £11,367 and the board of directors was enlarged during the year with the appointment of J E Hindle, a Vulcan director, and W Watson, a Rochdale grocer, who had both purchased blocks of shares.

Commencing in February 1926, the system of allocating chassis numbers was rationalized. Previously cars were numbered consecutively according to the date of sanction for the vehicle's initial assembly and irrespective of type of car. The new system gave a different first number for each basic type viz:

Type 'G'	Continuing in the 6000 series
Type 'J'	7000 up
Type 'K'	8000 up
Type 'L'	9000 up
Type 'M'	10000 up
Type 'N'	11000 up

Lea-Francis cars built in the Vulcan works did not follow any set pattern, Kirkstone cars commencing with Chassis No. 800 and the later 6-cylinder 14/40 model commencing with No. 1.

All the Meadows-engined cars were contined for the 1927 season without change although a Gordon England square-rigged but lightweight-fabric saloon was added to the range of 12/22 body styles. Prices remained broadly similar to the previous season.

The Vulcan concern was active during 1926 in the development of two new models, both of which, unfortunately, were to bear the Lea-Francis trademark.

The first car which was ready for production in March consisted of a standard 12hp Vulcan, into which was inserted another version of the 1½-litre Anzani power plant. Once again the right-angle drive magneto position was used but the induction arrangements were novel in that two Zenith carburettors fed into a common water-heated central induction pipe. The second carburettor came into use only at higher revolutions. Little was achieved by this design for power output was a mere 25bhp at 2000rpm.

A standard Lea-Francis gearbox was utilized and the brakes were assisted by the now popular Dewandre Servo. A typical Vulcan worm-drive rear axle possessed the depressing ratio of $5.2:1$. This car was built entirely at Southport and was given the name Kirkstone. It was soon dubbed 'Kerbstone' by the scornful folk at Lower Ford Street who regarded the sluggish machine, quite rightly, as inferior to their own products.

A total of 71 of these were built during 1926, 12 of which were fitted with standard 4ED Meadows engines. The majority of the bodies were four/five-seater tourers by Vulcan who also offered a strange conversion known as a Saloon-Tourer, a full saloon top secured to the waistline by dowells. This could be removed and left in the garage for periods of fine weather – what we should today term a detachable hard-top. Three such cars were built. Seven chassis were despatched to Coventry for the fitting of two-seater tourer bodies and one solitary coupé by Cross & Ellis. Prices ranged from £340 for the two-seaters to £425 for the saloons.

The second Vulcan project was more exciting and concerned a small-capacity 6-cylinder car of advanced specification. In February 1926, Messrs Lord-Six Motors of West Kensington offered a 1½-litre 6-cylinder engine with twin overhead camshafts for sale to manufacturers and it attracted the attention of C B Wardman who immediately bought the design outright. The engine was the work of A O Lord, who was previously associated with the Lloyd-Lord two-stroke car. He now transferred to Vulcan as passenger car designer to the company and continued development of the 6-cylinder engine in enlarged 60×100mm (1696cc) form.

The unit suffered from a basic lack of crank-case rigidity and also possessed some serious shortcomings in the lubrication system. A detachable cast-iron cylinder head with 90° valve layout and hemispherical combustion chambers was incorporated. The valves were operated from the camshafts through the medium of fingers pivoted on brackets which were bolted to the head casting. Valve clearance was adjusted by means of shims fitted inside the valve caps, a system successful on modern Jaguar engines but quite futile in the Lord design due to the minute size of the components concerned. The cylinder block, also of cast iron, was detachable being bolted to the aluminium crankcase along a flange placed at the base of the water jackets, the cylinder barrels extending deeply into the crankcase.

Connecting rods of duralumin with unduly slender big end bolts transferred power to a fully machined, circular webbed crankshaft which was said to run in four main bearings. However, only three bearings were effective for two were placed close together at the rear of the engine, separated only by the timing sprocket. A long duplex chain drove both camshafts and the oil pump which was placed high up on the rear of the timing case, and thus a long distance from the oil sump to which it was connected by external pipes. A further chain, but driven from the front of the crankshaft, drove the dynamo and magneto which were in tandem. Thermosyphon cooling was considered sufficient. Twin Solex carburettors were fitted originally and the induction pipe was water-heated. Power output was in the neighbourhood of 45bhp at 3750rpm, a figure which would have been attainable with a straightforward pushrod layout, and so the complicated and expensive design, resembling a racing-car engine in appearance, was futile. Furthermore, tuning efforts could not be undertaken with safety due to the inherent weaknesses previously mentioned.

The drive was taken via a single-plate clutch which appeared to be of Meadows manufacture to a gearbox designed by Lea-Francis which closely followed their standard practice. The chassis was of good design and owed little to previous Vulcan practice. Long semi-elliptic springs were fitted at front and rear and the final drive was by a conventional bevel gear type fitted in a Banjo casing. Axleshafts were semi-floating. The saloons were fitted with a 5:1 crown wheel and pinion whereas the lighter cars used 4·7:1 gears.

The brakes closely followed Lea-Francis practice but were of even more generous proportions with drums 14in in diameter. The handbrake operated an additional pair of shoes inside the rear drums. Tyre size was 28 × 4·95in and Rudge knock-off wheels were standardized. British market cars possessed a track measuring 4ft 4in but Colonial versions were widened to 4ft 8in. The wheelbase was 9ft 9in. The car was marketed as a 14/40 and the official factory designation was type LFS.

Two cars were completed late in 1926, a smart five-seater tourer, which was exhibited at Olympia priced competitively at £395, and a fully equipped de luxe saloon with Servo brakes, which was used as a demonstrator and was, at

The first 14/40 on test at the top of Kirkstone Pass

46

£550, easily the most expensive Lea-Francis car yet marketed. The coachwork was of outstanding quality and individualistic in appearance with a four-panel V screen, opening light in the roof and luxurious fittings within.

The chassis and bodies were built entirely at Southport and the Vulcan company offered a similar car under their own brand name. They also offered a lightweight version consisting of the 6-cylinder engine inserted in the worm-drive 12hp chassis and fitted with a Gordon England fabric saloon body. Very few of the latter model were produced.

Late in 1926, the motoring press carried a description of a new easy changing gearbox which was being developed by Lea & Francis and this was in fact another Vulcan project developed under licence from Humphrey-Sandberg. The design consisted of a constant-mesh arrangement in which the gears were held in the drive position by a series of clutches preselected by a short lever on the steering column and engaged by the normal clutch pedal. The clutches consisted of cones with rollers interposed between. After considerable experimentation, the project was abandoned. The rollers inevitably developed a series of flats, resulting in an appalling roughness. The problem was identical to that encountered with the Hayes transmission adopted by the Austin company a decade later, also quickly discontinued. The setting up and adjustment of the Humphrey-Sandberg gearbox was never satisfactory and the original demonstrator which was despatched to Olympia required readjustment after every single demonstration run.

The competition aspect of Lea-Francis underwent a complete change during 1926 with the decision to undertake a serious racing programme. The Society of Motor Manufacturers and Traders had, for some time, been voicing discontent about the way in which Reliability Trials had been exerting undue influence upon the car-buying public. The matter came to a crux in April 1926 when the SMM&T imposed a ban on manufacturers and agents from entering such events. A racing programme was, therefore, the only effective alternative left for makers anxious to seek publicity for their high-performance productions. Lea-Francis were soon to find out that by racing their sports cars, many valuable lessons were learnt in a very short space of time, and a host of improvements could then be built into all models. In short, they amply proved the well-worn adage that 'racing improves the breed'. The story will be traced in the next chapter.

The works continued to support Trials until the imposition of the ban, with Tatlow still driving the prototype 12/40. He gained a gold medal in the Colmore Cup Trial held in February and was backed up by Norman Norris and Frank Hallam, both of whom secured awards. Tatlow's car was fitted with Servo assistance for the brakes on this occasion. The success of this innovation led to the Dewandre Servo Motor being offered as optional equipment on the faster models shortly afterwards.

J P Dingle secured a gold medal in the Essex MC One-Day Trial while the Coventry and Warwickshire MC Manville Trophy Trial resulted in Norris gaining a gold and Tatlow both a gold medal and silver cup, the two 'Leafs' being the fastest cars in the acceleration test. This inveterate pair followed up this victory by securing the only gold medals awarded in both the Birmingham MCC Victory Trial and the Redditch MC and LCC Annual Spring Trial held on consecutive weekends.

The MCC London–Land's End Easter event resulted in three gold and two silver medals out of seven Lea-Francis entries. This was the last event supported by the works. Norris and Delaney claimed two of the golds, and Southport director, A S Fitch, entered a Vulcan 14 and achieved a silver medal.

Private owners, particularly J P Dingle, H S Stevens and G P Stevens, continued to compete throughout the year, and Lea-Francis cars gained a further seven gold, two silver and one bronze medals together with nine silver cups in major events before the end of 1926.

The year 1927 was indeed to see the pinnacle of success for the firm with the best financial results ever achieved, together with the largest number of cars built by the old company of Lea & Francis in any one year.

The Lower Ford Street works were humming with activity and an air of optimism was abroad. The departments concerned with service, development and competition were expanded and all available space was used to the full. No doubt the directors were giving thought to the acquisition of additional premises in the near future. Yet, sadly, no further extensions were going to be required, for decline was soon to follow in an almost identical reverse to the years of expansion.

The 1927 cars were all given new front wings neatly curved to meet the running boards, resulting in a much-improved appearance. A new dashboard fitted with quality instruments by Jaeger followed shortly afterwards (Cooper-Stewert speedometers had been used previously). The CAV headlamps were superseded by Lucas equipment at the same time, although they were retained for all of the 'Hyper' cars. The final mechanical improvement applied to the 1927 cars again concerned rear axles; axle-shafts were increased in diameter at the differential end for the final sanction.

Olympia, October 1926

While the majority of cars were still fitted with two-seater (Cross & Ellis) or four-seater (Avon) open-tourer bodies, the trend towards closed coachwork continued and a variety of styles by several makers were offered.

Fabric saloon bodies built on the 'Weymann' principle by high-grade coachbuilders were beginning to enjoy their short-lived vogue; certainly the smart appearance and silence of this form of construction had much to commend it. The type suffered, unfortunately, from cheap imitations fitted on popular chassis by the majority of manufacturers. Inferior materials were often used and nothing looked untidier than a fabric body that was coming apart at the seams revealing the cotton wool with which they were padded. This factor, coupled with the original laminated safety glass, also new on the market at this time, which soon starred and turned yellow, resulted in a sorry sight. These bodies soon came to be known in the trade as 'Rag Saloons'.

In addition to the Gordon England fabric saloon the firm of Cross & Ellis built a Weymann-type fabric four light saloon – complete with the usual false pram irons on the rear quarters – especially for Lea-Francis which was styled 'Leafabric'. Six 'J'-type cars were so fitted in 1927, together with 60 coupés of various types by the same firm.

The Avon concern also constructed a lightweight four light saloon which was of composite type, employing steel panelling below the waistline and fabric above, named the 'Warwick'. Thirteen were fitted to 'J' models with a solitary example being mounted on the 10hp 'K' chassis. Avon also built eight coachbuilt saloons for the 'J'-type during 1927, while the Vulcan concern was responsible for 49 saloons on the best-selling 'J' range, together with some 30 four-seater tourers which were very similar to the Cross & Ellis sports type in appearance. Vulcan disposed of these cars through their own depots of which there were several in the north of England and Glasgow.

A smart 'Duck's Back' two-seater body with the spare wheel slung underneath the tail and V windscreen was introduced for the 10hp 'K'-type. This model was advertized, unimaginatively, as a 'Semi-Sports'. It was built by Avon but only six were sold.

The total number of standard range cars delivered during the year was: 461 'J'; 86 'K'; 79 'L'; 134 'M' and a mere 33 basic 'G'-types. In common with several other manufacturers, Lea-Francis discovered that efforts to sell an ultra cheap car shorn of all accessories were to prove abortive.

A high proportion of 12/40 'M'-type cars were fitted with closed bodies, a total of four saloon types being offered by Cross & Ellis alone. Super sports styles were standard for the 12/50 'L'-type in four-seater or two-seater beetle back form although two special and distinctive two-door saloons were delivered, all 12/50 bodies being built by Cross & Ellis.

Scotland Yard bought seven 'L'-type, four-seaters in May, for the use of the Flying Squad, and one was purchased by the King of Iraq, the latter car remaining in Baghdad for many years – perhaps it is still there!

Three final 'N'-type cars were assembled, the last example (Chassis No. 11055) being fitted with a Meadows engine. The Vulcan concern managed to sell a further 21 Kirkstone cars, although they concentrated on the 14/40 Six. Some 340 of these cars bearing the Lea-Francis name were delivered during 1927, together with approximately five cars using the Vulcan radiator. A quantity of these cars were exported to Australia. The great majority of 14/40 models carried four- to five-seater tourer bodies, although 45 coachbuilt saloons, nine coupés and nine attractive open two-seaters were built, all by Vulcan.

Cross & Ellis were responsible for one solitary rakish four-seater sports body (Chassis No. 288), together with 16 fabric saloons, eight of which were of the recently introduced Lea-fabric pattern.

Soon after the early production 14/40 cars reached the hands of the public, the works at Coventry became troubled with a spate of guarantee work, which concerned big-end failures. Vulcans remained indifferent until the matter became so serious that a harassed George Andrews drove up to the Southport factory, and forced their directors to conduct an investigation, taking with him a good selection of damaged components.

The fact that Coventry were totally unfamiliar with the Vulcan designs caused some embarrassment. On one occasion an owner elected to wait sitting in his car while the brakes were adjusted, an operation taking only seconds on standard Lea-Francis cars. Consternation reigned while it took a long time to discover where and how to adjust them, the faithful George Andrews doing his best to make idle conversation with the owner, and at the same time conceal the fumblings of the nonplussed fitter.

C B Wardman who continued to have great, but misplaced confidence in the 14/40, organized a high-speed trial at Brooklands, under RAC supervision, in July. Six standard five-seater tourers, carrying driver and one passenger, thus weighing 27¼cwt, were required to average 60mph for six hours. The occasion was to be a Lea-Francis day with a party for agents and customers in the club house, while examples of all Lea-Francis models were made available for inspection and test. Mercifully Wardman's hospitality was so good that the guests on this beautiful summer day became rapidly inebriated and filled with *bonhomie*. Nobody, therefore, seemed to notice the six hard-pressed 14/40 cars, three of which succumbed to big-end failure, in addition to suffering valve gear problems, all due to inadequacies of the lubrication system. For an unexplained reason the cars were stressed further by running on the low saloon rear axle ratios of 5:1. Nevertheless, the three remaining cars completed the course in good order, and at over 60mph. The fastest averaged 63·3mph, no mean performance for a heavy car with the modest engine displacement of 1696cc.

Van Eugen designed a hasty modification by fitting an additional oil pump to look after the overhead gear, thus relieving the main pump which was adequate for the needs of the crankshaft alone. The improved engine was now reliable enough, but inherently noisy, and of course, expensive to build. Most of the early cars were modified free of charge, a costly business, since a complete overhaul was generally undertaken at the same time. Furthermore, considerable damage was done to the reputation of Lea-Francis.

An interesting side issue of the 14/40 concerned the fitting of a Ki-Gass hand pump. Some difficulties with cold starting were experienced with the engine and at this time C B Wardman travelled to Germany in connection with his concession for Mercedes-Benz lorries. He inspected the immense supercharged sports cars then being built by this famous firm and noted that Ki-Gass equipment was used to assist starting. Upon his return he purchased a licence to manufacture this equipment in England, a business which proved vital to

A Lea-Francis day at Brooklands, July 1927. The 14/40 cars are about to embark on the six-hour test

Britain during the Second World War, for every piston-engined aeroplane used by the RAF was so fitted. The business is still thriving in Leamington Spa, under the chairmanship of C B Wardman's son, Group Captain R B Wardman.

The Vulcan Co. embarked on a further and larger 6-cylinder machine during 1927, and while it possessed twin camshafts driven from the rear, together with 14/40-type accessory drives, there the similarity with the previous model ended. The new engine was to prove very good indeed, and it is sad that the record of the 14/40, together with a serious deterioration in the Vulcan finances was to prove too great a burden to overcome. Thus only a small number of 16/60 cars, as they were called, were built. Fortunately one example (Chassis No. 2/LFS/31) survives, and is in regular use, owned by Lea-Francis exponent Dr Robert Elliott Pyle.

The chassis was identical to the 14/40, but the new engine was given dimensions of 65mm bore × 100mm stroke (2-litre). The car was burdened by an absurdly low final drive ratio of 5:1 with an 8·45:1 third gear. A freewheel device of Humphrey-Sandbert type was offered as optional equipment. The new car was officially designated 2/LFS, and two prototypes were completed in 1927. Vulcan once again offered a similar car under their own flag.

C B Wardman took a keen interest in this model, and designed a most unusual fabric saloon body to be fitted to the first chassis for his own use. The principal feature of the new body was that it was built over the full width of the car enclosing the running boards and rear wings, possibly the first car so to do. An enclosed luggage boot and spare wheel compartment was included, and the whole outline of the body was rounded and smooth in

52

contour, although appallingly ugly. The white-enamelled steering wheel had the uppermost segment sawn off to aid forward vision, and this particular car was supercharged with a Zoller instrument driven from the offside front of the engine; a Vulcan radiator was also fitted. It was exhibited at Olympia as a production model, although it is believed that only the one car was built. Complete with free wheel, it was listed optimistically at £875. A similar body was, however, fitted to one of the prototype Lea-Francis 16/60 models (Chassis No. 2/LFS/1), and was duly exhibited at Kelvin Hall and styled the Gainsborough Saloon.

Perhaps obstinately the 14/40 was continued for 1928, and in addition Lower Ford Street were persuaded to use it in a virtually unmodified 'P'-type 12/40 chassis. Officially designated type 'T', this car was advertized as a Light-Six, and, of course, without the burden of the heavy Vulcan-built chassis, it possessed a good road performance. The first production drawing is dated August 1927, and three cars were completed before the end of the year. Two were fitted with Vulcan coachwork, with one Leafabric saloon by Cross & Ellis.

The drawing office at the Coventry works was at its most productive during 1927, with the design of a new range of 4-cylinder cars. They were, with minor improvements, to last until the end of motor car production under the aegis of the original company.

It was apparent to the designer that the old quarter-elliptic chassis had reached the end of its development, both as regards road handling and reliability. The latter quality had improved considerably, but premature failure of the spur gear differential could still occur with the combination of an unskilled driver and the rather fierce cone clutch. An embarrassing scene occurred on the company's stand at Olympia in 1926, when an owner produced a set of smashed pinions, and placed them on a nearby table in full view of the public. The offending pieces were quickly scooped up, while their bearer was ushered in to a private sanctum where he was assured that his was an isolated case.

In January 1927, Van Eugen prevailed upon his directors to allow him to commence work on a completely new chassis layout. Long semi-elliptic rear springs, together with lowered and widened frame, upswept at the rear, were adopted, and the car was enlarged in proportion with a wheelbase of 9ft 3in and track of 4ft 2in. A new rear axle embodying a bevel gear differential was used, and while the main casing was still of aluminium and split along the centre line, the outer extremities carrying the underslung spring attachments were of malleable iron. Torque was taken through the rear springs. The transmission brake was abandoned

TOP FAR LEFT
Wardman's Zoller blown 2LFS Vulcan; termed the Gainsborough saloon

TOP LEFT
A smart Cross & Ellis-bodied 14/40. Chassis No. 288

FAR LEFT AND LEFT
The two most popular models; a 1926 12/22 'J'-type and a 1928/9 12/40 'P'-type

in favour of a neat arrangement of four shoes in each rear-wheel drum, two being operated by foot and two by hand. The propeller shaft was of the recently introduced Hardy Spicer type, all of which were tested under load up to a speed of 5500rpm. The rear of all road springs now ended in a neat sliding and swivelling arrangement, embodying bronze trunnions, thus eradicating the side play of a conventional shackle. A similar layout was used by William Heynes for the SS Jaguar nine years later and by H N Charles at MG's.

The king pin thrust was now taken on ball-bearings, thus retaining light steering despite an increase in chassis weight. The radiator was enlarged once again, being wider and higher by 1in and 2in respectively.

The 4ED-engined cars were now fitted with a single-plate clutch of Meadows manufacture. This was a considerable improvement on the cone type, which was retained for the 12/22 touring models. This latter car retained Dunlop disc wheels, whereas the higher-powered types were all fitted with Rudge wire wheels. Detail improvements included a gear lever cranked to a more convenient position while the ignition, timing and hand throttle levers were positioned above the steering wheel. The whole car was finely engineered with extremely neat detail work reminiscent of continental practice. Every part was perfectly proportioned, and thoroughly sound in design, with the possible exception of the rear hub and axle shaft arrangements. Van Eugen was a staunch believer in semi-floating rear axles, but it was a fact that the spline fitting for the hubs was prone to wear, and eventual breakage with loss of a wheel, due to the difficulty of keeping the retaining nut tight.

The Alvis 12/50, always a direct rival of sporting Lea-Francis models, appeared heavy and clumsy in comparison with regard to the chassis, although both cars were often fitted with similar coachwork, Cross & Ellis supplying both firms.

The new Lea-Francis cars, ready in good time for the 1928 season, were as follows.

12/22 Type 'U'	Chassis 16000 up
12/40 Type 'P'	Chassis 13000 up
12/50 Type 'O'	Chassis 12000 up
1½-litre Supercharged Type 'S'	Chassis 14000 up
14/40 Light Six Type 'T'	Chassis 15000 up

The first drawing for these cars is dated 27 January 1927 (Stub axle, Type 'O') and the first cars were completed and on road test by July.

The development of the most famous Lea-Francis of all, the supercharged 'S'-type, which took place at the same time, will be covered in detail in the next chapter.

Touring models with 4EB and 4EC two-bearing engines were now being made in smaller numbers and the emphasis of production was switching to the 4ED-powered 12/40 car, although the former types were continued in small batches until late 1930.

Production of the new low-chassis cars got under way quickly and a sizeable batch of all models were despatched to Olympia and the Kelvin Hall for exhibition and demonstration. A short delay occurred in the delivery of the new bevel gear differentials which were 'bought out', produced by either ENV of Willesden or the local firm Gulson Engineering Ltd. Some early cars were fitted, perforce, with the old spur gear unit inside the new axle casings while a few 12/40s in the first batch were built with cone clutches, possibly to utilize old stocks.

By the end of 1927, a total of four 'O'-type 12/50s, 11 'S'-type Hypers, 65 'P'-type 12/40s and 75 'U'-type 12/22 cars were delivered, all with standard coachwork.

The financial year ending 31 August 1927, indicated a profit figure slightly improved over the previous year and the best result ever achieved by Lea & Francis with a surplus of £11,691. Good as this figure was, it did not reveal a true picture. The Vulcan Co. caused Lea-Francis to pay the Southport firm the sum of £20,000 as a development payment in respect of the 14/40 6-cylinder car. For some time this figure showed up as an asset in the balance sheet of Lea-Francis but it was, of course, valueless and the fact that the cash had been taken out of the business weakened the firm seriously. The old-established and well-respected Coventry concern might well have been able to pull through the economic depression which followed the Wall Street crash of 1929 if it had been allowed to retain the profits it had made. Certainly the new 4-cylinder engine that Van Eugen designed in 1929 would have gone into production thus taking the next logical step in the development of one of the finest British cars in its class.

The financial structure of Lea & Francis underwent a further change in October 1927. Conversion into a public company took place with an increased authorised share capital of £120,000 of which £64,000 was issued. The company secretary was now W G Rimmer of Southport.

While further improvements were to be made in the 1½-litre cars, weights had increased to a point where it could not honestly be called a Light-Car. These later developments will be followed in due course but in order to retain a reasonable chronological order, the formation and progress of the racing division is the subject of the next chapter.

CHAPTER SIX

Supercharged

The publicity obtained with trials successes had been largely responsible for the increase in sales which had taken place in 1924 and 1925. In order to remain in competition after the SMMT ban on trials entries by manufacturers, it became necessary to embark on a track racing programme. Accordingly, early in 1926, work began on the design and construction of a pure racing car. This machine was to retain a great number of standard parts including the faithful Meadows engine, although some consideration was given to the employment of a supercharged version of the side-valve Anzani unit, of which more anon.

The chassis bore a strong resemblance to the normal production touring cars, although it was lowered considerably, employed flat road springs and was given a new front axle with a deeper drop between its extremities and the spring pads. Brakes remained standard while the gearbox was given a set of close ratios and a central lever, various rear axle ratios were made available, the most frequently fitted set for long-distance events being 3·91:1. The old somewhat troublesome propeller shaft utilizing fabric couplings was discarded in favour of a Hardy-Spicer, while 'DuFaux' shock absorbers were fitted all round. A new radiator of striking appearance was designed, having a rearward slope of 15° with tapering sides and an under-bonnet filler cap. Cross & Ellis were commissioned to build a suitable body for Brooklands work and the result was a smart and distinctive polished aluminium structure with a low sloping tail which soon gave rise to the name of 'Lobster'. Although strictly a single-seater, the driver sat on the right-hand side while a detachable aluminium cowling covered the nearside cockpit. An undertray was fitted and the three-branch exhaust manifold protruded from the nearside bonnet panel feeding into the regulation 'Brooklands' silencer, a fishtail completing the system. Curiously, only the offside bonnet panel was louvred and Rudge wheels of a new dished pattern, to enable king pin centres to coincide with tyre centres, were used. A 16-gallon petrol tank was positioned in the tail and feed was by pressure from a hand pump.

The 12/50 engine was tuned further, BHB lightweight split-skirt pistons were fitted and the power output was coaxed up to 56bhp at 4400rpm.

The new car, given a chassis number in the 'L'-type range of 9030, was passed off test on 20 July, ready in time for the Brooklands August Bank Holiday meeting where it created a sensation with its fine appearance and by winning with ease the first event for which it was entered – the 75mph Short Handicap – at an average speed of 82·04mph with a fastest lap at 88·15mph. It was driven by Norman Norris.

The car reappeared later in the day for the 90mph Long Handicap and achieved third place behind a Salmson and the unusual supercharged EHP. The Brooklands handicappers hastily re-appraised the Lea-Francis.

A fortnight later the 'Lobster' returned to Brooklands for an Essex MC meeting and was rewarded with second place behind J Taylor's Bugatti in the Junior Long Handicap. It also won the Senior Long Handicap at 85.72mph and went on to win a 'Winners $8\frac{3}{4}$-mile Handicap' at exactly the same speed.

The Autumn BARC meeting saw Norris achieve third place in the '75 Long'. He also went extremely well in the '90 Long', but narrowly missed a place. The final Brooklands meeting in 1926 held by the Essex MC on 5 October yielded a second place to Norris in the Junior Long Handicap behind R F Oats (OM), then he went on to take first place in a standing-start one-lap sprint at 72·71mph. The car seemed to lack stamina, however, for although holding third place for a time in a 50-mile race during the day it gradually lost speed and finished well down.

During the latter half of 1926, Van Eugen began a study of forced induction and all the various superchargers then in existence were examined, including the Berk, Zoller and Cozette. The 'Lobster' racing-car was used as a test bed and the company entered this car for

The 'Lobster' chassis 9030 at Brooklands, August 1926

the JCC 200-mile race at Brooklands, at that time the most important event on the British motor racing calendar, the race in question being held on 25 September 1926.

A side-valve Anzani engine was fitted into the car at the instigation of Ernest Eldridge – who had been experimenting with this unit for some months – complete with a Berk supercharger driven from the nose of the crankshaft. The Berk instrument was manufactured by Pressure-Vac of Bradford, and had recently been introduced, primarily for fitting to existing touring-car engines as a means of increasing performance. It was designed on the Roots principle with three lobe rotors driven by spur gears inside a heavily ribbed aluminium casing, and drawing through a Solex carburettor. Power output of the Anzani engine so fitted was 88bhp at 4750rpm.

The 200-mile race was to prove a fiasco for Lea-Francis. Norman Norris was delayed shortly after the start by an oil-pipe breakage and forced to retire in the early stages of the race with a seized supercharger, probably due to expansion of the duralumin rotors. The 'Lobster' was hastily rebuilt with a standard two-port engine for the remainder of the season.

In addition to the racing-car, Lea & Francis ran a team of virtually standard 'L'-type 12/50 sports-cars during the year with varying degrees of success. Norris and Tatlow competed in the JCC Brooklands Spring Meeting in April with two carefully prepared cars but Norris tried too hard in the Short Handicap event bursting his engine with a most alarming bang, while Tatlow only managed a third place in the Stop-Start half-mile race. Curiously both these machines were originally built in March 1926 as 'N'-type Anzani cars but these engines were removed and replaced with two-port Meadows 12/50 units. The Norris car (Chassis No. 11005) was fitted with flat road springs and ran without front-wheel brakes for Brooklands work. Bodywork was the standard Cross & Ellis beetle-tailed polished-aluminium two-seater, virtually identical to that fitted to numerous 12/50 Alvis cars. Tatlow's car, a four-seater sports Cross & Ellis type (Chassis No. 11007), finished in blue with cream wheels, was only completed on the eve of its first race meeting.

Norris had better success with his two-seater at the Whitsun Brooklands meeting, finishing second to R F Oats (OM) in the 75mph Short Handicap. The energetic Essex Motor Club held another Brooklands event in mid-Summer

The Lobster in modified form with enlarged radiator

which included a 100-mile handicap event. Norris entered but was forced to retire with a sheared magneto coupling while private owner A G Armstrong in a standard four-seater 12/50 led the race for 20 of the 37 laps, but was forced to retire when the petrol tank succumbed to the rough pounding caused by the Weybridge track.

Tatlow and Norris entered the two sports-cars, both now minus wings and screens, in the BARC July meeting; neither gained a place, although Tatlow's machine ran extremely well. The redoubtable pair returned to Brooklands again during July for the interesting JCC Production Car Race for which an artificial road course was formed. The 'Leafs' failed on this occasion; Tatlow non-started and while Norris led at the start, he was soon overhauled by C M Harvey's Alvis. The Lea-Francis lost a sump full of oil due to a broken gauge pipe and it was this which eventually caused Norris's retirement.

The Ulster AC held a speed event at the Magilligan Strand Beach in Londonderry in July and private entrant A L Harvey achieved third place in the 1½-litre Sports Car class and fourth position in the unlimited event. A sand race held at Heysham and organized by the Bradford and District Motor Club in September gave a second place to T Northwood in a standard sports model.

Tragedy occurred in October 1926 when Norman Norris accompanied by works mechanic Jack Hewitson travelled to Northern Ireland to compete in another of the then popular sand races at Magilligan Strand. Two 12/50 sports-cars were taken, one being the faithful two-seater while a standard touring Anzani-engined car was included for Hewitson to drive in the touring-car event. The two-seater developed a jammed gear selector during practice and Jack Jewitson worked all night on the sands in a derelict tin shed to completely strip and reassemble the gearbox.

Repairs duly completed, the car started in a 10-lap event. But before one circuit had been completed, a giant wave caused Norris to swerve violently while travelling at a speed approaching 90mph. The car slid badly but the skilful driver was seen to correct it, then suddenly a tyre burst and the machine overturned pinning Norris underneath. He was killed instantly. Hewitson scratched his event later in the day.

The news came as a great shock to the Lower Ford Street works for Norris was a most popular figure who had done much to fly the Lea-Francis flag. The directors called a board meeting and quickly resolved upon a generous provision for the unfortunate widow while the badly damaged car was broken up (Chassis No. 11005).

During the winter of 1926–7, Lea-Francis cars continued to gain awards in long-distance trials although the number of entrants had dropped considerably, no doubt due partly to the SMMT ban, but perhaps this class of motor sport was beginning to lose popularity. K G R Bagshaw won a silver cup driving the only 'Leaf' in the London–Gloucester although five drivers entered the Boxing Day London–Exeter. G P Stevens non-started and H S Stevens retired after performing well on the hills, but Boyd-Harvey managed a silver medal and Gamble and W E Kendrick won golds.

The Easter London–Land's End run proved more popular with a total of nine entrants using various types of Lea-Francis cars and the Whitsuntide London–Edinburgh trial saw five 'Leafs' compete, although Podmore's 12/22 was eliminated in an accident at Stamford. F C E Cleaver ran a veteran 'D'-type, L W Turner in an 'E'-type 10hp car won a silver medal and H S Stevens and P D Walker took gold medals in their 12/50 sports models.

Many lesser trials continued to attract one or two Lower Ford Street machines during 1927 and they almost invariably figured in the awards lists, particularly the gallant H S Stevens who seems to have spent every weekend at the wheel of his polished aluminium 'L'-type.

The MCC staged a further high-speed reliability trial at Brooklands in October 1926 for standard touring cars and G T Gamble and K G R Bagshaw both gained gold medals in this interesting and informative event, Gamble managing a lap at 60mph.

During the winter of 1926–7, further work was carried on in the field of Supercharging and Van Eugen took a keen interest in the work of R J P E Cozette of Paris, a specialist in the field of carburation and induction systems. He had achieved considerable success with a vane supercharger of his own design which was being fitted to several small French sports-cars. A decision to supercharge the Meadows engine with a Cozette instrument fed from a Cozette carburettor was taken and L T Delaney managed to secure the British concession for these components which he marketed from his own company, L T Delaney & Sons Ltd.

The Cozette supercharger embodied six vanes, the rotor and the drum containing the vanes rotating at the same angular velocity. Cozette applied for a British patent for this device on 20 October 1925 and followed this with two further applications for cleverly conceived methods of driving the outer drum. Vertical drives were favoured by Cozette in order to avoid any rising induction pipes.

Cozette suggested to Delaney that a study be made of the SCAP sports-car then on the market in France and fitted with an 1100cc pushrod engine supercharged by Cozette. This was done and Delaney imported such a car, finding it highly effective. It passed to the Lower Ford Street works for a thorough examination and test and several ideas embodied in this French car were incorporated in the Lea-Francis conversion of the Meadows engine. Much testing of the SCAP was carried out at Brooklands and for this purpose it was fitted with a small radiator of Lea-Francis outline. This car was retained at the works until 1931.

The first experimental supercharged engine consisted of a standard 12/40 single-port 4ED unit to which was bolted a new timing cover, incorporating the bevel gear housing and horizontal flange to support the supercharger. Ample bevel gears were to drive the Cozette instrument at engine speed. No other alterations were made, and this first engine relied on thermosyphon cooling. The power output was almost doubled, and the 'Lobster' was tested at Brooklands in this form. Performance proved to be outstanding, but after a display of vivid acceleration, the engine burst with a very loud bang after approximately half a mile. The first modification was, therefore, a lowering of compression ratio!

The engine underwent further development, and was tamed to a point where it was considered suitable for use in a road car. The Lobster was then fitted with a rough-pointed-tail two-seater body for further running and assessment. Indeed, it was tested in this form by a motoring journal in March 1927. The car was well received, and recorded 83mph while it would throttle back to less than 10mph in top gear (3·91:1) and starting was found to be instantaneous.

The decision was made at this point to manufacture such a car for sale to the public, and an announcement was made to this effect – the car being called simply the Lea-Francis 'Special'. A further chassis (No. 9098) was put in hand, fitted with a rough-pointed-tail two-seater body by Cross & Ellis.

The public were informed that the production cars would be similar to the prototypes but the company had already decided to abandon the quarter-elliptic chassis at the end of the 1927 model year. The supercharged engine was really intended for the new semi-elliptic low frame which was already in the course of preparation. Understandably, the sales department did not wish to reveal their hand at this point – March 1927.

OPPOSITE TOP AND BOTTOM
Chassis 9098 on test during February 1927

60

The final specification for the 'Hyper' car was, in fact, decided by February and the first production drawing is dated 1 February 1927 (blower drive details). The official designation was to be type 'S' and the name of 'Hyper' was suggested by L T Delaney on the eve of its announcement in September. It was immediately adopted in preference to the hackneyed titles of 'Super Sports' or 'Special Sports' which were to have been used.

The engine specification for the touring 'Hyper' was standard, plain-bearing Meadows 4ED with single-port cylinder head. These units were stripped upon their arrival from Wolverhampton and carefully re-assembled in the competition department with particular attention to tolerances of bearings and pistons. New valves of slightly enlarged diameter were fitted together with duplex springs.

No. 8 Cozette superchargers with a carburettor of the same make were fitted in the manner previously described while a water pump was fitted on the timing cover driven by the dynamo pinion. Although a pump was initially installed on an extension of the crankshaft forward of the timing cover, this gave rise to sealing problems.

Supercharger lubrication consisted of a Best & Lloyd motor cycle oil pump mounted on the top of the blower for lubrication of the rotor drive and bearings. This was fed from a small tank on the dashboard although the main engine oil supply was linked to the system by a two-way tap and owners were urged to change over to this source for prolonged high-speed work for fear of exhausting the supply. The blower vanes were satisfied by an addition of 1 per cent to $1\frac{1}{2}$ per cent of Castrol XL added to the fuel and a neat 90cc measure was fitted into the petrol tank filler for this purpose. On no account was Castrol 'R' to be used in these engines.

The new 'O'-type chassis was altered only in detail for the 'Hyper'. Changes consisted of the fitting of the characteristic 15° sloping radiator which also tapered slightly towards the top, and a rear petrol tank of 10-gallon capacity fitted with feed by electric 'Autopulse'. The standard rear axle ratio was 4·27:1 which combined with the new gearbox fitted to the 'O'-, 'P'- and 'U'-type cars but with closer ratios gave a useful 5·56:1 third and 8·47:1 second gears. The lowest ratio was 14·23:1.

Initially, the new sports-car was offered only in open four-seater form. The coachwork, including the bonnet, made by Cross & Ellis, was covered in fabric and was of two-door type, very low in build, the waistline being only 38in from the ground. The two-panel windscreen, later hinged in the middle, was raked at the same angle as the radiator; two spare wheels were carried in wells in the swept front wings. The dashboard was of cream celluloid, similar to the old 12/50 but with re-arranged instruments including a blower gauge. Upholstery was in hide throughout with top-quality carpeting to match. A neat louvred valance covered the front dumb irons, hinged in order to gain access to the starting handle. The first production car (Chassis No. 14000) was delivered from the coachbuilders on 11 July 1927. This car, finished in black fabric with red wings and white wheels was revealed to the public in September and was retained as a works demonstrator for six months.

The machine created a sensation and still represents the epitome of the Vintage Sports Car. It must surely rank as one of Britain's best-looking cars and furthermore, was possessed of an all-round performance which was markedly superior to any other $1\frac{1}{2}$-litre British car in series production during the vintage years. A genuine 85mph was within the car's compass and given favourable conditions and top-note tuning 90mph could be achieved. Road manners, steering and braking were first class and the whole car felt right upon sitting behind the wheel.

The supercharged engine would behave with complete reliability if maintained correctly and not deliberately over-driven. The only penalty facing an owner, apart from the slightly irksome business of providing for the blower lubrication, was a thirst of about 18mpg of Benzole mixture.

Ten more cars were completed during 1927, including one special saloon (Chassis No. 14003), which was designed by general manager H E Tatlow for his own use. It was a close-coupled, four-door four-light fabric body of bizarre appearance with a high waistline and low roof of a type just coming into vogue. The Vee windscreen was raked back, again to coincide with the radiator slope, and false pram irons were fitted to the rear quarters. The imposing appearance brought with it a considerable restriction of visibility, and a certain amount of inconvenience was caused by the narrow rear doors. Nevertheless, the saloon, once more the work of Cross & Ellis, was offered as an additional body style at £595 against £495 for the standard four-seater.

Chassis No. 14004, supplied to managing director L T Delaney, created something of a sensation by virtue of being specially finished in gold fabric with wings and wheels to match, while the second car built (Chassis No. 14001) finished in blue fabric was taken over to France for the Boulogne Speed Week in September, and entered a Concours d'elegance, held at Le Touquet with Miss Doris Delaney at the wheel. She won first prize.

TOP LEFT
The first production Hyper; Chassis No. 14000

BOTTOM LEFT
Tatlow's saloon Hyper; Chassis No. 14003

No further technical changes were made during 1927, although the first five cars used the old cone clutches.

In view of the volume of activity involved in preparing a complete range of new production cars, the racing programme undertaken in 1927 was somewhat restricted. Two more specially tuned and prepared 'L'-type 12/50 cars were built however, and retained by the works for a season's racing. In addition, Tatlow's 1926 12/50 (Chassis No. 11007) was sold to S H Newsome, who raced it at Brooklands with some success.

'Sammy' Newsome, although brought up in the world of the theatre, was an enthusiastic motorist, and had been associated with a little-known motor-manufacturing concern called the Cooper Car Co. of Bedford, before forming his own firm of S H Newsome and Co. of Coventry. He became a Lea-Francis agent in addition to obtaining the distributorship for Standard, and later SS Cars.

The works managed to secure the services of Ronald Manners Verney Sutton – a cousin of the Duke of Rutland – as No. 1 driver and tester to take the place of the late Norman Norris. 'Soapy' Sutton was later associated with Alvis and Jaguar, and is best remembered for a notable run at Jabbeke in Belgium with an XK 120.

The first event in 1927 was the Brooklands Easter meeting, in which Sutton appeared driving the original Lobster in scratch position in the 90mph Long Handicap. He put up a display of vivid acceleration, but the race went to George Newman, in his highly effective Salmson, while the Lea-Francis finished the race with oil pouring from the bonnet.

The two new 12/50 competition cars were passed off test on 30 April, and were promptly entered in the Essex Six-Hour Event, held on the first weekend in May, backed up by Newsome in the old four-seater. Practice for this event passed off well enough, but the race proved a fiasco. Sutton suffered gearbox trouble after covering 26 miles, having to push the car for $1\frac{1}{2}$ miles in order to reach the pits, where he worked away for a long time without success, and thus retired.

Hendy, in the other car, suffered valve gear trouble in the first hour, but made a partial recovery, finishing the race, and covering 305 miles to average a dismal 51mph. Newsome was a little faster, averaging 54mph on the artificial course, until clutch slip forced his retirement in the last hour.

Press reports indicated that Newsome's pit work was terrible, taking $7\frac{1}{2}$ minutes to top up with fuel, oil and water, a task which the Bentley team accomplished in 85 seconds.

Upon arrival for scrutiny, Sutton and Hendy were advised that the single dickey seats in the tails of the two-seaters were smaller than stipulated by the regulations, and the cars were rushed over to the obliging Hoyal Body Corporation in Weybridge, where drastic surgery was performed. They were turned out, professionally finished, in good time for the race.

The Middlesex Club Brooklands meeting in late May was contested by R M V Sutton in one of the 12/50's (Chassis No. 9133) running in stripped condition. The car acquitted itself well by finishing second to J Fairrie in a Type 35 Bugatti in the two-lap Junior Handicap, after holding the lead almost until the end. A three-lap handicap event saw Sutton finish third, after a spirited duel with Eyston (Aston-Martin), this event being won by Campbell in a Bugatti. Newsome and Sutton drove in the 50-Mile Handicap later in the day, once more

The Works 12/50 team. Brooklands 1927

appearing evenly matched, but finishing behind Eyston's Aston-Martin.

The Whitsun Meeting at the Surrey track was to prove frustrating for Sutton. Two pistons melted in the Lobster during the Monday event, and the car was rushed back to Coventry for a complete engine rebuild, returning to Brooklands on Wednesday in time for the Gold Vase Race. On leaving the paddock serious plug troubles set in, and the car did not even reach the starting-line.

Kaye Don drove one of the 12/50 cars in the 90mph Long Handicap, and led for two laps before being overtaken by a bunch of larger cars. Nevertheless, he finished in fourth place, this being his first drive in a Lea-Francis car.

The popular JCC high-speed trial was the next event, and the polished aluminium Leafs of Sutton, Newsome and J H Whittendale – a Coventry estate agent – were generally reckoned to be the smartest cars entered. Newsome gained a gold medal, but Whittendale spun badly, losing an award. Gordon Hendy in a standard 12/50 tourer received a bronze medal, but Sutton retired.

The Surbiton Motor Club meeting was to see Sutton narrowly beaten in the first two-lap race, and he also finished third in a three-lap race behind Campbell and Mrs Scott in Grand Prix Bugattis.

The final 19-lap '52-Mile Event' saw Sutton finish fourth, after leading for 10 laps, but J V Livesey in another 12/50 retired.

The JCC *Sporting Life* trophy race, a four-hour event held in August, saw entries by Kenneth Peacock using Newsome's now 'cut about' four-seater (Chassis No. 11007), Sammy Newsome driving one of the works two-seaters (Chassis No. 9135), and Sutton in the hard-worked sister car (Chassis No. 9133). The

The staff of the competitions department with 9098 prior to the Boulogne trip, August 1927

latter ran consistently throughout to finish in third place, averaging 61·3mph. Newsome's car finished with some loss of tune, averaging 55·3mph, while Peacock suffered a fearful slide while trying to avoid a seized-up Senechal. He eventually regained the course and finished without further incident averaging 48·3mph.

The Surbiton Motor Club held an interesting 150-mile limited-fuel-consumption race at the track on 2 September, and both Sutton and Newsome entered the 12/50 two-seaters fully equipped with lamps and hood. Newsome's car ran well to finish in sixth position at 53·54mph, averaging 23·5mpg. The Sutton car fell out after 32 very fast laps with serious engine trouble. The mixtures seem to have been weakened to the limit, for Newsome's car proved difficult to start, and lost time as a result.

The race was won, incidentally, by a 2-litre Type-35 Bugatti, which averaged 24mpg with an average speed of some 70mph.

The French Automobile Club du Nord held a speed week in the Boulogne area, during the first week in September, and although an excellent time was had by the large Lea-Francis party, who travelled over, the main race for the Georges Boillot Cup was ruined by an absurd handicap system. It greatly offended the British competitors, who found they were without any hope of winning, and caused them to give voice, saying that the system was deliberately loaded against them. Sutton had entered the 12/50 two-seater, but unfortunately had to scratch because the car could not be rebuilt in time, following his blow-up at Brooklands the previous weekend. The other Lea-Francis entered was the rough experimental car which had been used extensively by Sutton for super-charger testing (Chassis No. 9098). This vehicle was duly shipped over to Boulogne, where it was to be driven by Kaye Don. Curiously, the Press went into raptures over its smart appearance. Maurice Harvey travelled over with a highly tuned Alvis, and with British drivers realizing that they had no chance of winning, elected to enjoy an all-out blind between themselves.

The race was to be run in two parts, commencing with an eliminating contest of 10 laps of the 23·2-mile circuit through the Forest of Boulogne, followed by a final of three laps.

Cars of all capacities started together, and the crowd was duly astonished to see Kaye Don leap into the lead, and draw away from Ariés and Lorraine-Deitrich machines, with engines of more than twice the size of the Lea-Francis.

Don was hotly pursued by Harvey and the two Coventry cars began lapping at over 63mph in conditions of torrential rain. Kaye Don suffered very bad luck for he led the race until the final lap, when the poor Meadows engine cried enough, forcing retirement. Harvey went on to finish in fine style, being the only 1½-litre car to survive. He was, as predicted, grossly out-handicapped in the final, and came in last despite impeccable driving.

Kaye Don's car was made good, and appeared at Shelsley Walsh a fortnight later, where it was driven by Newsome to win the 1500cc sports class with a climb of 59·6 seconds' duration.

The final track event of note during 1927 was the MCC high-speed trial for standard touring cars at Brooklands, held in October. Both H J Bacon and G T Gamble entered standard 12/50 'L'-type cars, averaging 61mph in pouring rain to win gold medals.

The 1927 racing season had been instrumental in forcing the development of the supercharged Meadows engine to a point where the cars so fitted were formidable opposition, quite capable of mixing it with complex 8-cylinder Grand Prix cars in short-distance events. The next season was to see an improvement in reliability, thus enabling Lea-Francis to win the most important race of the year.

The alterations carried out to the engine by Lower Ford Street, as a result of racing and testing at Brooklands, were concerned mainly with pistons, because the Meadows Standard Type broke up with the sharp power increase obtained. Several designs were tried, while the small end and gudgeon pin layout also received attention, culminating in a fully floating pin located with bronze end pads. Valve gear weight was lowered somewhat by the fitting of duralumin pushrods, while the racing cars ran with oil coolers.

It was realized that the standard plain-bearing big ends were dangerously overstressed when the engine was fitted with the large No. 9 superchargers used for racing, and late in 1927 the first engine was built incorporating tubular con-rods and roller bearings of German Baer design. The crankshafts for this type were made by Ambrose Shardlow of Leicester.

The 1928 season was undoubtedly the most successful of all for Lea-Francis although, ironically, it also heralded the beginning of the slide to receivership. There is no doubt, however, that the racing achievements helped the sale of cars considerably although whether the business thus accrued outweighed the cost of supporting a full programme is debatable. Certainly the production touring-cars all benefitted to a certain extent from lessons learnt in racing and the employees in this closely-knit and happy firm received a good morale boost as news of successes came in.

The whole outlook of the smaller-volume motor manufacturers was totally different in the halcyon days of the twenties from that obtaining today. First and foremost came the product and all effort and endeavour went into making it as good as was humanly possible. Secondly came the impulse to enjoy it all as much as possible. Certainly any thought of showing a profit came a poor third.

Perhaps the attitude of the times was a form of reaction resulting from the holocaust of 1914–18; certainly it could not last and all but the fittest and best were to face a trudge around the streets of Coventry looking for work in 1931 and 1932. When re-engaged, perhaps at Standards, the Humber–Hillman combine or Morris Motors (bodies and engines) they were to find that the old painstaking quality-first attitude had gone for ever.

In 1928 with a range of new cars selling well the design department were able to develop a competition version of the 'Hyper' and, in addition, evolve a new team of racing cars based on a revised quarter-elliptic spring chassis for the 200-mile race. The new sports-car used a similar chassis to the standard 'S'-type but with a repositioned outside hand-brake, large petrol tank inside the tail fed by hand pump, No. 9 Cozette supercharger and tubular connecting rods running on needle roller bearing using the Baer built-up crankshaft. The car was given neat and close-fitting cycle-type wings which were attached to flanges on the cast-aluminium brake backplates while a two-seater body covered in fabric and having a door on the nearside only was supplied by Cross & Ellis. A three-panel windscreen was fitted, the spare wheel was strapped into position on the side of the scuttle and the whole car bore an extremely businesslike and smart appearance. The first car (Chassis No. 14022), was completed in March 1928 and so impressed C B Wardman that he elected to enter a team of similar machines in the forthcoming TT race. The works were not in favour and argued that insufficient time was available for manufacture and testing but Wardman persisted and did in fact enter the cars in his own name. Thus a team of six cars were laid down on 16 May 1928. These machines were completely standard with the exception of sundry body details including gauze windscreens as directed by the race regulations. Identical cars were offered to the public and were officially designated as TT replicas.

The new 200-mile race cars (Chassis Nos. 9161, 9162 and 9163), were an improved version of the original Lobster design with quarter-elliptic springs raked upwards towards the rear in order that the frame should be kept as low as possible while a bevel gear differential of 'O'-type layout was utilized. A torque arm was fitted in a similar manner to the old chassis layout but cranked to clear a chassis member. A standard Hyper radiator was fitted and the body, again the work of Cross & Ellis, was panelled in aluminium and fitted with a rather high pointed tail in the manner of racing-cars of the day. Although the appearance no longer resembled a Lobster, it was still dubbed thus by the works personnel. These cars were, of course, somewhat lighter than the sports models and were possessed of a formidable performance and one car, driven by Kaye Don, was to achieve third place in the 200-mile event behind Malcolm Campbell's all-conquering Straight Eight Delage and the Eyston brothers' Type 39A Bugatti.

A new record-breaking car was evolved in 1928 and although carrying the Lea-Francis

9098 in its final form before sale to Frank Hallam in 1929. At this date it was fitted with an Anzani engine

TOP
Sutton on test at Brooklands with one of the 200-mile race cars

ABOVE LEFT
To Brooklands on the works Vulcan lorry

ABOVE RIGHT
Back to Coventry behind a hack 12/22

banner, it was the work of Ernest Eldridge who was commissioned by C B Wardman on this occasion. Eldridge had imported an American Miller racing-car for record-breaking purposes and the engine and transmission was taken from this car and mounted in a 14/40 Vulcan-built chassis. A Hyper radiator was added, together with monoposto bodywork. The works at Coventry never saw, and had no knowledge of, this machine. Driven by Harold Purdy, the car set the British Class E 2-Litre Hour Record with a distance covered of 110·63 miles, an improvement of some five miles on a similar record previously established with the straight-eight centrifugally-blown engine in its original chassis.

The first competition event held in 1928 was the postponed London–Exeter Trial. Six Lea-Francis cars entered, and all finished in good order, three competitors gaining gold medals. The Woking Motor Club held a trial in January, also taking the road to Exeter, but starting from Staines Bridge, and H Lawrence in a 12/50 tourer gained a silver cup. He followed this up with a bronze medal in the Sunbeam MCC Trials from London to Bognor, a few days later.

The Easter London–Land's End saw seven Lea-Francis cars enter and although G C Cobbold non-started, the remaining six all came home with gold medals. The indefatigable H S Stevens carried a course marshal on this occasion.

The NW London MC organized a trial in May, with a start and finish at the well-known White Hart at Hertingfordbury. H S Stevens introduced a comic element on this occasion by wearing a bowler hat and carrying with him a fishing rod; he had ample opportunity for employing the latter when he rushed a watersplash at too high a speed, soaking his magneto, and was marooned in mid-stream. He fared better in the London–Edinburgh event, winning another gold medal, as did five other drivers of the Lower Ford Street product.

The racing season for Lea-Francis should have commenced with the Brooklands Easter Meeting. Tatlow was to enter two cars but both were scratched, not being ready in time.

The May Shelsley Walsh meeting saw D W Parkes once again, trying out his 12/40 on this beautiful Worcestershire hill, only to achieve another dismal 79·4-second climb. J McVeigh and N Gordon fared better at the Ulster ASC Hill Climb a fortnight later, finishing second and third respectively in the private owners' handicap.

Tatlow entered for the popular Essex Six-Hour sport-car race, held at the Weybridge track in May. The car chosen to be driven by Frank Hallam, and partnered by Newsome, was the experimental machine of Boulogne fame, and a second machine, believed to have been a standard Hyper, was entered by L T Delaney for R M V Sutton to drive. E W Thomas, a private owner, also ran a Lea-Francis, but was disqualified for using the starting handle. The contemporary reports of this race all contradict each other, but what is certain is that Hallam lost control and shot through a barrier. He regained the course, but possibly some damage to the car was sustained, for a few seconds later, when coming off the members banking, the whole car burst into flames. Both the driver and mechanic were fortunately able to jump clear when the car had slowed sufficiently. The blaze lasted a good while before help arrived, and the machine was reduced to ashes. It was ultimately rebuilt with one of the experimental Lobster bodies

Hendy in the Miller-engined record breaker, while Colonel Lindsay-Lloyd looks on

67

and fitted with an Anzani engine. It seems that Newsome took over Sutton's car, when the latter was taken ill, and apart from a sheared magneto coupling at one stage, the car ran well and averaged 63mph. The Lea & Francis pit work was again criticized as being inefficient.

The Whitsuntide London–Edinburgh Trial was tackled by seven Lea-Francis owners, six of whom, including L Maxwell in a Hyper and H S Stevens with the faithful 12/50, gained gold medals, but W H Wilson was a non-finisher due to back-axle trouble.

The London–Holyhead event followed in June with two Leafs in the entry list, namely F Broomfield in a 12/22 who finished on time, and H S Stevens whose 12/50 was the only car to ascend all the hills.

The JCC held another high-speed trial for standard cars on the interesting Brooklands road circuit which included the test hill and entrance road combined with the outer circuit. P A Blooman entered his 12/50, but was forced to retire at three-quarter distance after covering 34 laps.

In July the Middlesex County AC ran a series of short-distance events at Brooklands in which L Maxwell driving a four-seater Hyper finished first while third place was taken by G E Maxwell driving an early example of the TT two-seater (probably Chassis No. 14022). The latter driver also recorded a notably fast time in a hill-climbing test. G E Took in a standard four-seater Hyper gained three awards in the Lewes Speed Hill Climb, also held in July, taking first place for 1500cc Super Sports Cars, third place in the racing-car class and second on Handicap.

The Surbiton MC held an event shortly before the 200-mile race, and the new Lea-Francis racing cars, which were built for this event, made their debut. On this occasion Sutton finished second in the Surrey Senior Handicap, being narrowly beaten by Kaye Don who drove his well-known 2-litre GP Sunbeam. Unfortunately Sutton was forced to retire when leading in the 50-Mile Handicap. The racing cars stayed on at Brooklands for the season, as the Lea-Francis Co. were now sharing Captain Miller's sheds at the track.

The 200-mile race which was held on 21 July, in an almost tropical heat wave, was to prove the last of the series. Although this event had been the major Brooklands event for several seasons, the popularity of long-distance races at the Weybridge Track was beginning to wane, and no longer attracted the public in large numbers, although the 1928 event was to prove an excellent race, despite the result being almost a foregone conclusion.

Malcolm Campbell's all-conquering Grand Prix Delage, the most advanced racing-car yet

A jubilant Kaye Don after a wet practice session

seen, and unsurpassed for almost 10 years, ran like clockwork to an easy win at 78·34mph, although it proved an uncomfortable machine for its driver, due to intense cockpit heat. The second car home was Basil Eyston's Grand Prix Type 39A Bugatti with a speed of 68·93mph.

The Lea-Francis entry, however, based on a modified version of the Hyper sports car as previously described, was to prove the most meritorious, for Kaye Don finished in third place at 68mph after a faultless run in Chassis No. 9163. The Brooklands silencer was emitting a strange note reminiscent of the squirt from a soda syphon, according to one reporter. Don made one pit stop at 18 laps for re-fuelling and a routine checkover. This race proved in a convincing manner that the sober-looking pushrod Meadows engine was not substantially slower than the enormously costly and complicated Grand Prix cars from the Continent. Additionally the roadholding and braking provided by Van Eugen's chassis design was second to none. Kaye Don's team mate, however, fared badly on this occasion. Chassis No. 9162 was driven by Philip Turner, an engaging and high-spirited character, who was forced to race under the pseudonym 'J Taylor' due to strong family opposition to motor racing. So determined were his next of kin, that on one occasion they travelled to Boulogne and belaboured Turner's Austro-Daimler radiator to prevent his appearance in the Boillot Cup Event. In the 200-mile race, Taylor set a cracking pace and mixed it with the Bugatti and Delage drivers for six laps, until he was forced to retire from lack of oil pressure and unseemly noises from the overstressed crankshaft bearings.

The Brooklands August Bank Holiday meeting was to prove a notable success for the

Kaye Don and Herbert Tatlow in the practice car (14056) at Belfast, 1928

200-mile race cars, for R M V Sutton won the 90mph Short Handicap in a convincing manner at 96·38mph, while 'J Taylor' managed fourth place, the car proving very difficult to start on this occasion.

The 75mph Long Handicap President Gold Plate was won by Kaye Don at 103·36mph, after one lap at 105·97mph. To round off this successful day Taylor managed third place in the Long 100mph Handicap.

The revived Tourist Trophy Race for production sports-cars was held on a road circuit in the vicinity of Newtownards in Ulster on 21 August 1928. The RAC and Ulster AC were jointly responsible for running this event, which was widely acclaimed as the most important motor race ever held in the British Isles, and the first real road race for six years. A system of credit laps was instituted as a means of handicapping, 750cc cars receiving five laps, 1100cc cars three laps, 2000cc cars two laps and 3000cc cars one lap.

Large-car manufacturers, namely Bentley and Mercedes-Benz, took exception to the system, and refused to enter, although their complaints that the event was loaded in favour of small cars did not seem justified. However, two privately entered 4½-litre Bentleys appeared in the hands of Henry Birkin and Humphrey Cook, together with a lone Mercedes-Benz driven by 'Scrap' Thistlethwayte. The other starters comprised teams of 3-litre Austro-Daimler, Type 43 Bugatti, 2-litre Lagonda, Amilcar Six and Frazer-Nash, together with five front-wheel-drive Alvis cars and hosts of Brooklands Rileys. There were also single examples of Stutz, OM, Salmson, Belgian FN, front-wheel-drive Tracta, Austin Seven, a somewhat outdated Gwynne, and a completely standard Ford Model A. The last-named was entered to gain some publicity for this recently introduced 'New Ford'. The entry list was completed with Wardman's four Hyper Lea-Francis two-seaters.

The race, therefore, had attracted the cream of the world's sports cars, and the victor stood to gain very valuable prestige.

The Lea-Francis team cars were all completed by the first week in July, and were despatched to Brooklands where a week's testing took place. The nominated drivers were Kaye Don, R M V Sutton, S H Newsome and George Eyston, and this team duly appeared at Weybridge to acquaint themselves fully with their engines.

The cars were scarcely modified in any way from the original specification, save for the fitting of 'André' shimmy dampers, and a change to Avon tricord tyres, in place of British Goodrich. Proprietary items included Terrys valve springs, Castrol oil, BP spirit, BBA brake linings, KLG plugs and a Lucas magneto.

The cars appeared satisfactory, and were duly shipped to Ulster a week before the race. The only incident during race practice concerned Sutton who rammed a bank near Ballystockart Bridge. The car turned over, and pinned the unfortunate mechanic by the neck, from which unpleasant position he eventually emerged without injury. Sutton, also trapped underneath, used all his power to lift the car in order to keep the weight off the mechanic until help came. Considerable damage was done to the steering gear and the machine was unfit to race, thus causing the substitution of one of the practice cars. Sutton also injured his hand, and was not able to compete, so his place was taken by Wilf Green of Derby. The Saturday of the

69

BELOW
In the 1928 TT, Don checks the coolant while Pellew re-fuels

FAR RIGHT
Van Eugen assists Don with refreshments; Wardman and Delaney are in the background

race dawned fine, the cars all warmed up in good time for the 'Le Mans Type' start at 11 a.m. Drivers ran across the road to erect hoods, a simple matter on the Cross & Ellis bodies of the Hypers, while the supercharged engines all started easily, and the whole team got away in good order, although the first to leave was Humphrey Cook's Bentley. Kaye Don completed his first lap, a distance of 13·6 miles, at an average speed of 61mph and was the first Lea-Francis to appear, in sixth place, behind the Bentley, Bugattis and Purdy's FWD Alvis.

A call at the pits on completion of their second laps to lower hoods, and all the Lea-Francis drivers got away well once more but Eyston was held up by the fire sweeping over the road from Campbell's Bugatti which ignited as he pulled into the pits, and became a blazing inferno within seconds.

The rival Alvis camp was going very well, particularly Purdy, who was lapping some 25 seconds faster than Don. For some 10 laps the going seemed constant with Green proving the second-fastest Lea-Francis pilot, while Eyston was gradually recovering his position. The small cars were still leading at this point although Harvey was now sixth overall behind the four Rileys and the Amilcar of Vernon Balls, Don having displaced Purdy for seventh place.

A local shower of rain near Ballystockart Bridge took Newsome by surprise, and he skidded broadside on, almost blocking the road, and damaging his car too badly to continue. He was about to be lapped by Harvey, now in second position, who, in avoiding Newsome, turned completely round, and crashed into the bridge. This put him out of the race, together with S C H Davis, who was following in a Riley. By lap 19, Don was in second place, and on the following lap took the lead when Dykes crashed badly in his Alvis. Don now led for the remainder of the race. Purdy was running second, but the cracking pace set by the Lea-Francis proved too much, and he retired with a broken piston, letting Balls into second place in the beautiful little Amilcar Six – unfortunately he crashed on the following lap.

The second Lea-Francis failure now occurred when Green was forced out with engine trouble, but Eyston was motoring at a tremendous pace, and covered one lap at 72mph, a speed which equalled that of Birkin's Bentley, and was a little faster than the Bugatti of Viscount Curzon. The fastest lap in the race was credited to Thistlethwayte in the Mercedes-Benz at nearly 75mph, but he spoilt his chances by leaving the road and lost much time in re-starting.

By lap 25 Eyston had achieved sixth place. Don made his only pit stop for fuel replenishment and a general glance over, but was off again in 67 seconds. Cushman was now following very closely in second place, and Eyston had moved up into fifth place, having taken Dutilleux in a 'works' Type 43 Bugatti. The Austro Daimlers of Mason and Paul were holding third and fourth positions.

Birkin forced past Eyston near the end of the race, and Cushman closed up to finish 13 seconds behind the flying Don, only to run out of fuel within a mile of the finish. His car was, incidentally, the only Alvis left in the race.

The winning Lea-Francis, watched by 250,000 people, sounded as healthy at the finish as at the start, and in fact, had averaged over 66mph for the last six laps achieving some 94mph down the Comber Straight. Don's race average speed was 64·06mph, and Eyston's 61·14mph. The fastest average speed for the six-hour event proved to be that of Birkin at 65·76mph.

The Lea-Francis car deserved its splendid victory for it proved, without doubt, a car of exceptional merit. Here was a 1½-litre sports car selling for a modest £495, which could equal the lap speed of the 4½-litre Bentley, could endure a six-hour race, and yet be comfortable and clean enough within for Don to drive back into Belfast, change into a lounge suit, and motor on to attend a civic function. It goes without saying that he followed this up by driving the car back to Coventry.

Apart from the magnificent RAC Trophy, the winner also received the £1000 *Daily Mail* cash prize. The Lord Mayor of Coventry gave a reception for the Lea-Francis, Alvis and Riley companies, and C B Wardman, his optimism so well justified, generously provided a lavish dinner and cabaret for all the Lea-Francis personnel involved, together with a gift of a gold or silver cigarette case. The works also presented Don with a new Hyper saloon in blue fabric, fitted with roller bearing engine and number 9 Supercharger (Chassis No. 14075).

The winning car duly appeared on display at

various agents' showrooms for the remainder of the year.

The Chassis numbers of the TT Team Cars were as follows:

14051	Sutton (damaged in practice)	
14052	George Eyston	
14053	Kaye Don	
14054	Newsome	
14055	Green	
14056	Practice car	

Chassis No. 14051 was despatched to Brooklands in September where it covered 961 miles in 12 hours, an average of 80·06mph in the hands of Sutton and Hallam, thus breaking a Class 'F' record. This achievement was short-lived, however, for the indefatigable Urquhart-Dykes husband-and-wife team put the record to over 81mph in their faithful Alvis in October.

The Lea-Francis team cancelled their entry in the Boulogne event on this occasion due to the time taken up by the personnel of the competition department with work connected with the TT.

The Essex Motor Club staged a meeting at Brooklands in October, and Wilf Green finished second in the acceleration race, having bought the car which he drove in the TT.

The final Brooklands event of 1928 was the MCC One-Hour Blind for sports-cars, which was held at Motor Show time. A minimum of 20 laps (approximately 58 miles) were required to gain an award, and all three privately owned 'L'-type 12/50 Lea-Francis cars achieved this goal, F Broomfield covering 64·9, P A Blooman 61·5 and G O T Gamble 60·4 miles. Urquhart-Dykes emulated his record-breaking performance, and his proved to be the fastest car entered, once again averaging over 81mph.

Interest in the traditional long-distance trial was not as strong as hitherto, only five Lea-Francis owners starting in the Boxing Day London–Exeter run, although three of the cars, including L Maxwell in his TT Replica, gained golds. The remaining two were awarded silver.

Hyper car production continued at a steady rate in 1928, 81 cars being completed, with the standard four-seater still being the most popular body style, although approximately 15 TT models, including the works team cars were built. A Weymann coupé version was added to the range late in the year, the first car being somewhat ugly with a vertical windscreen. This machine was used by the Press, and was well received, but 1929 cars were much improved in appearance by having the windscreen raked and the seating bettered. Approximately 10 of the striking saloons by Cross & Ellis were built, now termed Leafabric in line with the more angular 12/40 versions.

Gordon Hendy in 14051 during the 1929 TT

The only technical change during the year occurred with Chassis No. 14070, when compressions were lowered in the interest of less 'fussiness'. Maximum speed suffered a little as a result and the closed cars would now only achieve approximately 82mph.

The works, somewhat bemused with their TT success, decided to field a team of cars in all the major British events of 1929, and this was somehow achieved on a total budget of £1500. Additionally the competition department was to offer race-preparation service to all private owners. Any purchaser of a new TT model at £495 could now have his car prepared and delivered ready for any particular race, without any additional charge, and several sales and much goodwill resulted from this generosity.

The works cars used for the first half of the 1929 season were generally similar to 1928 models, but experience had dictated some improvements. The rather flimsy cycle wings had given trouble, and the cars were now to be raced with the wings attached firmly to the chassis, a change which was practical, but detracted somewhat from the car's appearance, due to the much greater clearance now required between the wing and wheel. Production two-seater cars, however, continued to be built with wings which swivelled with the wheels. The three-panel windscreen was dispensed with on the team cars in favour of one curved aero screen in front of the driver, while a much larger rev counter was fitted in an easily-read position on top of the steering column. Petrol and water caps were now both of a quick-release pattern, while a range of petrol tanks of varying capacities from 25 to 33 gallons was made available; 22-gallon tanks had sufficed for the 1928 TT.

The first event of note in the sporting calendar was the Double 12 Race in May – a new innovation by the BARC. Tatlow entered three cars to be driven by Shaw, Peacock and Green with Phil Turner, Newsome and 30/98 Vauxhall exponent E L Meeson as respective co-drivers. These cars were backed up by private owners G L Jackson and Gordon Hendy, partnered by motor cyclist Stanley Woods and T O Hodder.

Lea-Francis were to face competition from the advanced twin-camshaft Alfa-Romeos for the first time in the Double 12 and it was clear that both Lower Ford Street and Holyhead Road were no longer in a position of supremacy in the 1½-litre class. The Lea-Francis, costing less than half the price of an Alfa-Romeo was to put up a valiant show during the final vintage years, but if the British car was determined to hang on to the Alfas, rev limits were exceeded (the Meadows was safe to 5000) and reliability suffered.

Ramponi won the Double 12 on handicap in his 1500cc Alfa Romeo at 76mph from the 4½-litre Bentley of S C H Davis, which averaged 81mph. The Lea-Francis team on this occasion ran on standard Goodrich Tyres all of which gave continual trouble, stretching into grotesque shapes at high speeds, although mercifully never bursting. In the event some 40 sets of tyres were consumed, and the pit staff became so well practised that they could change all four wheels in 26 seconds. Shock absorber settings were also continually altered in an effort to alleviate the effects of the out-of-balance forces, but to no avail – Jackson had to change a broken front spring after six hours.

The second day's racing brought trouble for E L Meeson, when the exhaust system disintegrated, but repairs were effected and another stop was made to change plugs in addition to the inevitable tyres. Peacock also needed plugs, and once stopped to adjust tappets, but eventually retired.

Apart from these misfortunes the cars ran very well, and the results showed that, in Class 'F', Shaw and Turner achieved fourth place, with Green and Meeson fifth, both averaging 67mph, while Hendy and Hodder were seventh and Jackson and Woods eighth.

The cars used in the Double 12 were as follows:

Shaw	Chassis No. 14133
Green	Chassis No. 14130
Peacock	Chassis No. 14132
Hendy	Chassis No. 14051
Jackson	Chassis No. 14131

The Le Mans 24-Hour Race held on 15 and 16 June, was to witness a notable Lea-Francis success due to the solitary effort of a private owner – K S Peacock (later to become Sir Kenneth Peacock and Head of the GKN Group of Companies), assisted by his co-driver Sammy Newsome. Peacock purchased a new car (Chassis No. 14144) specially fitted with a four-seater, three-door fabric body suited to the Le Mans regulations and complete with slab petrol tank, P100 headlamps and a radiator painted black in order to reduce glare at night. The car was delivered on 6 June, fully prepared and all for £495. A few problems occurred in practice but the car ran extremely well throughout the race, moving up from twelfth to eighth positions during the night and holding that spot until the finish covering 1380·63 miles, thus averaging something over 57mph. One pair of tyres were replaced, and one front shock absorber anchorage gave way during the second day making handling difficult. The Leaf won the GP D'Endurance Prize, being the only 1½-litre car to finish, and was only beaten by cars of three and four times its engine size. The solitary Alvis, a supercharged straight eight, blew up during the night.

A fortnight after Le Mans, the BARC assumed the mantle of the defunct Essex Motor Club and held an event billed as the Six-Hour Race. In fact, it was a distance event on a handicap basis which was expected to last approximately six hours, the smallest cars were required to complete 314 miles and the unlimited class 457·8 miles. A Le Mans start was used, drivers and mechanics having to erect hoods and furl them again after 10 laps had been covered. This popular meeting attracted seven privately entered Hypers which were as follows:

R Childe – H Pellow	Chassis 14136
E. Thomas – H. R. Wellstead	Chassis 14105
G Hendy – T O Hodder	Chassis 14051
K Peacock – S H Newsome	Chassis 14144
G L Jackson	Chassis 14131
W H Green	Chassis 14130
Hon. A D Chetwynd – A Maclachlan	Chassis 14128

Incidents were plentiful. Childe, who fancied starting in gear with the clutch held out, thus hoping to gain a minimal advantage, jammed his starter in mesh and bent the Bendix shaft, necessitating the removal and fitting of a new assembly. He eventually got away only to find that gear-changing was very difficult if not impossible. He struggled on for several laps then discovered that the cause was a grease gun neck which was obstructing the gear gate. Childe now became excited and drove wildly, lap after lap the car executed alarming slides at the artificial corner placed at the end of the finishing straight. The driver eventually overdid things and came to rest on top of a marker barrel, the front axle being jacked high into the air. The car was pushed clear and apart from a bent dumb iron, no other damage was apparent. Pellew jumped in and finished the race without further trouble since the car seemed no worse for its misuse.

Gordon Hendy struck trouble early when his car ignited and for a moment the situation looked ugly. The flames were extinguished, however, but then the car retired on the following lap with a burnt-out piston.

Thomas and Wellstead enjoyed a long battle with the 1928 TT Alvis of Carr until the exhaust system disintegrated and Thomas had to break off for repairs. G L Jackson and Peacock both ran steadily averaging approximately 60mph but later Peacock suffered a blown induction joint and eventually ran out of water which damaged the engine and caused the Le Mans car to retire almost within sight of the finish. W H Green proved the fastest of the Lea-Francis drivers, having averaged 66½mph for the first four hours to lead the 1½-litre class. He was, however, later overhauled by the Eyston/Ramponi Alfa which speeded up towards the end to average 67·99mph for the full distance. Chetwynd's car frightened everybody with a monumental skid at one stage but he recovered to finish without further trouble as did all the other Hyper drivers excepting Hendy and Peacock.

July 12 and 13 were to witness a new race for sports-cars at Phoenix Park, Dublin, promoted by the Royal Irish Automobile Club and to be known as the Irish GP. It was to prove extremely popular and the entry list attracted the cream of British and Continental sports cars, the majority being works entries.

Lea-Francis entered three cars officially while Gordon Burney borrowed a new works car which subsequently stayed in Ireland. The cars and drivers were:

S C H Davis	Chassis 14132
W H Green	Chassis 14130
J W Shaw	Chassis 14133
J G Burney	Chassis 14138

The race was to prove one of the most successful events entered as far as Lower Ford Street was concerned. Preparation was good and all the drivers obeyed the strategy previously agreed upon. S C H Davis was to chase the Alfa-Romeos of Ivanowsky and Ramponi for all he was worth while Green and Shaw were to run at a set pace regardless of the leaders. Fortunately for Lea-Francis, perhaps, the Alvis concern did not enter the lists on this occasion. The race was to be a two-day event with cars up to 1½ litre running on the first day while the heavier machines ran on the morrow.

The weather was perfect and the race organization was first class. The four-mile course embraced a straight of two miles which tested power units to the limit while the back leg of the circuit was tortuous and exhausting for brakes and drivers. The start at 1.30 p.m. saw the drivers running across the road to their cars in Le Mans fashion. W H Green was first away but by the end of the first lap, Ramponi had forged ahead followed hotly by Green, Shaw, Davis and then Ivanowsky and Burney. Two laps later, the flying Russian had forced himself into second place behind his team-mate with Davis third, followed by Shaw and Green. At the first half hour, the order remained the same and it was clear that no other cars were anywhere near as fast as the leading five, Burney having slowed with some misfiring bothers. Both Alfas were lapping at 76·3, with Davis doing all in his power to keep in sight and returning 75·6mph.

The 1½-litre cars overtook the 1100cc cars on handicap after approximately 1½ hours. Ramponi and Ivanowsky came in for replenishment of fuel which was accomplished in 47 and 37 seconds respectively, but Ramponi who had been somewhat wild in his driving, overdid things at the Gough statue corner, turned round twice, then smote the wooden barrier with a mighty thump, bending both axles, and leaving his team-mate Boris Ivanowsky to fight on alone. The 300-mile race ended in victory for the Russian at 75·02mph with Davis 66 seconds behind at 74·65mph. Wilf Green followed in third place at 73·50 while Jimmy Shaw, the Irish Lea-Francis distributor, averaged 71·60 to finish fifth, not having quite enough time to overtake the handicap of Eyston's Riley 9 which was classified fourth at 68·40mph.

Burney, after a comparatively lengthy pit stop to change plugs, then enjoyed a good battle with Bertelli in the solitary Aston-Martin, but lost by a fraction to finish in 13th place with an average speed of 67·60mph.

All the Lower Ford Street cars, after a non-stop race, were running as well as ever at the finish, and Davis had been pulling over 5000rpm in the indirects and some 4900 in top, towards the end of the long straight.

Lea-Francis prizes in this event comprised the Team Prize, 2nd Prize in Class F (£500 and a gold medal), 3rd Prize in Class F (£200 and a gold medal), together with the Irish Driver's Prize, taken by Jimmy Shaw.

The 1929 TT took place on a slightly improved circuit at Newtownards on 17 August, and was notable for two reasons: the meteoric drive to victory of Rudolf Carrociola in a 38/250 Mercedes-Benz, and the dismal failure of the total Lea-Francis entry, 10 cars in all.

Three cars were fielded by the makers, although officially entered under the names of individual directors. They were fitted with new and lowered lightweight aluminium bodies of decidedly spartan appearance. Frontal area was reduced by virtue of moving the scuttle-mounted spare wheel into the tail, performance was slightly improved as a result and the cars would achieve close on 105mph. The total entry list consisted of:

ENTRANT	DRIVER	RESERVE DRIVER	CHASSIS NO.
Sir W Sinclair	Kaye Don	W H Green	14146
H H Timberlake	S H Newsome	W H Green	14054
H E Tatlow	J W Shaw	W H Green	14140
R Childe	R Childe	W H Green	14136
S Woods	S Woods	J G Burney	14138
G Hendy	G Hendy	R A Myers	14051
J W Ellison	J W Ellison	E Twemlow	14134
K S Peacock	K S Peacock		14144
D Higgin	D Higgin		14139
J W Shaw	E L Meeson	W H Green	14133

Opposition in the 1½-litre class was supplied by Alfa-Romeo with five cars, Frazer-Nash with two, solitary examples of Aston-Martin and Marendaz Special while the Alvis company entered three of their advanced straight eight supercharged FWD cars. These last machines were certainly not in the spirit of this contest for normal production cars, as they were not intended for sale to the public, and only the team cars were built, although listed in the maker's *Catalogue*. The race commenced in dry weather, but before long torrential rain began falling at various points on the circuit, which was to continue intermittently for the whole day. Childe, whose car sported a polished front axle, scratched due to illness.

At the end of the first lap, Kaye Don was seen to be the first 1½-litre car, closely following the Mercedes and Bentley giants, and Ramponi's 17/50 Alfa but Don was driving at such a pace that he was to provide the first disappointment when a piston melted after three laps.

This put W H Green at the head of his class, followed by the Alfa of Campari. Dan Higgin charged the sandbank erected outside Newtownards Town Hall on his 10th lap, managed to extricate himself, and continued, the car covered in piles of sand, but his front axle was found to be seriously bent, and he had to retire. Stanley Woods then suffered an accident, also bending his front axle, and had to retire, while Meeson fell out with engine trouble during the second hour. Shaw was badly delayed with carburettor float-needle difficulties, but Green was still travelling magnificently, and had worked up to ninth place overall, comfortably leading all the 1½-litre opposition. He had covered one lap at 71·48mph. Halfway through the race, however, he tried too hard, and followed the path of Higgins into the Newtownards Town Hall. His steering was too badly damaged to continue. Jimmy Shaw was the next to fail with a burnt-out piston, while Hendy was delayed when he had to change a wheel, due to broken spokes.

Campari was now comfortably leading Class F and for a time the race as a whole, until overhauled by Carraciola in the last half hour. The remaining Alfas followed, and all the Alvis Straight Eights were still running well, although unable to make an impression on the Italian machines. Minutes before the end, the final Lea-Francis catastrophe occurred when Hendy overturned, fortunately without serious injuries to driver or mechanic.

The race ended when Carraciola received the chequered flag after one of the finest drives in motor-racing history, averaging 72·82mph in heavy rain most of the way. The solitary Lea-Francis of private owner J W Ellison was still running at the end. Although unclassified he had a trouble-free run, but failed to make any impression on his handicap.

The last important event in a full season was the 500-mile race for stripped racing-cars on the outer circuit at Brooklands on October 12, organized by the recently formed BRDC.

Lea-Francis entered the pair of 1928 200-mile race cars (Nos. 9162 and 9163) with drivers Green and Pellew, to be assisted by Hallam and Margetts respectively – the latter was a Lea-Francis apprentice. Earl Howe had just taken delivery of a new TT two-seater (Chassis No. 14141) and he ran this car with Sir Ronald Gunter as co-driver.

The 500-mile race proved very popular and attracted an entry of 35 cars, ranging from Austin Sevens to the 4-litre Sunbeam Tiger and Tigress. The rough Brooklands track took a severe toll of chassis, aggravated by the very high speeds obtained.

Wilf Green was the first car to drop out at 12 laps with engine trouble, but Pellew and Earl Howe had really fine runs, mechanically entirely trouble-free, although a painful incident occurred when Humphrey Pellew was struck by a flying tyre thread. His car averaged 97·02mph for the first 54 laps, but the tyre trouble resulted in a certain loss of time, and the full race average came out at 89·19mph, giving Pellew seventh place overall, and first 1½-litre car, netting the Ferodo Cup. Earl Howe finished in ninth place at 88.37mph.

The lesser sporting events of 1929 witnessed many successes for Lea-Francis cars. Sixteen entered the London–Land's End Trial, 14 gaining gold or silver medals. The May Shelsley Meeting was contested by no fewer than 10 Leaf drivers, using 12/40's, 12/50's and Hypers. Allan Arnold achieved a time of 53 seconds in his ex-Kaye Don TT car (Chassis No. 14053), winning his class with E Thomas second in a similar car.

Allan Arnold, a Manchester coachbuilder, had previously achieved FTD at a CUAC Speed Trial, together with a real scoop at Southport in April with six wins out of eight classes entered in sprint events, and a third place in the 20-mile race held on this popular Lancashire beach.

The London–Edinburgh Trial resulted in gold medals for L Maxwell and G O T Gamble, with silver for F Broomfield and Humphrey Burman, the latter in his 14/40 car which he used regularly for some 40 years. This car has remained in good original condition to the present day (Chassis No. 132).

The Southport May meeting was marred by the TT Leaf of R Mellor (Chassis No. 14135) which, after initially leading the 100-mile race, indulged in wild cornering and eventually ran amok among the spectators, breaking the legs of three people. Mellor made amends at the Skegness races the following months, however, with a third and a second in the four-mile events.

The JCC High Speed Trial held at Brooklands in July was great fun as usual; six Hypers ran, and all averaged better than 70mph. The drivers included H J Widengren who had just purchased a very smart four-seater finished in cream fabric with green wings (Chassis No. 14143).

The MCC One-Hour Blind, held at Brooklands in September, resulted in four gold medals for four Hypers, the Hon. A D Chetwynd being fastest with an average of 79·83mph,

Don at Belfast Docks after the race

although beaten by the Hon. Max Aitken who achieved 82·03mph with an Aston-Martin.

The final Southport meeting in October resulted in a second place for J W Ellison in 14134, which had previously distinguished itself as the sole survivor in the TT. The season drew to a close with the 500-mile event, previously described. The year 1929 was destined to be the most active in the competition career of Lea-Francis.

The Hyper proved to be an outstanding performer, taking into account its modest cost, although clearly out of breath when pitted against the sophisticated and costly Alfa-Romeo in long-distance events. The first component to yield when over-driven was the piston and the works investigated and tested every type and make available. The best results, however, were obtained with their own design manufactured from chil-cast 'Y' alloy bars, heat-treated in the works laboratory to exacting standards.

Sixty-seven Hypers were built during 1929, of which 29 were two-seaters including the team cars while three competition cars were assembled with Le Mans-type four-seater bodies, each differing somewhat in detail. The Weymann Coupé found nine buyers but saloons only accounted for some five cars. The remainder were Cross & Ellis standard four-seaters similar to 1928 in outline but now with four doors. No technical change of any note took place apart from an alteration of road-spring rates and other minor details in line with the touring models.

A number of cars were exported to countries including Australia and Ceylon while Chassis Nos. 14162–4 inclusive, were despatched to Bombay and one car even found its way to Japan (Chassis No. 14094).

The Hon. Mrs A D Chetwynd opened the 1930 season by entering the Monte Carlo Rally in a new Hyper Sportsman's Coupé (Chassis No. 14174). The car ran in low-compression form in order to cope with poor Continental fuels and sported a pair of P100 headlamps. Finished in blue fabric it attracted great admiration. The leisurely character of the Monte in vintage years can be gauged from the fact that the Chetwynd party stopped near Thurso in order to photograph deer. This diversion resulted in late arrival at Inverness although the time was made up on the run down to London despite ice-bound roads. The Leaf ran the whole distance to the Riviera in trouble-free manner and tied for 57th place with Sunbeam sales manager Leo Cozens in his sumptuously equipped 20hp Weymann Saloon. Despite the de-tuned engine, Mrs Chetwynd won her class in the Mont des Mules Hill Climb which followed the rally.

J Allan-Arnold borrowed a 1929 team car from the works for the Inter-Varsity Speed Trials in March, the car ran well to record 24 seconds and second place in his class, while A D Chetwynd managed fourth, taking a second longer in his similar car. FTD was recorded by W B Scott in the GP Delage with a time of 20·05 seconds. One presumes that Allan-Arnold was well satisfied for he bought the car, while Lea-Francis took in part exchange his old mount – the ex-Kaye Don TT winner. This latter was rapidly overhauled, re-bodied and re-registered as VC 5461 for inclusion in the official 1930 works team.

The opening Brooklands meeting held in mid-March, was contested by the indefatigable Mrs Chetwynd in her husband's TT model which performed well but was beaten by the handicappers in both of its races. Gordon Hendy ran his faithful 1928 car in both Long and Mountain Handicaps gaining third place in the latter event behind Earl Howe in a 2·3 Bugatti and Ashby who drove his very special Riley. Hendy lapped at slightly over 60mph in this first Mountain Race, being beaten for sheer speed only by Howe. Pollack also raced a TT model in this event but was unplaced.

Allan-Arnold enjoyed a measure of success at the Easter Monday Meeting by finishing second in the Mountain Speed Handicap to Penn-Hughes (Frazer-Nash). A S Llewelyn, down from Staffordshire in a new car (Chassis No. 14175) and R E P Bliss (Chassis No. 14126) also ran at this holiday event.

The Double-12 race was held on 9 and 10 May and six Lea-Francis cars took part. The first three cars listed running as a team:

NO. 1 DRIVER	NO. 2 DRIVER	CHASSIS NO.
Gordon Hendy	T O Hodder	14051
G E Took	A N C Jameson	14147
J Allan-Arnold	A S Llewelyn	14141
A D Chetwynd	Oliver Bertram	14137
D K Mansell	Unknown	Non Starter
L K Driscoll	C W G Lacy	14176

The 1½-litre cars were set to run a minimum of 1296 miles (54mph) which compared with Malcolm Campbell in his Supercharged 36/220 Mercedes-Benz (Class B, 60mph) and all of the Bentleys (Class C, 59mph). The smallest cars, the unsupercharged Austin 7's, were given the reasonable goal of 45mph.

The winning Class 'F' car was to be the Aston-Martin of Bertelli which averaged a creditable 73·76mph. Driscoll and Lacy drove the only really successful Lea-Francis. This car, making its competition debut, finished in 11th place overall, averaging 68·17mph. Driscoll, a well-known motor cyclist, ordered his car at the 1929 Olympia Show and later travelled up to Coventry to collect it. Despite assurances that the machine had been very thoroughly tested and tuned with a view to racing, Driscoll found the performance somewhat lacking on the run home. He immediately stripped the engine only to find that it had been assembled with certain second-hand components, a shabby practice, not altogether unknown with small manufacturers in pre-war days. The matter was very quickly put to rights but Driscoll insisted on re-assembling and tuning the car himself. The results were highly satisfactory for the car proved to be faster than the works team on occasion while a high degree of reliability was also achieved. Driscoll's relatively good results in the Double-12 were achieved despite certain problems. The original works chassis erection chart shows that long rear springs were specified; these were not fitted, however, and Driscoll wasted valuable time on three occasions during the race when the incorrect short springs jumped out of their respective trunnions. He also suffered trouble with a faulty hand oil pump and broken exhaust pipes.

The first Leaf to drop out was that of Allan-Arnold which suffered a serious engine failure after 5½ hours. Took broke his exhaust pipe on the first afternoon and was forced to change his supercharger on the second, nevertheless, he proved to be the only other Lea-Francis pilot to cover the allotted distance and at the finish had travelled 1310 miles. Chetwynd had supercharger trouble followed by a collapsed rear wheel and finally retired with a cracked chassis frame. The Weybridge concrete caused the eventual failure of Hendy's car; a rear wing broke away at 6 p.m. on the first day then the petrol tank burst at 1.43 p.m. on Sunday while Hodder was driving, causing retirement.

A fortnight after the Double 12, the BARC held an invitation meeting and the hard-worked Hendy car was in action yet again. It netted a couple of thirds while W Y Craig using Pollack's car (14148) came home ahead of Hendy in the Sports Long Handicap to fill second place. The Novices' Handicap was contested by Pollack and E N Ward (14083), but neither were placed.

The Whitsun races were entered by six Lea-Francis drivers. A S Llewelyn managed third in the Devon Junior Short Handicap, while H C Spero in his first event with a Leaf turned in a good third in the Devon Long Handicap. His mount was one of the 200-mile race cars (Chassis No. 9161) which he had just purchased from Phil Turner.

The Mountain Race saw Hendy and S C H Davis going really well, both out in front until gradually overtaken by Campbell's Mercedes, and finally Aldington's Frazer-Nash managed to snatch second place from Davis.

Pollack enjoyed a successful June day on the sands at Skegness by scoring an easy win in a race for sports-cars of unlimited capacity. His car was an aluminium-bodied TT Replica (14148) which had originally graced the makers' stand at Olympia.

Kenneth Peacock and Sammy Newsome entered the Le Mans marathon yet again, and another car was specially ordered for the occasion. This machine (Chassis No. 14183) was fitted with a 3·91:1 crown wheel and pinion and Brooklands-pattern long rear springs. There was also an improvement to the overhead rocker oil supply and the regulation four-seater body was panelled in aluminium – the work of the Avon concern. Peacock obtained delivery on 4 June but upon arrival in France he became ill and missed a great deal of the practice period. Still far from well, he took part in the race and once again the pair achieved a most creditable result. Poor fuel caused a deal of plug trouble but the car itself gave every satisfaction and speed was increased by some 3mph compared with 1929, the distance covered being 1424 miles to average 59·44mph. Race position gradually improved during the 24 hours and once again the Leaf was the first small car to finish and was sixth overall.

July opened with the JCC members' day at Brooklands where an enjoyable series of events were contested by Dugdale, Hendy, Chetwynd and Ward. Ward achieved a gold medal, and Hendy managed second place in the Test Hill Sweepstake with a time of 11·2 seconds, being beaten by Earl Howe's Type 43 Bugatti (10·8 seconds).

Two Worcestershire events followed, the first Shelsley Walsh meeting attracting the following Hyper exponents:

Lindsay Eccles	Chassis No. 14157
I S Pollack	Chassis No. 14148
S H Newsome	Chassis No. 14171
J Allan-Arnold	Chassis No. 14141
K H Peacock	Chassis No. 14183

Newsome won the GP Challenge Cup for the fastest 1½-litre sports-car with a climb of 52·4 seconds while Peacock was third in 54 seconds. Tommy Wisdom filled second place in a Frazer-Nash (52·6 seconds).

Madresfield Speed Trials held on Lord Beauchamp's drive near Malvern (still used by the VSCC) resulted in A S Llewelyn securing fastest time of the day in Chassis No. 14175.

The Light Car Club held a series of races at Brooklands on 26 July for cars and three-wheelers up to 1½-litre capacity culminating in an event known as the Light Car Grand Prix. This consisted of 20 laps and a final of similar duration, both using the mountain circuit. Gordon Hendy entered his faithful machine while H C Spero used the 200-mile race car. Young Tom Delaney (now President of the LFOC) ran a works car (Chassis No. 14171) which had been used by several drivers during the season. These three were to do battle against the Frazer-Nash-driving Aldington brothers, H J in a supercharged machine. The remaining cars were a Bugatti entered by F G Van Horn and an unlikely device in the form of a Windsor driven by C A Paul, said to have been bought just prior to the race for a 'fiver'.

Spero enjoyed a terrific scrap with H J Aldington until the latter faded with ignition trouble; Spero went on to win comfortably followed by Hendy while the old Windsor, assisted no doubt by the handicappers, held third place. Tom Delaney was fourth.

The final resulted in a handicap win for the Morgan three-wheeler of Clive Lones while H J Aldington, equipped with a new magneto, just managed to turn the tables on Spero, beating him into third place.

Hendy ran a fine race in the Mountain Speed Handicap held during the August Bank Holiday meeting. He was extremely fast although Malcolm Campbell came through from scratch in his Bugatti and just caught Hendy to win almost at the finishing post. 'Sammy' Davis with Tom Delaney as passenger and using 14171 also enjoyed a fine duel, being evenly matched with the Hon. Brian Lewis in his Talbot. Davis eventually went ahead to take third place.

The Irish Grand Prix, held on 18–19 July 1930, attracted a Lea-Francis entry of six cars:

ENTRANT	NO 1 DRIVER	NO. 2 DRIVER	CHASSIS
Lea & Francis (L T Delaney)	R M V Sutton	S H Newsome	14053
Lea & Francis (L T Delaney)	Cyril Paul	S H Newsome	14130
Lea & Francis (L T Delaney)	Clive Dunfee	S H Newsome	14132
Dan Higgin	Dan Higgin	—	14139
Major R G Heyn	W Sullivan	R G Heyn	14138
J F Field	J F Field	—	14136

Spare Works Car: Chassis No. 14140.

The factory cars were entered under the names of managing director L T Delaney and the crew arrived a week in advance. The drivers and senior staff stayed at the Shelbourne Hotel. W H Green was originally nominated but illness supervened and his place was taken by R M V Sutton. The cars were modified in detail, the most significant being an improved exhaust manifold which was said to improve the power output, now approximately 82–85 bhp. Some impressive practice laps were driven and the cars were undoubtedly faster than in 1929, despite a drop in final-drive ratio. This change was difficult to explain when the

Phoenix Park circuit included a very long and fast straight.

The race was to be a two-day affair as in the previous year with cars of up to $1\frac{1}{2}$ litres running first. Lea-Francis preparation was better than before and all six cars were on the starting-line in first class order. When the flag fell, Higgin and Dunfee shot away ahead of the pack, followed by all but Field who let the side down by taking over a minute to start his engine. The end of the first lap saw Dunfee leading having averaged 68mph, followed closely by Higgin, Sutton and Paul with the Alfa-Romeos behind. Kaye Don in his Alfa forced past Paul on the second lap.

At 20 laps, Victor Gillow, faithful to Rileys as always, actually led on handicap with Cyril Paul in second place followed by Ivanowsky (Alfa), then Higgin, Sutton and Dunfee who had dropped back with mysterious overheating.

ABOVE
Peacock at Le Mans 1930, in 14183

LEFT
Newsome at Shelsley, July 1930, in 14171

Ten laps later Sutton forced himself into second place, Don, having bother with his car, now in fourth spot behind his team-mate Ivanowsky, while Paul had stopped for oil and water, being also bothered with overheating. Young Bill Sullivan was said to have broken a rocker holding down stud, a strange malady which caused his retirement at 21 laps.

Half-time was marked by a heavy downpour of rain which took Field by surprise, he skidded wildly at Ashtown badly damaging his nearside front wheel and this resulted in a slow drive back to the pits for a replacement and re-fuel.

Dunfee was out of the race after 48 laps with a sheared magneto coupling but Cyril Paul hung on grimly to fourth place. The Riley of Gillow was still leading on handicap with his team-mate Whitcroft now in third place, Ivanowsky running second. Captain Waite improved on his handicap to the extent of gaining third position at 50 laps in his Austin 7 followed by Archie Frazer-Nash on another Longbridge machine, Whitcroft having retired with a broken crankshaft. Paul, held back with serious overheating, was now lying fifth but retired just before the end with another magneto drive failure.

The cause of the gear failures was found to be due to the use of an experimental thin wall main bearing which soon hammered out, the resultant crankshaft thrash playing havoc with the timing gears. The overheating was caused by a partially obscured water outlet – the result of hasty modifications carried out by a Coventry radiator firm.

The first Lea-Francis to finish the 300-mile race was Sutton in 10th place with an average of 71·85mph, compared with 74·83 achieved by G E T Eyston in the fastest Alfa-Romeo. Dan Higgin followed at 71·21mph while Field completed the race in 15th place at a speed of 66·40mph.

The fastest laps by both Lea-Francis and Alfa-Romeo were identical at something over 75mph, the Italian cars gradually drawing ahead as the Lower Ford Street challenge faded.

The now traditional Ulster TT followed shortly after the Dublin races and was also contested by six Lea-Francis cars:

ENTRANT	NO. 1 DRIVER	NO. 2 DRIVER	CHASSIS
Lea & Francis (Sir W Sinclair)	S C H Davis	Frank Hallam	14130
Lea & Francis (L T Delaney)	C R Whitcroft	John Cobb	14132
Lea & Francis (H H Timberlake)	R M V Sutton	W H Green	14053
K S Peacock	K S Peacock	S H Newsome	14183
L P Driscoll	L P Driscoll	Dan Higgin	14139
Major R G Heyn	W Sullivan	—	14138

The early part of the race was run in dry conditions but clouds hung ominously above, which resulted in everyone driving flat out in the early stages in order to cover as much distance as possible before the inevitable downpour, which started after two hours of racing.

The 1½-litre cars all made an untidy start with Davis last away. He soon made up for this, however, by lapping faster than his team-mates. His best was 71·27mph compared with Don's fastest time of 72·85 in the Alfa-Romeo. Don was seen to be driving at a terrifying pace which he duly paid for by overturning the car. It burst into flames; Don and his mechanic were pulled clear to suffer only minor injuries.

The first Lea-Francis to fall by the wayside was Peacock's, which crashed into a butcher's shop in Comber village after 13 laps resulting in a badly bent front axle. C R Whitcroft gave up after 17 laps or some 1½ hours with what was described by the Press as 'gear trouble'. Sutton spent much time at his pit changing plugs and then a magneto which took 14 minutes. He lost yet more time by charging a sandbag at Newtownards and then began breaking valve springs, finally retiring at 23 laps. The tale of woe continued, for Sammy Davis also suffered plug trouble and valve spring breakages, giving up for good after 29 tours. Dan Higgins, in his privately owned, well-used and heavier car, ran through without trouble and finished in 16th place at an average of 64·26mph, a figure which compares with Kaye Don's winning speed of 64·06mph in 1928. The course had, however, been improved somewhat over the years. Sullivan was still running at the finish but was unplaced; he did, in fact, cover 355 miles, an average of 61mph.

The race was a sweeping victory for the 1750cc Alfa-Romeo driven by Nuvolari while his team-mates Campari and Varzi finished second and third, all three averaging 70mph. Fourth place was taken by the first 1½-litre car home which was a Straight Eight Alvis with a speed of 69·61mph and handled by Cyril Paul.

These dismal Lea-Francis exploits in the TT were offset a little by the results of the Craigantlet Hill Climb, near Belfast, which took place a week before the TT. Hugh McFarran took home two awards in a standard 12/50 model while W Gregg gained first place in the 1500cc sports-car class with his four-seater Hyper although he charged the bank on one of his runs. The same driver and car had previously made FTD at the Ballybannon Hill Climb, an exciting local event in which the cars were run off in pairs.

Encouraged by the popularity of the 500-mile race in 1929, the BRDC decided to repeat the performance in 1930. Lea & Francis were now in dire financial straits and works participation in motor racing ceased with the appointment by Williams Deacons Bank of a general manager on 31 August. Private owners, Driscoll Higgin and Spero, however, carried the Lea-Francis banner in the 500 event.

Spero set off at a great pace and led the $1\frac{1}{2}$-litre contingent for the first 100 miles when he burst a tyre. Scott then passed by in the Grand Prix Delage although he, in turn, fell out with a serious steering problem caused by the disintegration of the unusual three-piece front axle which was fitted to these cars. Spero was unable to recover and gradually faded out, although he did manage to complete 90 laps by the time the race was declared over. Driscoll also suffered many vicissitudes but nevertheless was still running at the finish of this gruelling event. Higgin retired with engine failure.

G E Took was enjoying success with his four-seater Le Mans-type car (Chassis No. 14147) achieving second place in the class for Super Sports-cars at the Lewes Speed Trials and a bronze medal in the MCC High-Speed Trials at Brooklands in late September. He held first place for the initial stages of this event despite continual spitting back, eventually finishing second at an average of 57·64mph, but E N Ward in a four-seater Hyper (Chassis No. 14083) was unlucky, breaking his propshaft after five laps. The Avon Standard of H C Hutchings turned in a speed of 60·69mph at this popular meeting, an astonishing gait for such a humble machine.

The sum total of awards in racing for Lea-Francis drivers during 1930 was completed by W Esplen in his late type TT Replica (Chassis No. 14181) with third place in a 20-mile race on the sands at Southport in October.

Owners still entered reliability trials, and the London–Land's End event held at Easter listed eight Lea-Francis cars. The drivers included C J N Tait, who non-started, H W Burman in his 6-cylinder car, L Maxwell with a TT machine, G H Seldon in a brand-new Hyper four-seater (Chassis No. 14179), and A A Mauleverer with his TT Replica. T W Drayton in a 12/40 gained a silver medal, but H Lawrence retired after failing several hills due to a poor steering lock on his heavy Ulster saloon.

H J Vidler won an award in the Brighton-to-Beer trial in June, while Maxwell, Burman and W E Holland netted gold medals in the London–Edinburgh. G O T Gamble also met with success and was awarded a silver medal. A D Chetwynd ran through the London–Gloucester run in December without any trouble, being easily the fastest competitor up all timed sections. The Boxing Day London–Exeter Trial was beginning to wane in popularity with a mere two Lea-Francis entries. W E Holland was forced to retire but Humphrey Burman won a silver medal in his immaculate 14/40.

Several famous cars were put up for sale at the end of the season including those of Bliss, Field and Peacock. The last-named was advertized from Sam Newsome's Coventry garage at £395. The economic climate can be judged by the fact that it remained unsold for some six months, eventually changing hands in the trade for well under £300 while Hendy offered his car for £215.

A mere 19 'S'-type cars were assembled during 1930, a clear indication of the impending financial insolvency. This total included eight T T Replicas, fitted with aluminium bodies. All were built with a single door on the nearside, although the catalogue specification states that no doors were provided. The last TT car (Chassis No. 14187) which was exhibited at Olympia in October, had considerably improved lines with a rounded tail, and heavily louvred valances, while a single pane, full-width screen was provided. It remained unsold until June 1934, and is happily still in existence, owned by Cameron Millar. Five Weymann Coupés were sold, but the standard four-seater tourer only accounted for three cars. Two or three saloons were completed, the final one (Chassis No. 14186) being despatched to Olympia for demonstration purposes. The total was completed with Peacock's Le Mans four-seater. No technical changes took place during 1930 on Standard Hypers.

The three works team cars were put up for sale by the factory in May 1931 for a purse of £900 but were in fact sold piecemeal, 14053 going to Tom Delaney, 14132 to A N L Machlachlan and 14130 to a Mr Whitaker of Wakefield, although it eventually passed into the hands of R C Vickers who raced it in 1933–4.

The spare car (Chassis No. 14140) was rebuilt and re-registered as 14149 and VC 9044 respectively and was prepared for Newsome to use at Shelsley in 1931, running with a 3·5:1 rear axle. This machine was later to achieve fame in the hands of Bill Sullivan in the 1932 TT by beating the $1\frac{1}{2}$-litre lap record.

The final modification carried out by the factory on the team cars concerned cooling. Thicker radiator cores were fitted while the system was pressurized. No further development was undertaken on racing-cars after the sale of the works team.

CHAPTER SEVEN

Decline

Sales figures during the 1928 season began satisfactorily but later in the season business became more difficult and a stock of finished cars began to build up. The company kept up a strong advertizing campaign with double pages being regularly taken in the motoring press. The racing and trials successes together with agreeable road test reports all helped prestige and the firm was assisted by some energetic agents. C B Wardman and Co. still took more cars than anyone else with their London and Home Counties distribution rights although they were greatly aided by the efforts of Eustace Watkins & Co., later to become well known as London distributors of Wolseley cars. The Central Garage of Bradford and Messrs Bayliss & Forbes of Nottingham put up the best performances among those representing the provinces.

The works were assembling cars quickly and efficiently with chassis frames in two rows placed upside down upon trestles at the commencement of their journey through the erection shop. The brake cross-shafts were first bolted into position and then the shackle eyes were aligned with the aid of long rods which were passed through from one side to the other. A certain amount of bending and twisting of frames was found to be necessary at this juncture before a satisfactory alignment was achieved. The springs and axles were then offered up, the latter sub-assemblies having been put together in the old building on the other side of the 'Arcade'. The frames were turned the right way up and were fitted with engines and gearboxes, followed by steering columns and radiators. A perfunctory chassis road test was undertaken before the cars were despatched to the coachbuilders, Avon (of Warwick) or Cross & Ellis. These two firms supplied 95 per cent of the bodies fitted. A quick turnround of chassis was achieved by these two concerns who maintained a good flow of production in readiness for the arrival of chassis and thus managed to return the completed car to Lower Ford Street within seven to ten days and in some cases in a mere 48 hours. Special orders and prototypes took longer – six to eight weeks.

The finished vehicle was then tuned and tested with some care although never enough to satisfy Van Eugen who always managed to find a few faults with a car which was alleged to be ready to hand to a customer – it was ever thus!

Competition cars were assembled on the same lines as their touring sisters but the built-up chassis was passed over to the racing shop for careful wiring and cottering of all vital components by Jack Lea, 'Plumb' Warner and Jack Hewitson under the watchful eye of Alec Taylor. At the close of a season the team cars would be stripped (they all suffered with cracked chassis in the vicinity of the rear engine bearer in 1928) and built up on to new frames in the erection shop alongside normal production cars. The mechanical components, having been overhauled in their respective departments, were then re-introduced to the cars although this system led to a certain mix up of components making it difficult to trace the history of individual machines. Original chassis numbers were, however, retained in most instances although they were sometimes re-registered with Coventry Council, no doubt to convey the impression to the public they were brand-new productions.

The financial results for the year ending 31 August 1928 were dismal and showed a loss of £17,175. The full effects of the disastrous 14/40 car were now being felt, with Lower Ford Street being forced to carry out a large amount of guarantee work on these Southport-built machines.

Several stormy board meetings took place and Wardman resigned on 19 October 1928; he did, of course, control the majority of the equity capital which was held by C B Wardman & Co. Ltd. As compensation for relinquishing his office as chairman he was presented with the lease of the London showrooms situated at 118–22, Great Portland Street, in former times the site of the residence of Boswell, Dr Johnson's biographer.

The board was strengthened early in 1928 with the appointment of Sir Walrond Sinclair, also chairman of the British Goodrich Tyre Co. which had become one of the principal creditors in Lea-Francis as the sole suppliers of tyres. H H Timberlake, a well-known motor agent from Wigan and a director of the Vulcan concern was invited to become chairman and W. Macdonald another Vulcan director also joined the Lea-Francis board. A S Fitch had resigned some time before in order to concentrate on his own Lea-Francis agency in Shaftesbury Avenue. G H Percival was appointed secretary having joined the company in 1924. He stayed until 1936.

The most popular model in 1928 was, predictably, the 'P'-type 12/40 and exactly 500 of these cars were delivered during the year. The vast majority were two- and four-seater tourers but approximately 50 of the heavy-looking Leafabric saloons were built, together with a similar number of coupés both fixed and drophead. A few cars were sold with Vulcan or Avon coachbuilt saloon bodies.

The smart 'O'-type 12/50 fitted with rakish Cross & Ellis coachwork accounted for only 38 cars, being overshadowed by the exciting Hyper which found 81 buyers. Surprisingly, 59 'T'-type 6-cylinder cars were sold, some being built at Southport and fitted with heavy Vulcan bodies. The Coventry examples generally received four-seater Avon or various patterns from Cross & Ellis. One car (Chassis No. 15005) was commissioned by Eric Findon of the Light Car, a keen Leaf enthusiast who previously ordered a special 12/50-engined 'G'-type (Chassis No. 7784) and later a Gordon England-bodied 12/40 'M'-type. His new 6-cylinder car with a special small-bore engine of 1½-litre capacity, thus qualifying as a light car, was fitted with a Lea-Francis freewheel and a Hyper-type blue-fabric saloon body complete with double row bumper bars of a type then coming into vogue. He wrote a glowing report of his first 2000 miles in this car, appreciating the ease of gear changing provided by the freewheel.

The popularity of the 12/22 model was beginning to wane. One hundred and ninety-nine 'U'-types were laid down although five were switched to 'P'-type specification during build, such alterations no doubt dictated by the state of the order book. Practically all of these two-bearing cars were fitted with Avon touring bodies, the Warwick firm now building two-seaters to the Cross & Ellis pattern. Two cars received Vulcan saloon coachwork and 14 final 'J'-types were assembled, nearly all were Vulcan saloons and the final one (Chassis No. 7970) was delivered on 10 July 1928. A few orders still came in for the economical 10hp cars and 11 more 'K'-types were sold, together with four 'G4'-types, all being Avon tourers. Production at Coventry for the 1928 season was completed with the assembly of the final 'L'- and 'M'-types, three and two cars respectively.

Continuous detail improvements to the production cars were made, amongst which was the main brake cross-shaft which was considerably stiffened, and mounted on large ball-races for all cars after mid-1928. The resulting reduction in frictional losses made the optional servo motor almost unnecessary, according to Van Eugen.

An interesting project undertaken late in 1928 concerned a rotary valve engine. The directors were impressed by a German layout conceived by Baer (of crankshaft fame) and Rommel, which embodied a rotating shaft placed longitudinally in the cylinder head, and which contained ports corresponding with those in the main head casting. The induction port leading from the carburettor was fitted with an inner sleeve which was spring-loaded against the rotating shaft to aid gas sealing.

Rommel tried to interest British manufacturers in this device and drove a Morris Isis so equipped which seemed to run very well. The conversion carried out for Lea-Francis was based upon a 14/40 engine, no doubt the drive for the overhead camshafts on this type rendered the rotary valve conversion easier to undertake. Initial tests revealed performance inferior to the normal engine while starting was very difficult. It was decided, no doubt wisely, that the risks involved in developing and marketing such an engine were too great, and the project was abandoned.

An additional model, known as the 'V'-type was introduced for the 1929 season, this consisted, to all intents and purposes of a Hyper Weymann Coupé without the supercharger. The standard two-port 12/50 engine, and final drive ratio of 4·7:1 were utilized, and a very pleasant car resulted.

Thirty-eight more 14/40 Lea-Francis models were built at Southport, production ceasing in September. Small numbers of the 16/60 2 Lea-Francis cars filtered through, 18 cars leaving the factory in 1928. A fair proportion were exported to Australia although the Lancashire factory had now discontinued the assembly of private cars bearing the Vulcan name. They received an enquiry from Australia for the production of an ambulance, and a long chassis version of the 14/40 car was designed for this purpose, but it seems doubtful if any were built.

Late in 1928, Sir Walrond Sinclair and L T Delaney began a series of talks with the directors of Bentley Motors, with a view to a merger. Lea-Francis were now freed from the Vulcan yoke, and it was considered that the range of cars made by Coventry and Cricklewood complemented each other. Lea-Francis were to be responsible for cars up to 14hp and Bentley would handle the heavy brigade from 16hp upwards, an arrangement which would have suited the agents very well. A close investigation showed, however, that both companies were identical in too many respects. Machine shop and engineering facilities were similar, neither possessed coachbuilding facilities, and both suffered from a shortage of cash. The talks were reluctantly abandoned.

It is interesting to record that a certain Bentley director, being rightly proud of his company's 4½-litre car, which had recently been introduced, spoke glowingly to the Delaney family of the fine performance of this model. He was invited to a match race against Delaney's Gold Fabric Hyper Lea-Francis, which he accepted in a somewhat patronizing manner. A rude awakening followed, for on a Sunday morning run around the roads of North London, the Bentley had the greatest difficulty in keeping the Lea-Francis in sight. The 1½-litre supercharged car proved markedly superior from rest to 80mph. A few days later a request came from chief designer Burgess for Tom Delaney to call round at Cricklewood with the Lea-Francis so that it could be examined at close quarters. There is no doubt that the performance of the Hyper Leaf caused a great many designers to give very serious consideration to introducing a mild boost to their touring engines.

Back at Coventry, Van Eugen began to think of the next stage in the development of his car, but clearly the chassis was still in the forefront of design and practice, considering the state of the art at that time.

Henry Meadows were approached concerning the re-design of their 1½-litre engine range. They refused to help, possibly suspecting that Lea-Francis would not survive to take advantage of any long and costly development that they would have to undertake. In any case, concern was felt at Coventry regarding the quality of Meadows engines, which had been deteriorating, resulting in dozens of 4-ED units being returned with complaints ranging from porous crankcases – found to be temporarily 'caulked up' – to poor power output. In one case power output was as low as 24bhp, while engines which were satisfactory with regard to power suffered from an unacceptable degree of vibration. The Wolverhampton firm, however, instigated a much stiffer system of test and inspection with the result that later engines were much improved.

Charles Van Eugen was, nevertheless, given the authority to design a new engine at Lower Ford Street, and work began in January 1929 on the first drawings of a 4-cylinder single overhead camshaft unit, still bearing the classic dimensions of 69 by 100. The assembly of the first and only engine was carried out by Messrs Coventry Climax, and it was placed in one of the new 'Francis' Fabric Saloons (Chassis No. 18055) in November 1929, for road testing. It performed substantially better than the standard Meadows 4-ED, and was obviously capable of considerable development. This engine was designated type 'TV'.

During this period, a vogue for small 6- and straight 8-cylinder engines was underway, and most manufacturers were determined to follow suit, ultimately to their great discomfort, and in some cases doom.

The directors considered that the reputation of Lea-Francis which had suffered severely from the 14/40 Vulcan might be put to rights by the introduction of a completely new and advanced Light Six, designed and built at Lower Ford Street, in addition such a car would satisfy the current dictates of fashion.

Further development of the ohc 4-cylinder engine was, therefore, suspended and in February 1930, Van Eugen received instructions to prepare a 6-cylinder version for production with all haste. Although he had, meanwhile, prepared a drawing for an improved 4-cylinder unit with single chain drive at the front for the camshaft and block and crankcase cast as one unit.

Orders for cars fell off badly as the year 1929 progressed. The dismal news from Wall Street destroyed confidence, and that economic barometer, the high-grade motor manufacturer, was, as usual, among the most vulnerable of industries affected.

The 'P'-type 12/40 was still the best-selling model, and 347 units were delivered. The loosening of ties with Vulcan saw a cessation in the use of Vulcan bodies. Only one chassis, which was supplied personally to C B Wardman in January 1929, had a Vulcan body, although several agents were still holding unsold Vulcan saloons built in the previous year, this model was thus still catalogued.

Cross & Ellis produced a suitable replacement six light body covered in fabric. Although somewhat angular, it was lower than its Southport predecessor, in height as well as price. This model was billed as the 'Ulster' Saloon at £395. The cumbersome Leafabric Saloon was phased out, while the demand for the four-seater tourer had also slackened. The two-seater, however, continued to be very popular and the recently introduced 'V'-type sold well with 85 cars delivered while Hyper orders totalled 67. Sales of that excellent, if sober 12/22, at £295 the cheapest model offered, were now very slow, and it was clear that this car was outdated. Nevertheless, 31 new cars found owners; almost all were Avon four-seater tourers.

There was concern about the number of sales for the lower-priced Lea-Francis models which were being lost to the Riley 9. This close-coupled and elegant fabric saloon seating all passengers within the wheelbase was gaining great popularity, and the nearby Foleshill factory, planned for large-scale manufacture by the standards of the time, was turning out ever larger numbers of these machines. It was ironical that the factory planning and organization of the Riley works for the production of the 'Nine', was the responsibility of George Leek, later to become head of the reconstructed Lea-Francis firm.

Van Eugen, determined to offer some competition, designed a lightweight fabric body for a modified version of the 12/40 car, during the summer of 1929. The result was a most distinctive machine following, but not slavishly copying, the lines of the 'Monaco' Riley.

The new Lea-Francis was to be known as the 'Francis' Saloon, and was officially designated as type 'W'. A new radiator of ten degree slope was evolved, with all facets slightly altered in a subtle manner, the result being most attractive. The windscreen sloped at a similar angle while a reverse ten-degree slope characterized the rear door shut pillar, and the body tail. A built-in boot was incorporated, 'à la Riley', but the six light styling avoided too close a comparison. Alterations to the chassis included the adoption of a rear petrol tank fed by an 'Autovac', while the dashboard and instrument panel were bolted directly to the chassis frame through the medium of stout steel pressings. The dashboard was now aluminium-faced; this new layout, being completely independent of the body, greatly facilitated production from the coachbuilders' angle.

Cross & Ellis were once more responsible for the new body, and the first one was built secretly at weekends, Van Eugen calling round at Dane Road on Sunday mornings to urge progress. Completed in September (Chassis No. 18000), it was shown to the agents for approval. The next car (Chassis No. 18001) was ready in time for the Olympia Show, and in fact, 48 cars were sold before the end of the year.

It proved impossible to get below a selling price of £375 and thus it was not directly competitive with the Riley at £295. It was, however, a most attractive car, and the faithful Meadows engine gave it a respectable performance; total weight was 23cwt.

Serious thought was then given to the manufacture of a genuine 9hp Lea-Francis car based on the 1100cc SCAP and it was considered that an expenditure of a mere £550 in machine tools would enable the firm to produce 25 9hp and 25 12hp cars per week, albeit with the assistance of night and evening shifts. The plan was abandoned after deliberation as it was felt that competition in the lower-priced market would become too fierce.

The remaining cars sold in 1929 were the result of special orders. In total, seven 'O'-type 12/50's and two 'G-4' 10hp cars were ordered, and one final 'K'-type was assembled in July. A number of Coventry-built 'T'-type 14/40 chassis were still in store and 21 of these were completed and sold during the year, mostly with Cross & Ellis or Avon coachwork, with the exception of Chassis No. 15071, which was given a fabric body by Morgan Hastings.

June 1929 witnessed a serious financial crisis at Vulcan motors. The majority of their workforce was laid off while their unsold stock of 16/60 2 LFS cars were taken over at 'bargain basement' prices by Rosenfields of Manchester. This concern succeeded in re-selling them within a short space of time, no doubt aided by a lowered price.

Lea-Francis financial results for the year ending 31 August 1929 made dismal reading with a loss of £15,418. The continuing difficulties with the 14/40 car were blamed. There were now some 350 of these vehicles in use.

The remaining three Southport directors, namely Hindle, Rimmer and Macdonald, retired at the time of the Vulcan difficulties in June. Their place was taken by Charles Turner, an accountant from Sheffield. He was appointed by Williams Deacons Bank, who held debentures in the Vulcan business.

Herbert Tatlow complained that the fall in sales was due to a lack of effort on the part of the sales force. He was therefore offered a chance to put matters aright and moved down to the London sales office in 1930, Gerry Becker looking after production at Coventry. Tatlow was unable to effect any improvements in sales and he left the company, moving to the Beatenson windscreen firm.

The most important event of the year 1930 was the introduction of the new 6-cylinder car. The first example, a brown fabric Cross & Ellis Saloon was through final inspection and test on 5 June, an outstanding effort by a handful of dedicated enthusiasts and craftsmen under the guidance of Van Eugen who first put pencil to paper on the 'Ace of Spades' project only four months before. The chassis, it is true, was entirely unaltered excepting an increase in wheelbase from 9ft 3in to 9ft 6in. The engine was, however, completely new and all the work

ABOVE AND OPPOSITE
The 'Ace of Spades' engine

was carried out at Lower Ford Street.

This power unit embodied many advanced features and showed much original thought. The first requisite of the designer, no doubt influenced by the basic weakness of the 14/40 car, was to ensure a stiff and well-supported lower half with an adequate lubrication system free of untidy external pipes. A respectable power output was also sought with careful attention to porting and valve layout.

The classic dimensions of 65×100mm were chosen giving an RAC rating of 15·7hp and a capacity of 1991cc. The crankshaft was of very generous proportions and fully counterbalanced, running in four main bearings of 55mm diameter with big ends of a similar size – very large by the standards of the time. The crank was balanced statically and dynamically, a vibration damper being considered unnecessary. Certainly the unit was very smooth-running; despite the length of stroke it would 'rev' happily up to a maximum of over 4000rpm. The connecting rods were of duralumin, a material then very popular although this feature was to result in the scrapping of numbers of engines with breakages in later years due to age hardening. Pistons of 'Bohnalite' Invar-Strut pattern were fitted.

Both cylinder block and crankcase were of integral construction and cast in iron. This main component being of great rigidity. The cast-iron cylinder head was most interesting and unique in respect of the method of attachment to the block. Short studs were screwed into the lower face of the head, the free ends passed through the top face of the cylinder block and into recesses underneath for the attachment of holding down nuts. These recesses were covered by neat plates bearing the Lea-Francis monogram. The whole effect was very neat and achieved the worthwhile object of water passages and ports being totally unobstructed by bosses for conventional studs. A possible drawback which may have become apparent if the engine had been developed and subjected to higher pressures was the positioning of these studs which were towards the outside faces of the engine (in order to gain spanner access to the nuts), thus the support between cylinders was limited and may have been insufficient to prevent gasket leakages. The engine as built, however, was quite free from trouble in this respect.

An overhead camshaft arrangement embodying operating fingers running on needle bearings was adopted utilizing the layout of the experimental 'TV' 4-cylinder engine. Combustion chamber shape was almost hemispherical and the head diameter of both valves was 1·41in. The camshaft was driven by a two-stage roller chain of Duplex type while the camshaft sprocket could be detached and placed on a ledge cast into the timing cover which enabled the cylinder head to be removed without disturbing the valve timing. One wonders if Wm Heynes of Jaguar consulted Van Eugen (his Mentor at the Coventry branch of the IAE) about this feature when laying out the XK engine; perhaps Van Eugen also influenced Heynes with regard to the sliding block spring shackles found on SS chassis from 1936 onwards.

The new Lea-Francis engine made much use of the magnesium alloy electron; sump, valve cover, engine bearers, sundry small castings and the timing cover were cast from this metal. The timing cover closely resembled an inverted 'Ace of Spades'; the works personnel quickly coined this phrase, and it was adopted by the company as the official name for the new model within weeks of its initial announcement. Originally however the car was advertized both as a '2-litre', '16/60', and later 16/70, with chassis numbers in the 20,000 series. The official drawing-office title was also type 'AS', after the two draughtsmen responsible, W S Ainscough and F R Smith.

The distinctive timing cover shape was necessitated by the lower timing chain which also drove the accessories passing over a sprocket on the offside, which drove the magneto, and another on the nearside, which rotated the dynamo armature and water pump which were in tandem.

The sump held 14 pints of oil and the submerged pump was driven from the rear of the crankshaft and fed oil through a 'full flow' detachable filter to all points under pressure. The crankcase was drilled for oilways and only one external pipe was to be found, this latter to pass lubricant to the camshaft and valve gear.

Carburation was by downdraught Stromberg which fed mixture into a tubular manifold with a hotspot warmed by exhaust heat via a pipe passing through the centre of the cylinder block. Two water outlet branches were fitted, one on each side of the front of the cylinder head. A new departure for Lea-Francis concerned fuel delivery which was by AC mechanical pump.

The whole engine was very neat in appearance and bore every evidence of being a production of the highest grade. The works costing of the complete engine when in production came out at £84. The valve gear and cylinder head attachment layout were both the subject of patents and a Borg & Beck clutch was specified, possibly the first British car so fitted.

A new gearbox was evolved concurrently with the Ace engine, known as the 'Duo' by virtue of the fact that it consisted of two separate boxes bolted together. The forward part housed third and top speeds with dog engagement, the gears being in constant mesh while the rear gearbox contained first, second and reverse together with the speedometer drive. The gears in this section were of normal sliding type. The complete assembly held the liberal quantity of five points of oil. The object of the new gearbox was to shorten the unsupported length of the shafts and thus with less distortion achieve a reduction in noise. Despite all this good sense the indirects were still comparatively noisy, although, like its predecessor it was an extremely robust unit with a very quick change. Time was to prove that it was almost indestructible. The Duo gearbox was patented and adopted later on for the 12/40 range as well. Ratios as standard on both 4- and 6-cylinder cars being 4·7, 6·45, 9·4 and 15·01:1 with a 20·4:1 reverse.

Official launching of the Ace of Spades took place in September 1930 and the car was offered with six different body styles, all the work of Cross & Ellis and ranging from a standard two-seater with dickey similar to the 12/40, a four-seater tourer. Both these open cars were priced at £445 followed by two attractive styles of fixed-head coupé known as the 'County' and the 'Sportsman' to a rather long and cumbersome six light saloon panelled in aluminium, although one could specify a fabric roof and rear quarters. All of these closed cars were listed at £495.

The 4-cylinder range of cars continued almost unchanged during 1930, the only noticeable difference concerning a new arrangement of throttle and ignition levers at the top of the steering column complete with a horn push and bakelite surround.

Production figures for 1930 relate a further reduction of business. The most popular model proved to be the 'W'-type Francis saloon with 118 cars delivered. Thirteen Aces were delivered before the end of the year, six of these were built with 10° sloping radiators, all were Cross & Ellis saloons. The faithful 'P'-type found 107 buyers, most were two- and four-seater touring cars, although a small number of coupés and Ulster Saloons were delivered. The old Vulcan saloon was still listed well into 1930, although none had been built for some 18 months. 'V'-type Weymann Coupés accounted for 17 sales. The final drive ratio on these cars was lowered to 5·1:1 in the majority of cases, while one was ordered with a TT two-seater body (Chassis No. 18121). Hyper sales dropped to 19 cars.

The total output was completed with several odd special orders. The final 'U'-type 12/22 orders totalled seven; these were converted from 'P'-type chassis, mostly with wire wheels, and the last car (Chassis No. 16312) was despatched without an engine on 1 August. Five 'O'-type 12/50's were assembled. The open two-seater Avon bodies reserved for this model were sleeker than the standard 12/40 type with lowered windscreens, front opening doors with raked shut pillars. One car (Chassis No. 12051) of this rare type has fortunately survived in very good order. Four-seater cars in this series utilized the Cross & Ellis design.

The final 'T'-type 14/40 car was completed and sold on 19 February without guarantee, this was fortunate because it ran two big ends on 22 February.

The little 'G'-type 10hp car was still remembered, and two more cars were assembled, the final one (Chassis No. 6825) to the order of racing shop foreman, Alec Taylor. Both these cars were built with front-wheel brakes, ball-bearing brake cross shafts and 12/50 Brooklands engines.

The financial results for the year ending 31 August 1930 made poor reading. The year's trading resulted in a deficit of £12,164 and the overdraft stood at £41,858. The economic depression was held to blame, but the board had high hopes of regaining prosperity with the Ace of Spades. The directors underwent considerable privation in order to help the firm as much as possible during these difficult days, for emoluments of all six totalled a mere £300.

The firm's bankers were not satisfied, however, and although they had insisted on representation on the board through Charles Turner, they now instructed that the day-to-day running be put in the hands of a general manager, Bert Ware. L T Delaney therefore resigned as managing director, but retained his seat on the board.

The company put on a brave show at Olympia in October. All the exhibits were attractively finished in Wedgewood Blue with cream wheels and consisted of a Francis Saloon, 'P'-type two-seater, Ace of Spades semi-panelled saloon, the final TT two-seater (Chassis No. 14187) and a polished and plated Ace Chassis (No. 20003). These cars were backed up with a team of demonstrators. Orders remained scarce and the Hyper series failed to find a single buyer.

The Ace of Spades met with a very good reception by the Press, *The Autocar* testing the model on three occasions. The semi-panelled saloon (Chassis No. 20002) which they handled in February 1931 was commented upon most favourably. This large and comfortable car was found to be smooth and lively, recording a maximum of 74mph with 60 available in third, together with steering and road holding of a very high order. The creditable figure, for a car weighing 25½cwt, of 24mpg was averaged for the whole test.

An enlarged version of the Ace engine was now evolved, work beginning in November 1930. The bore size was increased to 69mm giving a capacity of 2244cc and an RAC rating of 17·7hp. A new cylinder head was produced with enlarged valves, while the ports were increased initially in diameter by 5mm to 35mm, although later reduced to 33mm. No power curves for these engines appear to have survived, but it is probably that the 2-litre engine delivered some 60bhp at approximately 4000 rpm with the enlarged version providing 70bhp. The compression ratio was 6·1:1. The first engine was installed into Chassis No. 20049 in April 1931.

The economic depression reached its nadir in the Spring of 1931, and the old firm was now at the point of insolvency. The company secretary, G H Percival, a man of considerable commercial ability had always insisted on prompt payment being made to all small creditors, thus putting as much load as possible on to the firm's bankers. Together with

ABOVE
Olympia, October 1930

LEFT
The sole surviving 'O'-type 12/50; now converted to independent front suspension

Delaney-Galley and British Goodrich, they were, after all, in control of a great majority of the equity via the Vulcan shareholding and that of Delaney and Sinclair. Thus it was that Lea-Francis enjoyed a good relationship with suppliers which proved very valuable in ensuring technical help and quick delivery of material during these difficult years.

The end came at the beginning of March. Avon bodies were presented with three cars (Chassis Nos. 18163, 18174 and 19034) as payment by contra for a batch of two-seater bodies. This practice was common to many manufacturers in pre-war days.

On Friday morning, 6 March, the bank appointed Charles Turner as official receiver. An immediate cut back in staff took place, and it was agreed that the day-to-day running of the firm be left in the hands of Van Eugen (works) and Percival (commercial), while Charles Turner travelled down from Sheffield for a weekly meeting. The only immediate outside effect concerned Cross & Ellis, who took fright and impounded all the Lea-Francis cars in their body shops – they were eventually re-assured with much anxious telephoning – after all, one is always secure when dealing with an official receiver.

On 18 March, Sir Walrond Sinclair and R H Lea both resigned. Lea was now over 70 years of age. The weekly wage bill was reduced immediately from approximately £500 to £250, and before the end of 1931 it had fallen to £200. The insistence of cash payments for all goods started to yield results immediately and trading for the year from 5 March 1931 to 5 March 1932 resulted in a surplus of £3200.

The receiver continued to sanction the erection of chassis in batches of 10, and a full range of new cars were held in stock at the factory.

The London showrooms were closed in September and retail sales were then handled direct from the factory, although Messrs L T Delaney still continued to hold a small stock at their Calton Vale Service Depot. Relieved from the necessity to hand over large discounts to agents proved beneficial, and some profitable deals were made with both new and second-hand cars.

During the year 1931, Lea-Francis were approached by Sir Denistoun Burney for the supply of engines for his highly unorthodox rear-engined car, then in the process of development. The Burney had utilized straight eight Beverley-Barnes Twin-camshaft engines but these were proving troublesome, and were outrageously noisy. Van Eugen told the author that if pedestrians passed by, they were alarmed by the noise of these brutes even when ticking over by the kerbside.

Van Eugen and Percival offered to supply Ace of Spades engines at £125, but the order went to Armstrong-Siddeley, although the entire project faded out soon afterwards.

A decision was made to fit the 16hp Ace engine into the standard 'P'-type chassis, the result being a less-cumbersome and slightly livelier car. This model was advertized as a '2 Litre', and was given a chassis number in the range of 18500 up. Messrs Carbodies were responsible for the saloon bodies fitted to these cars, styling being basically similar to the Cross & Ellis pattern. The first sample (Chassis No. 18500) was completed in August, and was used as a demonstrator and press test car for 11 months.

Detail improvements to the 4-cylinder cars took place in readiness for the 1931 model year. Chromium plating was adopted for radiators and sundry fittings, while an elegant and shallow four-eared cap bearing the Lea-Francis monogram was evolved for use on radiator and petrol tank. This pattern was retained with a change of thread by the re-constructed company for cars built up to 1954.

All 12/40 models were now given rear petrol tanks and the rigid chassis mounted dash and instrument board, together with smarter front wings embodying a longer sweep, while the lighting system was modernized. These changes were also embodied in the Ace of Spades. The Duo gearbox gradually replaced the older pattern on all models, but a batch of 'P'-type cars were fitted with close ratio gearboxes, thus using up surplus Hyper stock. No supercharged cars were sold in 1931, apart from a store-soiled Hyper saloon demonstrator (Chassis No. 14186) which had been completed in the previous October. Cross & Ellis produced a modernized fixed-head coupé body for the 'P'-type 12/40 and three or four examples were sold.

The depressing habit of lowering final drive ratios, prevalent in the early thirties was also gaining ground at Lea-Francis, and nearly all the 12/40 cars were now being fitted with 5·1:1 crown wheels and pinions, albeit with a tyre size increase from $4·75 \times 19$ to 5×19.

Production figures became difficult to determine from this point onwards, and some finished cars were in stock for several years, but actual sales during 1931 consisted of 41 'P'-type cars, 18 'W'-type and three final 'V'-type coupés (Nos. 17099, 17101 and 17104) fitted with 'W'-type 10° radiators and bodies built by Cross & Ellis to the Weymann design. Twenty-five more 16/70 models found buyers, which included two Avon two-seaters, one of which must have presented a unique appearance being fitted with a 10° sloping radiator. Three four-seater tourers by Cross & Ellis were also built using sloping radiators with door pillars and windscreens angled to suit. Two of the attractive County coupés were delivered, and one machine bore a saloon body which was the work of Carbodies. The remaining cars were Cross & Ellis saloons, one example being fully fabric covered.

The first sale of a short chassis Ace (No. 18504) was effected on Christmas Eve.

Scrutiny of the repair department records, *circa* late 1931, provides an indication of the service problems that were encountered with the Ace of Spades of which some 50 cars were now in use. Chassis No. 20000, in the hands of Van Eugen and works testers had covered 40,000 miles and a total engine strip for examination was carried out at 38,739 miles. Maximum cylinder bore wear of 0·005in was discovered at the top of all cylinders, a figure then considered very good, while the condition of the crankshaft and all other major components showed virtually no deterioration.

Cars in private use were all proving free from major headaches and the basic 'correctness' of the design was proved. Certain shortcomings were, however, manifesting themselves which caused the re-design of the parts concerned. Several cars visiting the works for routine service were found to be suffering from cracked

W Graden of Whitehaven with 14187 and Ace of Spades 20003

rear-engine bearers, a stiffer pattern still cast from elektron was introduced and fitted retrospectively under guarantee. Dynamo drive shafts were breaking and water pumps were leaking, but both problems were overcome. A new type of pump with an adjustable gland was developed. Some trouble with sticking valves occurred but boring out the guide where it protruded into the port cured this complaint. The downdraught Stromberg carburettor was never quite satisfactory, since it was too easy for an inept owner to overchoke the engine. This meant having to change plugs, which was not easy, although a special spanner was provided.

A number of complaints about boiling were received and always after the cars in question had been to the service depot for work involving the removal of the radiator. This was found to be due to water pump grease blocking the matrix and an immediate end to this problem was effected by filling the radiator with water and blanking the outlets while this component was detached, thus keeping the grease in suspension. A camshaft-bearing modification completed the development changes and all were incorporated in cars built during 1932 and subsequently.

Competition activity was much reduced during 1931, primarily as a result of the withdrawal of the works team. A few private owners, however, began modifying their cars with a view to extracting more performance and often with surprising success.

The most consistently successful contender over the next few seasons was Tom Delaney. He carefully tuned his car and ultimately fitted a No. 11 Cozette supercharger resulting in some 18lb of pressure. Despite strenuous racing, no major breakage ever occurred; the only real problem was a tendency to crack cylinder heads in the vicinity of the exhaust ports. Driscoll's car was also considerably faster than standard; alterations included raised compression using Martlett pistons, Scintilla Magneto and very careful balancing of crankshaft and connecting-rod assemblies. In this form the car would reach 5850rpm in top gear equivalent to approximately 115mph while a lap of the outer circuit was timed at 112·8mph.

Alan Machlachlan, who purchased a four-seater Le Mans-type car (No. 14128) and then a works team car (Chassis No. 14132) also indulged in some special tuning and very careful assembly. He eventually lowered the radiator and body considerably on the latter car. Both were very fast and reliable.

The opening Brooklands meeting held in March saw a third place for Driscoll in the

Lincoln Senior Short Handicap and another third for Tom Delaney using a works car (Chassis No. 14171) in a Mountain Speed Handicap after a duel with A P Agabeg in a Salmson, the latter perhaps better known as A F P Fane. The Easter meeting was spoilt by atrocious weather and although contested by Leaf owners Allan-Arnold, T G Clarke, the Hon. A D Chetwynd and L P Driscoll, no awards were gained although Driscoll almost certainly forfeited a place in a mountain race when he stopped to render assistance to S C H Davies who had crashed badly in his Invicta.

Lea-Francis entries in the Double-12 were confined to G C Dugdale partnered by Delaney in a 1929 works team car (No. 14144) and E N Oetzmann assisted by F Ivins, their mount being Kenneth Peacock's 1930 Le Mans car (No. 14183). Bad luck supervened, for Oetzmann broke a gudgeon pin after 60 laps. He pushed his car a considerable distance to the pits and promptly stripped and rebuilt the engine, but gave up the struggle at 4.15 p.m. without rejoining the race. The Dugdale/Delaney car suffered a bad radiator leak causing retirement at 9.15 a.m. on the second morning. The engine had actually been rebuilt on the eve of the race following damage caused by a loose sleeve and it also ran throughout the race with no oil pressure whatsoever registering on the gauge, seemingly without any ill effects.

Tom Delaney now purchased the old TT winner (No. 14053) from Lea & Francis and entered it for the Irish Grand Prix. It was the only Lea-Francis in the race in 1931 which, as usual, saw the smaller cars on the first day. Pit management was in the hands of L T Delaney, who was assisted by his daughter Doris, while H C Spero was to be co-driver. Spares and equipment were all carried in the family Francis saloon (No. 18096). The racing car behaved well in practice and turned in some impressive lap times. Racing began at 3 p.m. and torrential rain fell for most of the time. Delaney shot into the lead as the flag fell pursued by A C Taylor in an Alfa-Romeo. The end of the first lap saw Delaney out in front undeterred by the miserable conditions and after another round the position was still the same. Yet Victor Gillow was on his heels and by a display of somewhat wild driving managed to force past; but then he spun off the course and Delaney was in first place once more. Meanwhile the Riley was building up a commanding lead on handicap. This unsupercharged 1100cc car proved quite outstanding and managed one lap later in the race at 77.8 mph while Tom Delaney's best was 76.7mph. Taylor's Alfa-Romeo kept station with the Lea-Francis for most of the race, but Delaney's hopes were dashed when the supercharger casing burst. He limped to the pits and changed the complete blower, but with so much time lost, all hope of a place vanished.

The race was ultimately won in convincing fashion by MG Midgets followed home by Rileys. A C Taylor covered 64 laps to finish in 11th place while Delaney completed 56 laps when racing was declared over.

The Light Car Club held a relay race at Brooklands in July and several teams entered. Mrs Chetwynd's team comprised herself in a 'C'-type MG Midget, her husband in the well-used 'TT Leaf' (No. 14137) and A P Hutchings who drove a Wolseley Hornet. J C Elwes ran an Ulster Austin in league with M B Watson (Brooklands Riley) and Alan Machlachlan made his debut at the wheel of his four-seater Lea-Francis (Chassis No. 14128). The Elwes team finished in second place largely due to the amazing speed of Machlachlan, who averaged 95·3mph for 29 laps. The Chetwynd team secured fifth place although the Coventry car in this triumvirate misfired badly until its plugs were changed.

L P Driscoll indulged in a three-lap race against C B Bicknell on a 500cc JAP-engined motor cycle but the 'Leaf' threw a fit of temperament on the second tour and came to a halt. The next event in the busy mid-summer Brooklands season was the popular JCC meeting comprising the Hour Blind contested by Dugdale, Oetzmann and Chetwynd. The latter two were awarded silver and gold medals respectively while Oetzmann won a one-lap sprint with a speed of 70·44mph, beating Baker's big Minerva and Donald Munro in an MG 18/80.

J K Whittaker in his recently purchased works car (No. 14130) entered the August sand races at Southport but was unplaced, and the first Shelsley Walsh meeting saw Kenneth Peacock in another machine which he had spirited out of Lower Ford Street. This car was one of the old 200-mile race machines (Chassis No. 9162) and a climb in 52 seconds was recorded, S H Newsome needing 54.4 seconds in the standard TT car (No. 14171). T G Clarke and J Allan-Arnold also ran but did not record impressive times.

W Gregg was still active in Ulster events and gained two awards in the Croft Hill Climb held in the province in July.

August proved dismal from the point of view of Lea-Francis drivers: T G Clarke, Machlachlan and E J J Leatham were at the Brooklands Bank Holiday meeting but no successes attended their efforts while Clarke entered the ex-Hendy car (No. 14051) in the TT but scratched at the last moment. Thus the marque was unrepresented at Ards in 1931.

Peacock persuaded Sutton to undertake a

rebuild of Chassis No. 9162 involving some extensive modifications including the removal of the power plant to a point some 8in further back in the chassis. An attempt at lightening was made while the shapely pointed tail was displaced by an ugly flat panel and the front brakes were removed. The car was duly entered for the Shelsley September meeting to record 52.4 seconds on its first run. Peacock determined to try very hard on the final ascent and shot off like a rocket but the car proved extremely difficult to control in its new guise and was seen to hit the bank in the vicinity of the crossing. The car seemed distinctly unstable as it climbed to the Esses, then suddenly the nearside front wheel and stub axle became detached completely. Peacock continued to press on until he saw the wheel travelling alongside, and miraculously came to rest without further damage. This car had, nevertheless, shown its paces by winning two events and proving fastest sports car at the Madresfield Speed Trials held on the previous weekend, road equipment being in place for the occasion.

Brooklands was chosen by the Brighton & Hove Motor Club for some interesting races in September which included one of the ever popular Hour Blinds. A N L Machlachlan won this event in a convincing manner with a very fast drive aided by some skilful pit work.

The MCC held yet another One-Hour High-Speed Trial in late September in which W G Wolff averaged 75·46mph in a TT Replica to gain a gold medal while G E Took experienced some difficulties and covered a mere 46 miles.

Morris-Goodall, with an Aston-Martin, proved fastest in the 1½-litre class with a speed of 78·55mph. G E Took recovered to average 75·80 in a one-lap race and finished third behind the Aldington Brothers.

The recently opened motor cycle course at Donington Park was the venue for an experiment to see if cars might be suitable for the rather narrow track. Wilf Green took his TT Replica round at a speed not far short of the motor cycle record but considerable improvement was deemed necessary before cars could be safely used.

The final design work undertaken at Lower Ford Street concerned an entirely new chassis to suit the enlarged Ace engine. Known as the 18hp car and begun in October 1931, the solitary example completed was on the road by the following April.

This car represented the next logical step in development, and was, without doubt, a very fine machine. A wheelbase of 9ft 11in and track of 4ft 6in resulted in a comparatively large car, while the chassis frame was entirely new and represented an attempt to lower the centre of gravity still further. All four cross members were cranked downwards towards the centre while the front member was a tube of 2in diameter. The side members differed in shape from previous designs with a straight run down from the tubular cross member to the front dumb irons. Large gussets resulted in increased stiffness while the road springs, wider than hitherto, were almost straight in the unladen state. Extended spring trunnions similar to the racing cars were employed. Brake-drum dia-

Sutton in 9162, re-built for sprint work. 1931

TOP
Heston in 1931. A Blackburne aircraft with Delaney's sales fleet

ABOVE LEFT
Light-hearted moments at Heston

ABOVE RIGHT
Sutton in 9163

meter was increased to 13in and all chassis components were scaled-up compared with previous models.

The final drawback of Van Eugen's semi-floating rear axle was eliminated by the use of a split taper collar behind the hub which effectively locked this component on to the axle-shaft. This feature can be seen on the post-war Morris Minor and others of that family which were the work of the same designer.

The propeller shaft on the 18hp car passed over the central cross members while as on all models, the engine/gearbox unit was angled to achieve a straight transmission line. A 12-gallon petrol tank was fitted between the rear dumb irons on a new three-point mounting while an electric gauge was utilized in place of the 'Nivex'-type used on standard Ace of Spades models. Wheel size was reduced to 18in, the tyre section being 5·25in.

New and yet stiffer engine supports were evolved, still in elektron while Silentbloc flexible mountings were fitted at a later date. The radiator was entirely new consisting of a film-type block surrounded by a new cowl much slimmer in outline, thus following contemporary fashion for the ribbon-type to a degree. A false honeycomb was employed which extended well below the real radiator. The total height of the cowl was 30in with a backwards slope in characteristic Lea-Francis fashion, this time of $7\frac{1}{2}°$. The radiator had lost the beauty of former designs and was, perhaps, the least-attractive feature of the new car. When completed, a stone guard was fitted, once again following the dictates of fashion for these useless ornaments were fast becoming the hallmark of the pseudo sports-car, fitted of course to every Austin Greyhound, Morris Ten-Six Special and the like.

Cross & Ellis mounted a full five-seater saloon body on to the new chassis which embodied louvres to the tops of all door lights. A division was later fitted to this car in order to separate Charles Turner from his chauffeur, the receiver having taken it over for his Coventry–Sheffield commuting.

The costs involved in the manufacture of this one-off motor car, the chassis of which was almost tool-room built, are interesting. The cost, including patterns and the relatively expensive coachbuilt body, totalled a modest

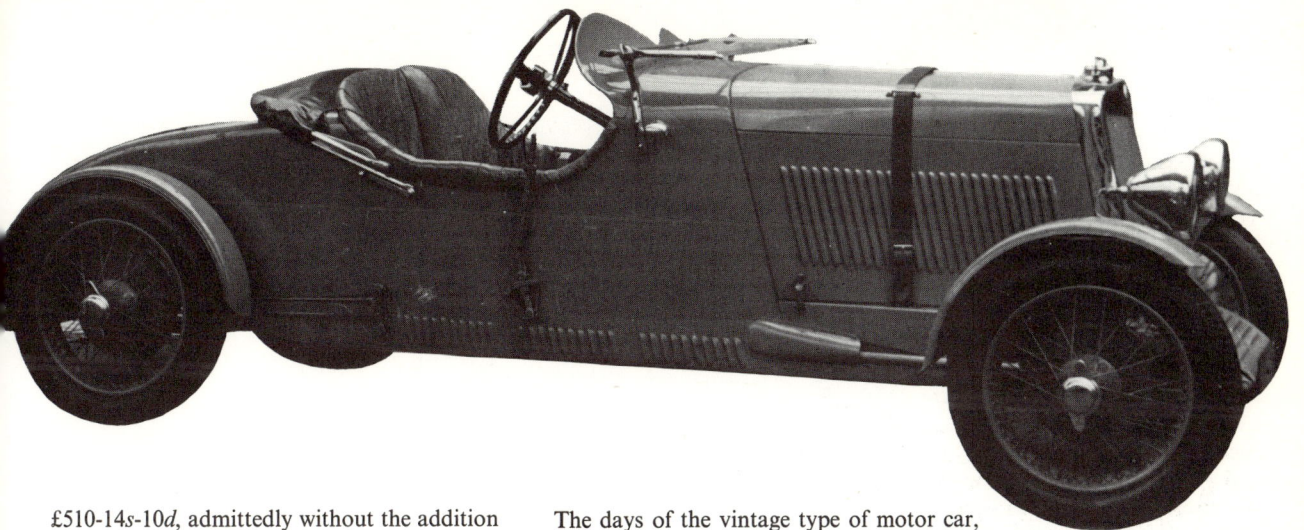

Final TT replica 14187

£510-14s-10d, admittedly without the addition of factory overhead expenses. The machine was, unhappily, but understandably, never sanctioned for production due to the continuing receivership, although it was hoped that this modernized car, ready for demonstration, would assist in the sale of the business. Turner, with some feeling, still hoped to find a buyer for the complete running concern rather than dispose of the assets in piecemeal fashion.

It is interesting to consider how this car would have fared in the market of 1932–3 had resources been found with which to back it. Luxuriously equipped and with a chassis finely finished almost to Bugatti standards, it would have been listed in the £550–£600 bracket. Maximum speed approached 80mph and the efficient engine enabled the use of a 4·27:1 rear axle ratio, refreshingly high by the standards of the time. Rivals from nearby Holyhead Road were assembling fair numbers of Silver Eagle saloons which sold at £700 and were slower and comparatively cumbersome to handle. The Sunbeam Co. offered a beautifully built, but none-too-happy, scaled-down version of their larger models rated at 18.2hp. This car, considerably heavier than the Lea-Francis, was compelled to adopt a dismally low top-gear ratio and could neither better 65mph nor 18mpg. The London partners of the STD Combine were more competitive. The Talbot 75, capable of 75mph, was interesting technically and sold for a mere £495; once again final drive ratios were comparatively low resulting in a certain loss of the high-speed cruising gait of the Lower Ford Street car. The Talbot utilized a pre-selector gearbox and great interest was now being taken in various forms of easy gear-changing mechanisms, no doubt Lea-Francis may well have been compelled to offer an alternative transmission system if production had got under way.

The days of the vintage type of motor car, however refined, it seemed were at an end. The public were now more interested in the latest and lowest type of coachwork and relief from the need for any skill or effort in gear changing. Roadholding, long life and high-grade engineering mattered little.

A total of 29 new cars were sold in 1932 of which 11 were 'P'-type 12/40's; several were fitted with coil ignition and steel con-rods. Four final 'W'-type saloons were sold, three of which carried Carbodies coachwork. The short 'Ace' accounted for seven cars, one example was endowed with a Cross & Ellis four-seater touring body of a type normally intended for the Alvis Silver Eagle. Six more 16/70 cars were despatched including drophead coupés by Carbodies (20040) and Tickford (20047) while one very smart close-coupled coupé was built by Cross & Ellis (20039). The sales total was completed by the disposal, to a Scottish gentleman, of the final four-seater Hyper (14188) finished in blue fabric and happily this car still exists.

Business done during 1932 included the sales of used and reconditioned cars which kept the factory busy. The year's working showed a further surplus of approximately £2000 although a gradual wind-down had taken place with the result that the weekly wage bill had fallen to £120 by December.

Henry Meadows Ltd, no doubt feeling concern about the fall-off in orders for their smaller engines, now produced an entirely new 10hp power plant (Type 4EJ) with which to woo the specialist light-car makers but in this they were totally unsuccessful.

A single overhead camshaft with two-stage drive was specified, the lower chain being of single width while the upper was duplex. The crankcase and cylinder block were cast in one piece. Dimensions were 63mm bore × 100mm

ABOVE AND OPPOSITE
The 18hp car, 1932

dale and Whittaker ran their TT cars 14156 and 14130 respectively, Miss Enid Fawcett used a 14/40 and Charles Turner entered the new 16/70 Foursome Coupé (20039) nominating R M V Sutton as driver. The system of marking heavily favoured cars which had fluid flywheel transmission systems, and were able to cope well with the slow-running test upon which undue emphasis was laid. In order to put up a reasonable showing in this event, Sutton's car was fitted with the lowest axle ratio of 5·1:1. His final placing was 84th out of a total of 232, but the other cars fared badly, largely due to the aforesaid slow-speed test. The final positions were: Whittaker 191st, Dugdale 221st and Miss Fawcett 230th. A minor benefit enjoyed by Sutton occurred when he hit a pheasant which he promptly despatched to his wife.

A coachwork competition held after the rally should have merited an award for this immaculate and stylish new Lea-Francis but the judges apparently placed great store on the ability to enter saloons with top hats in position, resulting in further successes for the Daimler-Lanchester-Armstrong contingent.

The JCC held a rally at Brooklands in March, resulting in second-class awards for 'Leafs' by J W F Windrum and J W Drewett. Afterwards Driscoll and Delaney staged a match race against two Velocette motor cycles around the Mountain Circuit but, in spite of a five-second start, the cars were both soundly beaten.

The BARC Easter Monday races were contested by three Leaf owners: T G Clarke (No. 14051), Tom Delaney, in scratch position in one event and very fast, and R C A Thompson, who shot through barriers in a mountain race. The Whitsun meeting saw Delaney active again and while unplaced in a Short Handicap, he found form in the Nottingham Junior Mountain Race. He led initially then held second place, after being overtaken by Featherstonehaugh in his Alfa-Romeo. Bad luck intervened towards the end, when Delaney cooked a plug and allowed Dr Roth (Talbot) to force by just before the flag. T G Clarke also entered two races in his TT car but was unplaced.

C T Osborne raised a few eyebrows at the BARC Inter-Club meeting held at Brooklands in June by winning the Sports Short Handicap at 83·43mph and despite re-handicapping went out again to win the novices' handicap at 83·72mph.

R Evans ran an old 'L'-type 12/50 at this meeting and set off in limit position in the Sports Car Handicap. He held his lead until three-quarter distance when he became submerged by other competitors. Then again in the Sports Long Handicap he enjoyed the lead for two laps before his torque arm snapped halting further progress.

stroke while the maximum output of 37bhp was delivered at 4000rpm. Curiously, the output at 2000rpm was 20bhp which exactly equalled that of the original 4EB unit designed 10 years earlier. The crankshaft ran in three bearings of 1½in diameter. Coil ignition was adopted with the distributor high up above the valve cover and driven by vertical shaft forming an extension of the oil pump drive. The engine appeared cheap by comparison with previous productions. Pressed steel was used for timing cover and sump although cast-aluminium was retained for the overhead valve cover. Valve angles were unusual, inlets being vertical while the exhausts were sharply inclined resulting in a somewhat untidy appearance. Little seems to have been heard of these engines although they were extensively advertized for a time.

Lea-Francis cars were not conspicuous in the sporting events of 1932, but four examples entered the well publicized and equally well criticized RAC Rally held in February. Dug-

The Ulster AC Croft Hill Climb saw Montgomery tie for FTD in his Hyper with Sloane in a highly tuned Wolseley Hornet Special. This latter model was enjoying a great vogue. The first Shelsley meeting was contested by Peacock in the single-seater (9162) which R M V Sutton had repaired. It failed to leave the line, however, and Newsome in a works TT car (Chassis No. 14140) had trouble on his second run although he managed 52·6 on his first. Tommy Wisdom won the class in his Frazer-Nash with a time of 52 seconds.

The JCC organized a race meeting at Brooklands in aid of Guys Hospital in July. The first race, a one-lap handicap for medical students, was won by J M Lees starting from scratch in the Chetwynd car (14137) at a speed of 76·39mph. Mrs Chetwynd also used it for a ladies' race which she promptly won at 76·73 mph. Back in the hands of Lees for a two-lap handicap the Leaf, still in top form, almost scored a hat trick, finishing a close second behind Wilson (Talbot).

The BARC August Bank Holiday meeting saw Tom Delaney really trying in the Senior Mountain Handicap. The track was very wet following heavy rain and he arrived at the fork on his first lap going much too fast. He went into a complete spin. He managed to keep going, however, and won by one-fifth of a second from Raymond Mays in his white Invicta. Delaney's speed was 59·49mph.

William Sullivan borrowed a works car (Chassis No. 14140) for his entry in the TT and surprised everyone by taking the 1½-litre lap record for the Ards course, previously held by Don in an Alfa-Romeo. Sullivan's speed was 74·06mph. The car ran without road equipment in this race which probably helped. Sullivan drove with great skill throughout the race only to break down on the penultimate lap with a comparatively trifling fault. While the car was in Ireland, Sullivan entered it in the Craigantlet Hill Climb where he recorded FTD together with three class wins.

A programme of races in the Phoenix Park saw Sullivan competing in a 50-mile race where he came within one second of Cyril Paul's 1½-litre lap record, also with a Lea-Francis in 1930. Sullivan finished this event in fourth place. This car was to return to Coventry and remain at the works until 1936. The axle ratio selected for the Irish expedition was 3·5:1 and one wonders whether the reliability record of the Hyper in long-distance races would have been improved if this high ratio had been specified at an earlier date. F A Gannon in the ex-Allan-Arnold car (14141) also ran in the Phoenix Park races, but while in third place in an amateur event, the car caught fire. Fortunately the damage was not extensive.

The final Brooklands BARC meeting saw Delaney out again and although unplaced in the Junior Short Handicap, he secured third spot in the Senior Mountain Race behind Machlachlan (Austin) and Shuttleworth (Bugatti).

The classic reliability trials held during 1932 saw further Lea-Francis successes. A total of eight cars entered the Land's End event; while W S Perkins and C A Gray retired, the other six all gained awards including J F Lamb from Coventry who was fast in his 'Ace of Spades' (20031) as was H J Vidler in a Hyper saloon (14048). H W Burman using the faithful 14/40 tourer gained a silver medal in company with Vidler and F G Sturgess.

The London–Edinburgh Trial saw Burman gain yet another silver medal. C H Wagstaffe won a gold in this, his first outing with his recently acquired four-seater Hyper (14089). It is interesting to record that up to this day Wagstaffe has remained faithful to Lea-Francis

99

cars and still uses a 12/40 saloon as daily transport in addition to appearing in Lea-Francis club events. W E Holland in a well-kept early 12/40 also won a gold medal in the Edinburgh while H S Linfield of *Autocar* took the short chassis Ace demonstrator through the trial in the course of a road test and gained a silver medal. Holland also won first-class awards in the Buxton and Derbyshire Trials, while H Bolton in a 10hp car and Wagstaffe both achieved golds in the Scarborough Trial held in August.

The final event of 1932 was the London–Exeter run in which Humphrey Burman won his customary gold medal, F P Baker took a bronze but on this occasion Wagstaffe and Vidler failed.

The years 1933 and 1934 passed quietly: operations continued under the protracted receivership, new cars were still listed in the various buyers' guides and occasional half- or full-page advertisements were taken in the motoring press.

The Ace of Spades was the subject of further road tests, *The Observer* reporting in February 1933 and *Autocar* in the following May. Once again the motoring journalists were rapturous in praise. John Prioleau described the handling and steering as 'if not the very best that I have known, certainly at least one of the three best'. This opinion was shared by Messrs Linfield and his team, who summed up the short-chassis Ace as 'a car of strong character, having a very good performance'.

Unfortunately, one finds difficulty in accepting without question the reports of the day, for the ultimate in dreadful cars of the period, such as the Austin Twelve Six, were also able to bask in paeans of warm appreciation by the road testers.

Lea-Francis tinkered with the carburation of the cars used for these 1933 tests; a Carbodies Short Chassis Saloon (No. 18517) was fitted with non-standard jets for the Brooklands Speed Tests, in order to improve performance. Judgement was duly wrought for this rather dishonest trick, for in the event the maximum speed recorded was 72·58mph, lower than that obtained with the heavier long-chassis car in 1931.

The final chassis were assembled in July 1933 to be despatched to the coachbuilders as and when required; actual sales of new machines totalled 12 'P'-types in 1933 with a further three in 1934. These cars included one Carbodies saloon (Chassis No. 19083) and two or three f/h coupés, the remainder being standard two- and four-seater tourers – the latter now looking distinctly dated in appearance. Short-chassis Aces accounted for five cars in 1933, and a mere two in 1934. All except one car were standard saloons, the odd machine (Chassis No. 18514) was equipped with an 18hp engine, together with 4·27:1 axle ratio, while Carbodies were responsible for fitting a smart four-seater body. A solitary 16/70 model fitted with a sloping radiator and special open coachwork embodying a built-in luggage boot, rear windscreen and bench seating in the front was ordered by a Leamington Spa owner and delivered in August. This car, also built with an 18hp engine, was duly featured in *Autocar* and the writer well remembers seeing the car in Warwick up to about 1952, still in mint condition. Alas, it seemed to disappear and one wonders where it is now. The chassis number was 20048. The two-seater Hyper (Chassis No. 14187), which was exhibited at Olympia in 1930, was finally sold to W Graden of Whitehaven in July 1934.

Prices were once again revised for 1934; 12/40 Tourers were increased to £315, while Hyper Saloons were a little more realistic at £550. The dismal new car sales figures were fortunately augmented by second-hand and reconditioned models which seemed to average 30 to 35 per year. A certain amount of sub-contract machine work was also undertaken which, together with the receipts of the repair and spare parts departments, resulted in a surprising surplus of approximately £6000 per annum for the 1933–4 seasons. This satisfactory performance enabled a payment of £8000 to be made over to Williams Deacon Bank, in addition to a fee of £2000 for the receiver.

The racing season opened with a 1¼-mile sprint at the March BARC Meeting which Delaney won easily on limit position from C G H Dunham (Alvis) and Kaye Don in the fast, but difficult Type 54 Bugatti. The Lea-Francis was unplaced, however, in a mountain race held later in the day.

Easter Monday saw Tom Delaney out again, unplaced in the Addlestone Senior Short Handicap, but managing third place in a Mountain Handicap. The track at Donington Park had been altered, and was duly demonstrated to various officials by Wilf Green in his TT Leaf, recording a lap of 54½mph for the 2¼-mile circuit. The May meeting held at this venue, fast becoming popular, included entries from R C Vickers in the ex-Whittaker Team Car (Chassis No. 14132) and C H Wagstaffe who had purchased the re-vamped racing car from Peacock (No. 9162). Vickers managed to lead one heat for five laps, but he was passed by Wagstaffe who, despite losing his exhaust system, continued unabated to win. However, Vickers managed third place in the final of this event behind the Rileys of E K Rayson and John Eason-Gibson.

The BARC Whitsun event provided another

outing for Delaney and this time he finished second in the Cobham Mountain Handicap, behind R Morgan in an Invicta. The important British Empire Trophy Race held in mid-summer was preceded by two 50-mile handicap races; one, the Canada Trophy Race, saw yet again the partnership of Delaney and the old TT car proving mettlesome, for they averaged 95·41mph to take second place behind Frank Hallam driving an FWD Alvis TT car.

The following weekend at the Weybridge Track was the occasion of the BARC Inter-Club meeting. Mrs K N Roe won a two-lap race in an alloy-bodied TT Lea-Francis, at an average of 81·23mph; her speed on the second lap was 85·13mph.

August Bank Holiday Monday provided yet another opportunity for Tom Delaney to have a crack at the Mountain Circuit, and he finished second in the Byfleet Lightning Handicap behind Wolverhampton garage proprietor Harry Attwood in a blown MG Midget. R C Vickers (14132) contested an earlier mountain race at this meeting, but somehow found himself in neutral for the corners, which were, therefore, negotiated in a somewhat untidy fashion.

Vickers also ran in the August Donington Meeting, but his driving still caused some alarm; and he passed Smithson (Frazer-Nash) in a heart-stopping fashion, but nevertheless won one heat at 56·90mph. This event witnessed two of the old 200-mile race cars reunited, for Wagstaffe entered 9162 and A S Mazengarb brought out 9161, although neither achieved distinction.

Wagstaffe did well in the Hour Blind of the MCC Brooklands meeting in September, when he averaged 75·4mph, thus tying for fastest 1½-litre entrant with C H Wood in an Aston-Martin. Later in the same month, Delaney and F Connell competed in the Brighton Speed Trials, while at the October Southport meeting George Mangoletsi in his TT model (14138) scooped the pool, winning a flying-kilometre event for 1½-litre cars at a speed of 81·64mph, in addition to recording fastest 1½-litre time in a One-Mile Spring, and finishing second overall. He also won his class in a Seven-Mile Event, and was only beaten in the unlimited class by two Mercedes-Benz 38/250 supercharged giants.

Mangoletsi, still a force to be reckoned with in the tuning world, had converted this 'Leaf' to run on alcohol with a boost pressure of 17lb/in . A 40mm Solex carburettor was utilized, while much attention was given to ports, valves and exhaust system. The car would hold 110mph in this form and went on to win a total of 30 races on the sands of Southport during the next three years. Mangoletsi was aided on these occasions by Joe Williamson, later to become service manager at Rolls-Royce, Crewe. Countless Rolls-Royce and Bentley owners owe a debt of gratitude to 'Uncle Joe', for his unfailing help and sage advice, always so cheerfully dispensed.

The final Donington Park Meeting held on 7 October was contested by Wagstaffe, Mazengarb and the indefatigable Delaney, the latter finishing second behind E R Hall in a K3 MG Magnette, with S S Tresilian, another Rolls-Royce employee, close behind in a Type 35 Bugatti. Mazengarb crashed his car badly, almost shearing the front axle clean off when he hit a tree.

The racing season ended with the BARC October races duly contested by Messrs Vickers, Delaney and Mrs Roe, all in their alloy-bodied TT cars, identical in appearance, but success eluded them on this Autumn day.

Messrs H J Vidler and H W Burman were successful in the Land's End Trial, winning gold and silver medals respectively, while Wagstaffe and Bolton both took premier awards in the London–Edinburgh. The Ace of Spades Coupé (20039) used in the 1932 RAC Rally, was seen again in the Scottish Rally of June 1933, when it did duty as an official car, driven by its first owner, a Glasgow businessman, who fitted three SU carburettors. One wonders if this car still exists, perhaps languishing north of the border to this day. The registration number was KV578.

The name of Ken Riley first appears when he secured an award in the Brighton Trial of July 1933. Riley was the proprietor of a specialized Lea-Francis repair business which he operated until his death in the early sixties.

C H Wagstaffe fitted road equipment to the 200-mile race car and used it in trials which must have been enormous fun, securing awards in the Scarborough, London, Gloucester and MCC Sporting Trials – the car positively leaping up the hills at a prodigious pace.

Yet another name which figured in the trial awards for at least 25 years, at the wheel of Lea-Francis cars, was that of A L S Denyer, who began with a bronze in the 1933 London–Gloucester.

Motor Sport road tested Machlachlan's car (14132) in June 1934 and enthused over the delights of this 'real sports car which allied tractability with a 95mph maximum'.

The ranks of Lea-Francis trials entrants had now thinned to three or four stalwarts and this enjoyable form of motor sport was fast becoming the province of new small sports cars, in particular MG and Singer.

The most successful man in 1934 was L Mills who competed in the Colmore, London–Edinburgh, MCC Welsh, JCC Lynton and London–Exeter to gain four awards. His car was an Ace of Spades four-seater tourer (20046) which was always fastidiously maintained.

Kaye Don's sister, Rita, drove Tom Delaney's car at the Whit Monday Brooklands meeting and while she held the lead in the early stages, was gradually swamped by the opposition. Tom rode as mechanic and despite earnest exhortations says that he could not prevail upon the nervous Rita to keep her foot down hard enough.

The Leinster Trophy Race held near Dublin and of 100-mile duration, was contested by F Pearson in what is believed to be the ex-Allan-Arnold car (14141) but, running unblown and with a standard 12/40 cylinder head and carburettor, he finished the course in 15th place.

Lord Avebury had recently purchased a TT replica (14185) and ran it in a highly tuned form with No. 10 blower, SU carburettor and a high-compression cylinder head. He competed in the LCC Relay Race with the Driskell team but the other two cars, a BNC and a Ford V8, both gave trouble and the team's chances were ruined. Lord Avebury was later responsible for the production of the Lammas Graham car.

Tom Delaney managed his usual place at the August Bank Holiday meeting at the Weybridge Track with a second spot in the Short Junior Handicap, while his final appearance with this successful car was at the Brooklands Speed Trials in September where he averaged 53·63mph for the standing half mile. He sold the car back to the works in November and it was eventually re-sold to the trade in May 1936.

Charles Van Eugen left in late 1934. He had been approached by Victor Riley to help manufacture a top-grade luxury car utilizing a V8 engine built on Riley principles which then existed in prototype form. Van Eugen was thus engaged to design and build the Autovia car, a venture which was to be entirely unconnected with Riley Motors, apart from the supply of engines, and was to be wholly owned by the Riley family and Gordon Marshall. It is fairly certain that the project would have found great difficulty in surviving as a commercial proposition. It eventually failed with Riley Motors, who were found to control the majority of the shares in March 1938; this fact caused bitterness to Van Eugen, for he then unexpectedly found himself out of employment.

The Autovia car was interesting in many respects and in view of the coincidental matter of the old Lea-Francis Co. being taken up by ex-Riley men, it can be regarded as a perfect cross-pollination between the Lower Ford Street régime and that of Much Park Street.

The 90° V8 engine had dimensions of 69mm bore and 95·25mm stroke, giving a capacity of 2849cc and an RAC rating of 23·8hp. It was built on Riley lines embodying high-set camshafts and short pushrods. A pre-selector gearbox was standardized although a manual ZF box became optional at a later date. A wheelbase of 10ft 9in and a track of 4ft 8½in resulted in a large car capable of accepting commodious seven-seater limousine coachwork although the most popular style was an elegant four light sports saloon, all bodies being the work of the Northampton Mulliner concern. The actual chassis will be of interest to Lea-Francis enthusiasts for the family re-

The office staff with 9163 at Lower Ford Street in 1929–30

semblance is most striking. The sliding spring trunnions appear to be almost identical, while the front dumb irons were joined by one long pin which also located the road springs; all detail work was well proportioned and reminiscent of Lea-Francis practice.

Van Eugen was always keen on achieving a low centre of gravity and his efforts in this direction with the 18hp car of 1932 were taken a step farther with the Autovia which utilized an underslung worm-drive rear axle while the chassis frame side members passed under this unit. The front axle was particularly interesting and embodied boxes through which the front springs passed 'à la Bugatti' although secured by 'U' bolts to a conventional axle pad. The remainder of the chassis followed Riley practice to a degree, with Girling brakes and automatic one-shot lubrication, together with a torque tube drive. The forward end of the latter consisted of a wide fork, the extremities of which were hinged to a cross member. This layout was geometrically imperfect but no doubt the 'Silent Bloc' bushes interposed

TOP
Tom Delaney with 14053 in about 1934

BOTTOM
A V8 Autovia fitted with a body of rather more rakish lines than standard

103

coped with the irregularities that would result when one wheel encountered a bump.

The radiator, which was equipped with thermostatically controlled shutters, was very similar to the 18hp Lea-Francis while other typical Van Eugen features included elektron back plates for the brakes and a cast-aluminium dashboard.

The first car was completed in late 1935 and by the time of the closure two years later, approximately 40 cars had been built. The chassis was listed at £685 while the sports saloon retailed at £975, later reduced to £800. The limousine also cost £975. Despite the all-up weight of 35¾cwt a speed of 91mph was recorded by *Motor* allied with a fuel consumption of 17–18mpg.

The original development work was carried out in a separate bay of the Riley works in Durbar Avenue but a factory in Midland Road was taken over and remained as the official address for the life of the business although assembly was transferred next door to the old Coventry Ordnance works for a time.

Shortly after the demise of Autovia Cars, Van Eugen met Miles Thomas (later Sir Miles Thomas of BOAC fame) while he was walking through Coventry. Thomas was, at that time, managing director of Wolseley Motors and he persuaded 'Van' to join the technical staff at Ward End. The Dutchman expressed reservations about his fitness for such a post since he had no experience of mass-production engineering. Miles Thomas dismissed this notion and his choice of staff was soon vindicated.

Towards the end of 1934, negotiations began between the Lea-Francis receiver and a consortium headed by George H Leek, but due to a series of setbacks, the old firm was to continue trading for a further two years.

Business in 1935 continued quietly with a turnover of approximately £9000 which resulted in a further small surplus while a sale of surplus machinery in November realized £330. Charles Turner died in July and was replaced by H C Hepworth, a Manchester accountant.

New-car sales included the clearance of two final 'P'-type 12/40's, a semi-panelled Carbodies saloon (19069) and a coil ignition two-seater (19088). Three more short chassis 2-litre cars found buyers, one of which was fitted with an attractive Cross & Ellis golfer's coupé (18524), of a type normally found on Alvis Firebirds. This car was depicted in *Autocar* as a new model; it has survived and is at present undergoing restoration.

A stocktake carried out on 31 August disclosed that 12 new cars were still in stock, together with approximately eight second-hand vehicles, while the old works truck DU40 was still in use and receiving regular servicing.

The marque had now virtually disappeared from the racing scene although Denyer and Burman continued in trials gaining gold and silver respectively in the London–Exeter, while L Mills managed a third-class award with the Ace of Spades in the Colmore Cup Trial. In 1936 George Mangoletsi climbed Shelsley Walsh in 48·2 seconds in his highly tuned TT car (14138).

Geoffrey Smith of Evesham purchased one of the 200-mile race cars (9163) from the works for £100 in November 1935 and proceeded to enjoy two trouble-free seasons' competition, the car always proving very fast in the dry but showing a disinclination to run well in wet weather. A second place was achieved in a Berkhampstead MC Speed Trial, together with a third at Wetherby. Smith also enjoyed Donington Park, although clearly outclassed when entrants included Charles Martin in a P3 Alfa-Romeo and Whitehead and Tongue driving ERAs. The Southsea Speed Trials held in August was contested by M W Sheppard and R Cooper, the latter finishing second in his class with the ex-Hendy TT car (14051).

J M James, better known for his post-war exploits with the Sunbeam Tiger, also campaigned a Leaf in 1936 but without notable success.

A total of nine new cars comprising three 16/70 and six 2-litre models were disposed of in 1936, all saloons except for a solitary f/h coupé (18503). The 18hp experimental car was also sold, after recording a mileage in excess of 40,000, to W Creak-Davies of Milford-on-Sea. It does not appear to have survived.

The weekly wage bill had dropped to an average of £58 per week by the early part of 1936 and although the intending purchasers were unable to produce the cash required for purchase, they were allowed the use of the works and drawing office once a deposit had been paid. This resulted in an increase of activity for a period from April with a total of 41 people employed.

However, the receiver was clearly unable to allow this state of affairs to continue indefinitely and the Leaf Engineering Co. Ltd of Leek and his colleagues was given notice to quit and the business was once more put up for sale. The General Electric Co. became interested and purchased the freehold, together with the remaining machinery and plant, for £22,000, taking possession in February 1937 and remaining to this day (1976).

The final new car, a 2-litre, still in chassis form (18525), was disposed of in March 1937 to Messrs Gardiner and Towers of Rugby who fitted a four light Avon saloon of Waymaker styling, soon to be adopted as standard for the new 1938 Lea-Francis.

CHAPTER EIGHT

Reconstruction

The Autumn of 1934 found intending purchasers for the Lea-Francis assets in the form of two stalwarts from Riley Motors. George Harold Leek, who had served 10 years with the Humber Co. and no less than 23 with Riley, was an energetic and colourful character of no mean ability, although occasionally a little unstable and held back somewhat by his love of the turf. Leek had passed through the Riley concern in various capacities; he had been chief buyer for a time and was then given responsibility for planning the production of the Riley Nine, a task he carried out with outstanding success resulting in his appointment as general manager of the whole business in 1932. He then began to experience difficulties with his chief, Victor Riley, and resigned in the summer of 1934.

Raymond Hugh Rose, son of an engraver, had embarked on an engineering career against parental advice and first became apprenticed to the Humber concern, as did so many men destined for prominence in the motor industry. Rose found that his immediate superior was the renowned Louis Coatalen. This eccentric soon gave Rose his first lesson in which he asserted that the only way to achieve success in the fledgling motor industry was to marry the chairman's daughter. As the chairman of Humber had no daughters. Coatalen told Rose that they would soon be going to work for Mr Hillman who had three!

The efforts of Coatalen while at the Hillman works led to a very successful motor car but failure in the marital stakes – the latter may have been partly due to the strange habits of the Continental genius which included an insistence on wearing his bicycle clips all day and every day, whatever the occasion.

The pair then moved on to the Sunbeam concern. Coatalen's exploits at Wolverhampton are well known and while Hugh Rose remained with him for some years, he eventually followed ex-Sunbeam works manager Sydney Guy, to be responsible for the design of Guy lorries. Then came a time as chief designer with Crossley Motors, followed by similar posts at Belsize and Calthorpe. After this he returned to Sunbeam and designed a bus with an interesting OHV engine, reminiscent of later BMW and Bristol practice, together with the 'Silver Bullet' with which Kaye Don attacked the world's land speed record.

Victor Riley commissioned Hugh Rose to design a new 4-cylinder 12hp engine based on established Riley principles in 1933. This unit was successful and continued in production with but minor modifications until 1954. The main change was the adoption of chain drive to the camshafts in place of gears during the Nuffield era.

George Leek persuaded Hugh Rose to join him in the 'new Lea-Francis project', the intention being to build a car aimed at the traditional Lea-Francis market utilizing an improved engine of the 'Riley type' which Rose had in mind.

The principal change in this concerned the high-set camshafts, which were placed at the top of the crankcase in the Riley, some 4in below the cylinder-head face, whereas the projected Lea-Francis engine was to have camshafts just below the cylinder-head face in cavities provided. This resulted in the tappets being disposed in the cylinder head, while the pushrods were a mere 2in in length achieving the ultimate in reduction of valve gear weight without resorting to overhead camshafts with attendant problems of lengthy drive and relative inaccessibility, an important feature in the days of frequent decarbonization and amateur owner-mechanics.

A provisional patent for this feature was taken out in the names of Leek and Rose on 5 February 1935 and initial design work on the new car was carried out by Hugh Rose at his home, 'Red Roofs', Penn, Wolverhampton. George Leek, being responsible for the commercial side of the new enterprize, busied himself with the task of approaching various financial supporters and appeared to have found the answer in Edwin B Bott of Victoria

ABOVE
The Lower Ford Street entrance, now occupied by GEC. 1968 photograph

OPPOSITE
The feminine influence in advertizing: 1928 'U'-type, and 1938 drophead coupé

Street, London, SW1. The motoring press announced in December 1934 that Bott had purchased the business outright, but this was false and no monies changed hands until February 1935 when the receiver obtained a cheque for £3150 from Coventry Holdings Ltd in payment for 'forfeiture of non-completion of contract'. The aggrieved Bott ultimately issued a writ against Lea-Francis Engineering (1937) Ltd, but the case was dropped when war began in 1939.

John Scott, OBE, a former postmaster, then came on the scene, and in April 1936 the new Leaf Engineering Company was formed with Scott as chairman. The other directors were George Leek and Charles Follett, the latter agreeing to take the initial production of the car in return for distributors' rights for London and the Home Counties. The new company paid a deposit of 10 per cent on the assets (£2700) on 31 March 1936 and were then allowed the use of the drawing office and works in order to get things moving. Herbert L Read financed this part of the transaction.

A body of people now left Riley Motors and joined Lea-Francis. These included Messrs Nall, jig and tool designer, Ingram, progress, Twyneham, machine shop superintendent, and Compton and Ward in the purchase department. An additional works in Holbrooks Lane, formerly occupied by the Midland Light Body Co., was taken over but finance was slow, resulting in serious difficulties when the unfortunate new concern was unceremoniously bundled out of Lower Ford Street by the receiver of Lea & Francis Ltd.

John Scott and Charles Follett withdrew from further participation and Leaf Engineering Co. was later wound up, but Leek commenced negotiations to purchase the Triumph Gloria works in Much Park Street from E W D Scott for the sum of £20,000. A new company was formed for this purpose on 16 July 1937, entitled Lea-Francis Engineering (1937) Ltd, which was converted to a public company on 22 July 1937 with a share capital of £150,000 split into 2*s* shares of which 720,000 were to be issued to the public while a quote was sought on the Birmingham Stock Exchange. Messrs Leek and Rose were to receive 380,000 shares and £8500 in cash in exchange for the assets and designs which they held.

The prospectus was wildly optimistic and spoke of production of 1000 cars in the first 12 months; the number actually built during this period totalled approximately 35. The profit forecast of £31,000 also proved a shade off target for the first balance sheet revealed a deficit of £16,360 for the first 18 months of trading up to 31 January 1939. The flotation was hardly a success with the majority of the shares being left with the underwriters, five out of six of whom defaulted almost causing an early collapse. A mortgage of £8000 was negotiated, however, and somehow the business managed to get under way.

The factory in Much Park Street was hardly ideal, although the main machine shop and tool room comprising some 20,000 sq. ft. were reasonable shops. The remaining space comprised a series of small and badly placed buildings reminiscent of rabbit warrens. The front office block facing the street was a four-storey building of Victorian appearance. Total ground floor area was originally approximately 35,000 sq. ft. but the very old property to the west, a relic of the lace and ribbon industry days, was later acquired and an extensive modern building for car assembly and finishing was erected.

Premises on the opposite side of Much Park Street were also acquired and this effectively almost doubled the original 1937 works area. These buildings originally housed the Standard Motor Co. at its formation in 1903 and were latterly occupied by Charlesworth Bodies, who were taken over by Lea-Francis for production of the six light streamlined body in 1948.

General engineering sub-contract work was undertaken as soon as George Leek had organized the factory, having to wait until the Triumph Co. cleared a stock of cars, while Hugh Rose and his team pressed on with motor-car development.

The new cars were originally described in the first prospectus as 12/50 and 14hp types with the option of a six light body by Avon or a four light by Charlesworth. The engine, as already mentioned, followed Riley practice very closely, almost a 'Chinese' copy with the exception of the improved valve gear. However the drive now consisted of a first stage by duplex chain, the top sprocket being attached

107

to an idler gear which meshed with the camshaft driving gears. The distributor was driven by skew gearing from the forward end of the inlet camshaft, a Weller blade took care of chain lash and the entire system was quiet, trouble-free and capable of an immense mileage between overhauls. The oil pump was driven by a vertical shaft from the exhaust camshaft and the body of this component was of iron, contrasting with the Riley which utilized aluminium, although this material was used on the first trial Lea-Francis units. The counter-balanced crankshaft was inserted from the rear of the crankcase and the front main bearing of 1¾in diameter was in the form of a bush. The centre main bearing was a split circular diaphragm located by a dowell, while the rear main housing, also split, was attached to the rear of the crankcase with 12 studs, rather stiffer and more positively attached than in the case of the Riley. The first six engines, however, used the Riley pattern housing. A 9in Borg and Beck clutch was used and a water pump of Lea-Francis manufacture was located centrally on the front of the cylinder head to be driven by the dynamo belt. Combustion chambers were fully machined and hemispherical. The ports were also fully machined and an exhaust-heated hot spot was arranged. The engine was offered in the form of a 12hp type with the usual dimensions of 69mm bore × 100mm stroke (1496cc), while the 14hp was bored-out to 72mm giving a capacity of 1629cc and an actual RAC rating of 12·9hp power output at 48 and 53bhp respectively was delivered at 4700rpm. The engine bearers were flexible, consisting of rubber blocks at the front and a bonded-rubber mounting under the gearbox at the rear.

The tops for the crankcase breather pipes were made from surplus Ace of Spades valve cover nuts and all covers on the engine were of cast aluminium attached by ¼in studs and set pins; the whole power unit was neat and attractive in appearance. It was a well-engineered high-grade production and probably the most efficient private-car engine available in the immediate pre-war period.

The chassis, although thoroughly sound and using well-tried components, did not reveal any particularly outstanding features and was typical of British sporting-car practice. The Alford and Alder front axle, Burman-Douglas steering box, Girling brakes, ENV rear axle and Luvax-Bijur chassis lubrication system were familiar enough and the brief specification read rather like that of an Alvis 12/70, SS Jaguar 1½-litre, Riley 1½-litre or Triumph Dolomite, all honest, elegant and lively cars from the City of the Three Spires.

The size of the new Lea-Francis closely followed the old 12/40 with a similar wheelbase of 9ft 3in, although the track at 4ft 4in was 2in wider. The chassis frame with side members running to a maximum depth of 5in was underslung at the rear, while a diamond form of bracing surrounded the engine and gearbox location resulting in good stiffness in this area. A total of six cross members were employed, one of which was bolted into position. The springs were all of semi-elliptic form, the rears being of reverse camber. The rear-axle ratios were of 5 or 5·25:1 as standard, with 4·75:1 specified for sports models. A Wilson pre-selector gearbox and centrifugal clutch was an optional extra for a surcharge of £30. The petrol tank held 11 gallons with feed by electric pump.

All spring bushes were of bronze, lubricated together with all the king pins and steering ball joints by the Bijur system. Two silencers were fitted while these pre-war cars used flexible exhaust down pipes; 42mm Rudge hubs were

1947 sports engine, CE2089

fitted, tyre size was 5·25 × 17in, and brake drums were 13in diameter.

The initial batch of six chassis were hand-assembled by C V Ridley, another ex-Riley man, later in charge of the progress department. Laid down in October 1937, these prototypes were fitted with a divided propeller shaft and Singer gearbox, all of which were rejected on account of noise to be replaced with a Standard 12 unit and single propeller shaft. Two or three differing radiator cowls were fitted to these early cars, one having a false honeycomb with two vertical bars, while another utilized fine vertical strips. Wider chromium-plated slats were standardized for the production version. Rounded valve covers were also used on two or three of these cars but the design was altered to a flat-topped pattern with shallow grooves running longitudinally for noise reduction.

Chassis numbers commenced at 50 with the prefix 'A' being applied to the larger-engined version. The first completed car (Chassis No. 55), was returned from the New Avon Body Co. on 23 December fitted with a four light saloon of the good-looking 'Waymaker' pattern. This was standardized as a production type at £395 and must have been useful for the Avon concern, since they had a stock of this type which were previously built on Standard 20hp chassis and made redundant following a disagreement with Standards.

The next car (Chassis No. A54), was fitted with a six light saloon body of Carbodies manufacture. This type was not adopted for production and the chassis was rebodied before sale with an Avon-built six light saloon which was designed exclusively for Lea-Francis, and also priced at £395. Chassis No. 53, back from Avon on 6 January 1938 was endowed with a d/h coupé, once again of a pattern formerly built on Standard chassis and priced at £410. Chassis No. 52 was despatched in chassis form

The 'Lea-Francis' body shop at A P Aircraft

109

110

to Charles Follett, who commissioned the Carlton Carriage Co. to build a very striking and graceful 2/4-seater sports body, which was later listed as an additional model to the range at £475.

This particular car, fitted with a highly tuned 69mm bore engine, twin SU carburettor and a rear axle ratio of 4:1, was to provide useful publicity for Lea-Francis when it showed amazing speed at Brooklands. The car is still in existence owned by Michael Perkins of Henley-in-Arden. The first car sold to a private owner in April 1938 (Chassis No. A50) is also still extant, although no longer fitted with the original coachwork.

A sanction for 1000 sets of parts was issued in January 1938 and orders were placed accordingly. Very few modifications were found to be necessary in the production cars and changes were mainly concerned with facilitating ease of production or machining. The Midland Motor Cylinder Co. supplied the cylinder-block castings at a price of £3-7s-6d each, while Henry Meadows Ltd were responsible for machining both block and crankshafts for the pre-war engines. Riley Motors undertook the machining of con-rods and cylinder heads, their machine shop being well placed to carry out work on Lea-Francis engine components due to the similarity of design.

A total of 62 production models were built during 1938 of which 44 utilized the larger engine. Eleven d/h coupés were built, while one four-seater touring-car by Avon Bodies was sold to Humphrey Burman who kept it for his lifetime (Chassis No. A65). It is still in first-class condition. This body was then offered as an additional model but no orders were taken.

Only one chassis was fitted with a Wilson gearbox (Chassis No. A64). Strikingly finished in ivory and with hosts of extras, this d/h coupé took a first prize in the Ramsgate Concours D'Elegance in July. The owner of this car, T Loftus-Tottenham, ordered a replica of Charles Follett's sports model. The body for this car (A115) was built by Corsica and a lowered radiator was fitted. The three standard types (Nos. 114, A116 and A117) graced Stand 165 at Olympia, backed up by the Corsica with a further six light saloon (Chassis No. 110) for demonstration purposes. The latter car was subjected to an *Autocar* road test in December; 600 miles were covered and the New Leaf made a good impression, being described as 'thoroughly honest in a British engineering sense'. A speed of 75·63mph was recorded, 0 to 50 took 18·1 seconds, and the first-class brakes stopped the 26½cwt car from 30mph in 29½ft. Fuel consumption ranged from 23 to 28mpg.

Another body type was listed for production at the time of the Olympia. A de-luxe four light saloon priced at £485, it was to have been supplied by Charlesworth and was of the pattern used by them on the Alvis Speed 25, albeit slightly smaller. Only one demonstration car was built (Chassis No. 109).

Sales during 1939 fell off, while the company switched the emphasis to subcontract engineering work, most of which had a military significance as Britain made a belated effort to expand

ABOVE
The 1960 Lynx

TOP LEFT
Corsica Sports, 1938. Chassis A115 and George Leek watching the proceedings with interest

BOTTOM LEFT
Six light saloon interior, 1938

Sunbeam bus engine, 1930. Designed by Hugh Rose

its armed forces following Munich.

Cars assembled in this last pre-war year totalled six with 72mm engines and 12 of the 69mm type. This total included two coupés, one four light saloon and two more Corsica sports models, while a solitary f/h sports coupé was built by Corsica (140). Little is known about this car but it would probably rank as the most elegant Lea-Francis of all time, the lines following that of the sports models. This particular car was last heard of in 1955.

Car production virtually ceased in September 1939 and while the service department remained open and a small amount of car-development work continued, the works were almost wholly engaged on Air Ministry contracts. Major A E Allnatt, OBE, acting for a debenture holder, joined the board during 1939 and the results for the year ending 31 January 1940 were to show that a further loss had been made but this was down to the manageable amount of £3964. The total development costs of the new car were calculated at £9870. Officials of the company were still busying themselves with the unproductive task of suing the various defaulting underwriters but with the vast amount of profitable business about to be undertaken, the matter was to become insignificant.

While the City of Coventry suffered badly during the war, the premises in Much Park Street survived virtually intact and were it not for the business which hostilities brought in its wake, the recently formed business of Lea-Francis would undoubtedly have foundered.

War contracts included several large orders from Shorts of Belfast including throttle boxes, oxygen-bottle racks, tank-cover lids, together with a flash eliminator for the Browning gun which was developed by Lea-Francis. Various other projects including work for BSA and A V Roe were undertaken.

Trading for the year up to 31 January 1941 revealed a turn round in profit, the surplus amounting to £3115, while Major Allnatt's seat on the board was now taken over by Alan H Perkins. The following year, a satellite factory in Leicester now in operation, saw a leap in profits to £17,619 after allowing for the write-off of all car development costs. The year ending 31 January 1943 revealed an astounding result with a profit figure of £82,404 and a payment of 8 percent dividend while the debenture and mortgage holders were both paid off. A quote on the Stock Exchange was obtained in 1943 and the 2s shares were changing hands at over 3s.

H L Read now resigned from the board, while the profit figure for the next year was £51,855 which permitted another 8 per cent dividend, and the remaining unissued shares were offered at 2s-3d each.

C W Hayward became interested in Lea-Francis cars and through his company, Electrical and General Industrial Trusts Ltd, purchased a considerable block of shares.

Hayward was also a director of Brooklands Aviation and as such, was at the centre of the controversy over the sale of the Weybridge Track after the war.

Three new cars were completed during the early part of the war, and were all bought by directors. Chassis No. 134, a d/h coupé, went to Major Allnatt in January 1940, while a six light (136) in matt-black war finish was taken over by Col. Symons in December 1941. H L Read purchased Chassis No. 135, which was fitted with the Carbodies six light saloon, which had been in store for four years.

Development work on motor cars went on quietly and included the manufacture and test of a centrifugal supercharger, a revised induction system with a carburettor on the exhaust side. Hydraulic zero-lash tappets were also appraised and tested on several engines, in the quest for improved silence. Difficulties with maintaining sufficient cleanliness in the oil supply for efficient operation led to abandonment, however. The most interesting development concerned a system of 'Oleo' leg suspension which was tried on one car, while an epicyclic overdrive was built and patented in 1941 – very similar to the Laycock unit which followed 10 years later.

An auxiliary 2-cylinder engine was developed for the Air Ministry in 1943–4. This unit of 90×90 bore and stroke, together with a single-cylinder version, was completed and tested, but orders were cancelled and the project was dropped.

A further chassis (137) was erected for Hugh Rose in April 1944 and fitted with a second-hand six light Avon saloon for use as a test bed for the 'Oleo' suspension, overdrive and a special 78mm bore engine.

Preparations for the post-war car began in mid-1944, and while the basic layout was to follow the pre-war design, many detail changes were to be made. A decision to increase the size of the larger engine to 75mm in the bore (RAC rating 13·9hp) was taken, and this engine was to prove most popular. Demand for the 11·9 version fell off, especially with the introduction of the flat rate of taxation in 1947. The main engine modification concerned the crankshaft which was enlarged to 2in diameter for both the big ends, and front and rear main bearings. The rather complicated breather and drain plug arrangement was abandoned, perhaps the stock of Ace of Spades valve-cover knobs had been exhausted! The hotspot arrangement was now water-heated, the old recirculatory exhaust gas arrangement being abandoned, while a new and flexible engine mounting arrangement was evolved. A Moss four-speed gearbox was standardized initially, and although strong, it was somewhat noisy with a rather indifferent synchromesh mechanism.

The old Luvax-Bijur chassis lubrication system was dropped in favour of grease-gun application for king pins and steering ball joints, while 'Claytonrite' rubber bushes were now used for all spring and shackle pins. Pressed-steel wheels replaced the Rudge wire pattern. Curiously the chromium-plated hub cap was impressed with a Lea-Francis monogram which was incorrectly drawn, the L and F being incorrectly superimposed, a fault which was never put right. The new car had a two-spoke steering wheel, while the handbrake was now of the pistol grip type mounted under the facia. New instrumentation was evolved which did not include a rev counter, and was not too well positioned, some instruments being partially shrouded by the steering wheel. Other changes included the fitting of Luvax piston-type dampers, while unsprung weight was increased by the fitting of a DWS built-in jacking system. The rear axle ratio was originally 5:1, later standardized at 4·875:1 for the 14hp car, with a 5·125:1 set for the smaller-engined type.

The first two chassis, Nos. 200 and 206, were laid down in November 1944 with 202 and 204 following in July 1945. They were initially assembled with several 1939 features which were changed before eventual sale. Chassis No. 200 was taken across Much Park Street to Charlesworth Bodies, who built upon it a rather ungainly six light saloon which was not approved. This firm also purchased Chassis Nos. 204 and 206, to which they fitted f/h and d/h coupés respectively, again of a type which was not repeated.

Messrs Perkins and Austin, formerly engaged in the production of Riley bodies had formed their own sheet-metal business titled A P Aircraft Ltd, and occupying the former Cross & Ellis works in Dane Road, Coventry. This firm was engaged by George Leek to manufacture a lightweight saloon body, suitable for the Leaf chassis, and No. 202 was duly sent along, to return in September 1945 with the first prototype body, none-too-well finished and with imperfect proportions. The outburst from George Leek when first he saw it in the works yard has been indelibly imprinted on the memory of those within earshot. The works register covering this car, written in George Andrew's hand, merely bears the cryptic words 'not approved'. This four light saloon with slight alterations and brought up to an acceptable standard of detail was nonetheless adopted as the standard type. The next body mounted on Chassis 218 and completed in December 1945 was passed and resulted in sanction for production.

The 'APA' coachwork was of an interesting

TOP
The engine shop at Much Park Street, January 1946

ABOVE
Early post-war cars bound for Copenhagen, March 1946

construction. The floor, bulkhead and rear-wheel arch assemblies were of steel, while the remainder was almost entirely of aluminium, and of a partially stressed-skin construction. The wings, bonnet and running boards were also of aluminium; only a small amount of ash was used, particularly for screen and cant rails. This body, mounted as it was, on a relatively harshly sprung chassis was never really satisfactory, structural cracks and rattles developing in service. The total weight of the car was kept to a reasonable 24½cwt and the performance, especially that of the 14hp version, which delivered 55–65bhp according to actual specification was extremely good; 75mph was easily attainable, good acceleration and a petrol consumption of 24–26mpg. Compression ratio was now standardized at 7·25:1. The new car was listed at £750 to which was added a purchase tax increment of £209-1s-8d. Extras soon to be made available included a Clayton heater-demister unit, and an HMV Model 100 radio. Work on a left-hand-drive version commenced in November 1945. One further chassis (234) was built to show-finish standards in 1945 which passed around the agents before recall in 1947 when it was fitted with a standard saloon body before sale.

The first post-war car sold (208) left Much Park Street on 23 January 1946 bound for Copenhagen. This particular vehicle was fitted with a gearbox of Armstrong-Siddeley manufacture evolved as an option to the pre-selector transmission for their recently introduced 16hp car. This unit was more refined and quieter than the Moss gearbox, and was adopted as an alternative by Lea-Francis superseding the latter entirely by late 1947. A neat horn push embodying the Lea-Francis monogram was added before the end of 1946 and later a nitride hardened crankshaft was standardized. Various rear spring ratings were also tried, but the axle movement was really insufficient, a penalty of the underslung chassis, and the rear suspension was never really satisfactory. Perhaps understandably Charles Follett always wanted a softer spring for London and Home Counties cars, while Messrs Rossleigh specified the stiffer pattern to cope with Scottish roads.

In 1946 production really started in earnest with the despatch of 326 cars, of which 27 were left-hand drive, and a mere five were fitted with 12hp engines. Export markets were pursued resulting in sales to Switzerland, Iceland, Malta, Australia, Belgium, Persia, Nigeria, Denmark, India, Portugal and Egypt.

Chassis No. 248 was despatched to Riverlee Motor Bodies of Birmingham who constructed the first estate car to be built on a Lea-Francis chassis. A good market then existed for this type of vehicle, which enjoyed purchase tax immunity, and plans were made to introduce a car of this type as a standard model. The Southern Caravan Co. of Yapton, near Chichester, built the early cars and a total of 54 chassis were sold to individual coachbuilders who built 'one-off' variations on this theme during 1946.

An attractive two-door saloon was designed by Arthur Keene, the manufacture of which was entrusted to the Westland Motor Co. of Hereford. Panelled in aluminium on an ash frame, and with flowing wings continuing into the running boards, the proportions of this type were excellent, while thin chromium window frames resulted in good all round visibility. The first car (348) was completed by the end of 1946.

Avon Bodies built one d/h coupé of pre-war design (404) but this design looked less attractive on the post-war chassis, and no further examples were constructed. Messrs Helliwells Aircraft built their own body on Chassis No. 488, titled 'Swallow' following that firm's purchase of the Swallow Sidecar trademark from SS Cars. One further chassis (400) was

Westland coupé, Chassis 348

equipped with a six light Charlesworth saloon. Messrs Cowell & Whittet purchased a special short chassis version of a type later standardized for the '14 Sports' upon which they constructed a lightweight and spartan competition two-seater body, styled by Denis Jenkinson. This car (442) was duly described in the press, and was intended for production, but no further examples were built, although a similar inspiration by the Connaught concern met with greater success later on.

The remaining cars sold during 1946 were all standard four light saloons, and among prominent local owners were the Earl and Countess of Warwick who purchased three such cars during the year (Chassis Nos. 250, 456 and 592).

Hugh Rose used a Riley 16-4 Blue Streak saloon for most of the war period, and this car may have influenced his thinking when he laid out a 2½-litre engine for Lea-Francis, work commencing on this project in September 1946.

With dimensions of 85 × 110mm bore and stroke, the new engine, while embodying the patent Lea-Francis high camshaft arrangement was entirely different in every other respect. The three-bearing crankshaft of cast nickel iron and of generous dimensions with main bearing diameters of 2½in and big ends of 2⅜in was inserted from below in the conventional manner, thus the engine was far easier to assemble than the 14hp type. The crankcase extended 4½in below the crankshaft centre line.

The drive to the camshafts consisted of one long duplex chain, passing over a jockey pulley which originally embodied a patent 'Renold' automatic adjuster. This was not entirely satisfactory, and soon gave way to an eccentric manually adjustable type, which could be easily set from outside without the need for any dismantling. In order to achieve accurate valve timing, each camshaft sprocket was slotted to enable its position to be rotated in relation to the camshaft with the aid of two slotted eccentric dowels, which when turned with a screwdriver caused movement of the sprocket. The whole was locked with four ¼in diameter pins, indeed, all post-1937 Lea-Francis engines were assembled mainly with set-screws, nuts and bolts of this diameter, all threads being BSF. The cylinder head of the 2½-litre engine followed the layout of the smaller engines, but four rocker boxes were used, very similar in outline to the pattern used on early Riley Nines. The distributor was situated on the upper end of the oil pump drive, which again was driven from the exhaust camshaft. The water pump was now placed on the nearside of the engine, and was also driven by skew gears from the rear of the exhaust camshaft.

The inlet manifold was water-heated and consisted of an aluminium casting which bolted along the centre line of the main intake gallery. Half the inlet tract was therefore formed by a recess in the cylinder head.

A single SU carburettor was fitted to the standard engine, intended for saloon cars, while twin carbs were used for sports cars. The standard delivered approximately 90bhp on a 6:1 compression ratio at 4000rpm, the normal sports engine delivered 98–100bhp at 4000rpm on a compression ratio of 7:1. The adoption of 9:1 compression, high-lift camshafts, deletion of the air cleaner, and AQ needles in the H4 carburettors resulted in a further useful increase in power.

The first unit was completed in September 1947, and was later mated to the standard Armstrong-Siddeley Mark IV gearbox via a special bell housing, to accommodate the large-diameter flywheel of the big engine. The Mark IV gearbox, designed as it was for a 2-litre 6-cylinder engine of fairly modest power, was dangerously near its limit when applied to the rigorous 2½-litre Lea-Francis, which delivered an abundance of torque in the pounding manner of all 'Big Fours'.

A good driver taking moderate care when starting in bottom gear could make a gearbox last for up to 70,000 miles. More forceful types were breaking the teeth from the Layshaft bottom pinion within a few months of taking delivery, while mainshafts also began to shear across a circlip groove. Nevertheless no modifications of any moment were made, apart from a change in first-gear teeth profile, which affected but a small improvement.

A further important development began in 1946 with the design of an independent front suspension system using double wishbones, the upper being combined with a double acting Luvax damper, while the lower and longer wishbones were splined to a torsion bar of 27in length. The steering arm was spigoted into the stub axle, while a new divided track rod was coupled to an idler arm bolted to the centre of a new front cross member. A further new 'bolt in' cross member located the rear ends of the torsion bars, and their attendant height adjustment levers. The remainder of the chassis frame was unaltered, the dumb irons remaining although their only duty was to provide an anchorage for the front bumper assembly.

The first prototype IFS Chassis (No. 198) was assembled in the service department, and fitted with a four light saloon body – this was ready in April 1947. Hugh Rose took his wife on an extended Continental tour in this car, which gave no sign of trouble and proved to have a good tyre life. The ride was still very firm and the layman could be excused for thinking the car still had a rigid axle, although the new system eradicated the tendency to scuttle shake, prevalent in the older design. The inspiration for this form of IFS was in some part due to the Citroen Light 15. Hugh Rose bought a new car of this type, which he kept for many years.

A reconditioned 1½-litre engine was loaned to Follett's in November 1946 for testing and appraisal by the HRG people who fitted it into one of their sports cars. It was not adopted, however, and was returned two years later. The HRG concern ordered another 1½-litre engine and gearbox assembly in March 1950, to be built to sports specification, and including dry-sump lubrication, but the order was later cancelled.

The post-war competition scene began to gather momentum in 1946, and one or two Hypers emerged, Denyer securing a second place in a VSCC Sprint with a time of 21·6 seconds for the standing start quarter-mile. E G Pool ran at Brighton and Prescott. G R Baird also ran the 'Triangle Special' at Prescott, but took the rather lengthy time of 64·76 seconds, although Pool was even slower in 71·64 in the old Chetwynd car. The 'Triangle' was built by Ted Lloyd-Jones and consisted of a Hyper engine, gearbox and back axle combined with a Lombard chassis.

A new four light saloon won the Grand Prix D'Honneur and Engelbert Cup in a Concours in Brussels, while the works fielded a team of three new four light saloons in the cavalcades held in various cities to mark the 50th anniversary of the motor industry. George Andrews backed up the new cars with his 12/40 Francis saloon (No. 18165).

New staff engaged by the works during 1946 included Albert Ludgate in the drawing office, who ultimately became chief engineer, leaving late in 1952 for a post in Australia. The drawing office staff also included J Gannon and Peter Nottingham. Ken Rose, son of Hugh, was employed in engine and road test capacities, leaving in December 1951 to form Cosmic Car Accessories of Walsall. The service department was maintained by the Fowler Bros. under the direction of George Andrews, and using premises in Parkside for a period.

Production for 1947 rose to 553 14hp cars and chassis, of which 25 were lhd versions. A

ABOVE
The first post-war demonstrator. Chassis 218

LEFT
The Yapton estate car, Chassis 486

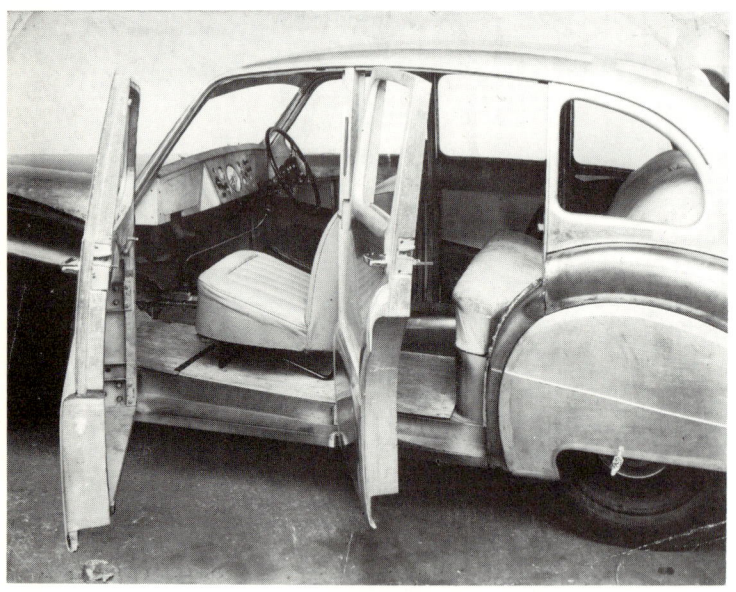

further eight 12hp cars were built including one lhd (No. 788). Most of these cars were ordered by Messrs Rossleigh for Scottish owners.

Special cars included a hideous wooden saloon by Messrs Joel Ltd (No. 1784) while Southern Caravans made two copies of the standard four light saloon on Chassis 1844 and 2062. Two more Westland coupés were delivered, and Jensen Motors built an Estate Car (No. 1616). Yapton estate cars and vans totalled 44, while some 80 chassis with prefabricated dashboards and front wings were supplied to various agents, most were completed as shooting brakes, although one or two ice cream vans appeared for service in due course.

A prototype sports car was built in the service department and despatched to Abbey Parts, for two-seater sports coachwork, completed in July 1947. This car was also fitted with the new IFS and a highly tuned 12hp engine was installed (Chassis No. 196). The body was adopted for production with a few modifications, which included remodelling the radiator grille, lowering the windscreen and evolving a remote-control unit for the gearbox in place of the long and rather 'woolly' saloon-type gearlever. A new four-spoke steering wheel was also fitted to the later production car. A further prototype was completed in September 1947 (Chassis No. 1300), utilizing the standard solid front axle, which was to be retained almost for the entire production run of the '14 Sports'. This second car also used a 12hp engine.

Various experimental schemes were drawn up for changes to the 14 sports body, including electrically operated hood mechanisms, and wind-up glass windows in the doors. Experiments were carried out with road springs 3in longer than standard at the front and 4in at the rear and one or two cars were so fitted.

The only production changes during 1947 covered inlet valves, which were enlarged for all engines, and this appeared to provide approximately an extra 4hp.

A few sales of second-hand Lea-Francis cars were still made by the works, indeed a 1927 12/22 (Chassis No. 7370) was bought and sold in 1947, together with several 1938–9 models.

Production figures for 1948 ran to a total of 551 standard 14hp cars, of which estate cars and vans accounted for 243, while 25 Westland coupés were completed.

A new saloon body by Minnion & Keene was evolved in 1948. A visit to the Geneva Show resulted in the design of an up-to-date streamlined six light saloon devoid of unnecessary ornamentation, with a crisp and pleasing appearance. The front end treatment comprised a narrow grille with the traditional Lea-Francis outline in vestigial form. Headlamps were shrouded into the wings, while the bonnet top was of one-piece construction (apart from one or two exceptions, built to special order), and hinged at the scuttle with a normal release cable operated from within. All doors trailed, and the interior layout and fittings were far better than in the case of the four light model. Indeed one might say that the new car, to be known as the 14/70, was sumptuous. It was also less prone to structural cracks, although still not faultless in this respect; both bonnet and wide boot lid were flimsy, and with no stiffening behind the back seat squab the whole body could be seen to be vibrating gently at the rear, if one looked into the mirror. The front doors were also unduly heavy, and could not hold up under their own weight, thus a small roller was built into the door bottom, which travelled up a slope attached to the concealed running board to ensure that the door would shut reasonably well. Constructed in the traditional manner with an ash framework mounted on a steel floor, all panelling was of aluminium, rear wheels were spatted, and the new coachwork was fitted on IFS chassis only; 600 × 16 tyres were specified in place of 550 × 17 used on other models.

The Charlesworth bodyworks were taken over for the manufacture of this coachwork, which was, therefore, the first bodywork ever built by Lea-Francis.

The car was priced at £1150 for the standard Mk V and £1250 for the deluxe Mk VI with radio and other extras as standard. The first car (Chassis No. 3668) was completed in September 1948, and was exhibited at the first post-war Earls Court Show, together with the third example (Chassis No. 3688), while the second car (3670) was to be Follett's demonstrator.

Production of the '14 Sports' was underway in 1948 with 89 units completed, and starting with a 12hp example (1302). Eleven cars went to the USA of which five were built in lhd form, while one example went to Uruguay where there was an active Lea-Francis agent.

Sir Clive Edwards, Bt, a keen Lea-Francis devotee, bought No. 1372 (at present undergoing restoration in the author's ownership) while Prince Jaideep Singh took delivery of 1394. Continental Cars purchased six chassis fitted with competition engines, which became famous as Connaught sports cars. The first chassis delivered in March 1948 (1356, 1358 and 1360) were actively campaigned in sports-car races in 1949. Connaught experienced difficulty with body production, resulting in a failure to complete the cars for the '48 season.

Autocar duly road tested one of the Lea-Francis demonstrators (1320) and were enthusiastic, speaking highly of 'this well-built and exciting British sports car'. They recorded 87mph, together with an 0–50 acceleration figure of 13·3 seconds. The '14 Sports' was arguably the best post-war Lea-Francis, featuring an excellent driving position, light, quick, and accurate steering, first-class brakes and pleasing lines, although the cowled-in frontal treatment could, perhaps, have been happier.

There is no doubt that the works should have done far better with this model than the actual production figures bear out. The car was virtually without a competitor, being in a higher bracket than the MG TC, and more powerful and sophisticated than the only other British sports car in this class, the HRG also distributed by Charles Follett. The early cars delivered close to 80bhp on a 7·25:1 compression ratio, while later examples went up to 8:1 resulting in peak power of 87bhp at 5200rpm. A final drive ratio of 4·55:1 was specified, although the smaller-engined car utilized a standard saloon 4·875:1 axle. The car was priced at £998 plus purchase tax of £278, a

ABOVE
Albert Ludgate and Ken Rose before leaving for the USA sales trip in 1949

TOP LEFT
The new finishing shop, 1947

CENTRE AND BOTTOM LEFT
The prototype six light. Chassis 3668

much higher rate of tax applying to cars of £1000 and over at this time of Cripps' austerity. Modifications proposed, but not adopted, for this model, included a tubular chassis by Ludgate.

The first 2½-litre sports-car was on the road in May 1948 (Chassis No. 5000), and consisted of a '14 Sports' body mounted on a new 8ft 3in wheelbase chassis with independent front suspension. These cars were finding buyers at up to £1600 on the flourishing 'black market'.

The company's auditors discovered certain indiscretions concerning the sale of new cars which had avoided the payment of full purchase tax, indeed some 70 cars were sold as second-hand demonstration models in 1947 alone, amounting to over 20 per cent of the total production. It is fair to say that the engineering integrity of both Charles Van Eugen and Hugh Rose was not matched on occasions by those responsible for the commercial direction of Lea-Francis.

Financial results for the 18 months ending 31 July 1946 allowed a dividend of 6 per cent following a useful profit of £33,214, assisted by recoverable excess profits tax, while the following 12 months resulted in a surplus of almost £18,000 upon which a dividend of 4 per cent was paid.

Charles Hayward now resigned from the company, and George Leek was once again chairman. The directorate was now reduced to three. Sub-contract work for the Ministry of Supply and the general engineering industry continued, while the 1949 car programme underwent several changes.

A much better-looking shooting-brake body was now standardized, built by APA, and using the four light scuttle and windscreen. A van on the same lines was also available.

The independent torsion bar suspension was now standardized for all private cars, excepting the Westland coupé, while practically all the saloons built in early 1949 were of the new six light pattern, four light production building up again later in the year, although now glazed and trimmed in the enlarged Much Park Street plant. This style was now given a lower roof line at the rear.

Production for the year 1949 totalled 25 sports 14's, 84 six light saloons, 122 four lights, 238 estate cars and vans, 10 separate chassis and three final Westland coupés. Left-hand-drive chassis accounted for a mere 20 of this total, mostly six lights.

The 2½-litre range was also launched during the year. The big engine in single-carburettor form appearing in the six light saloon, and lustily pulling a 4·1:1 top gear. The ample high-geared performance resulted in a most restful car to drive. Designated as the 'Eighteen' or Mark VII saloon, the first car (5002) was ready in December 1948, and was retained for many years as a development car by Hugh Rose. A total of 21 more were delivered in 1949, and one 2½-litre sports car was completed. This car (5026) was exhibited at Earls Court and Kelvin Hall, while the following season

'Midget car' engine despatch

found it competing in production sports-car races with Ken Rose at the wheel. The new sports car was considerably more sophisticated than the '14 Sports', embodying a fixed three-panel windscreen and generally larger dimensions, enabling a small seat to be fitted in the rear. The doors, now trailing, contained wind-up glass windows but these were never really satisfactory.

The two original Connaught sports cars made a real impact on the competition scene in 1949. Rodney Clarke and Kenneth McAlpine ran these cars in sports-car races and hill climbs, achieving a first and second place in a five-lap handicap at Goodwood. They repeated this performance in a similar event at Blandford, together with second and fourth places in scratch races at MMEC and BOC Silverstone meetings. Bob Spikins installed a 1½-litre Lea-Francis engine in his well-known Spikins Special, which he tuned himself, resulting in a Class win at the Brighton Speed Trials (29·16 seconds) among other successes.

G R Baird, in conjunction with Ken Rose, built a special all-independent racing car equipped mainly with Lea-Francis material, including the engine and gearbox, the former with the recently introduced aluminium cylinder block. This car known as the RBL, was not particularly successful although Baird achieved the creditable performance of climbing Prescott in under 50 seconds (49·43), as did Spikins in his special (49·53). The old short course then in use. Sir Clive Edwards installed one of the aluminium Leaf engines in his HRG to make an effective competition car, ascending Shelsley in 45·03, and Prescott in 50·60. McAlpine won his class at Prescott, with a time of 53·05 in the Connaught. Rose took the RBL over to the Isle of Man, and drove in the Manx Cup Races without success, although Kelly using yet another competition Lea-Francis in his special, which was named, rather astonishingly, an 'IRA', held third place until forced to retire with mechanical troubles.

Denyer and Burman were active again in the trials world with first- and second-class awards respectively in the Land's End event, Burman now using his 1939 car (A61). Denyer also achieved distinction at the Great Auclum speed hill climb, while H H Mayes won a first-class award in the Sturgess Trophy Trial in his post-war car.

Racing in 1950 saw a string of successes for Connaught sports cars, principally in the hands of Kenneth McAlpine, and in 1951 by K H Downing using MPH329 or MPH995 (Chassis Nos. 1356 and 1358); the pair also won a total of 10 races at Goodwood, Silverstone, Gamston and Winfield. W J Skelly from Motherwell purchased a '14 Sports' chassis, together with a highly tuned engine (Chassis No. 7098) to which he fitted a rudimentary sports body for competition work north of the border. The first outing for this car was the August 1949 Boness Hill Climb, and it finished second in the 1½-litre class. a third place in a three-lap race at Winfield followed, while Ted Lund won the

Six light demonstrator at Coventry

TOP
Rose at Goodwood in 5026

ABOVE
Ken Rose and the 2½-litre sports (chassis 5026) at Silverstone, followed by Spikins in an 18, Chassis 5022

Blandford Trophy in his Lea-Francis special in May at an average of 77·70mph.

H Thornton entered a '14 Sports' (No. 3420) in the MCC one-hour speed trials in October 1950, averaging a dismal 51·26mph, but A S Steven in the first '14 Sports' to be fitted with independent front suspension (No. 7100) did better in the '8 Clubs' one-hour trial in June 1951, qualifying for an award, as too did E J Chandler in the ex-Cowell special (442).

Jack Turner from Wolverhampton became interested in tuning the Lea-Francis engine, and prevailed upon Hugh Rose to make an aluminium, twin-plug cylinder head. The first engine so fitted was inserted into a Turner Special to which Abbey Panels fitted a very good copy of a Ferrari 166 body, marred somewhat by the Morris Minor radiator grille! Ken Rose drove this car in several races and hill climbs, recording 52·35 seconds at Prescott.

Ken Wharton tried out the 'Spikins' car, now known as the Cromard Special. The Goodwood meeting in September 1951 saw Wharton win a five-lap handicap at the respectable average of 81·29mph, and the car was later put up for sale at £1500.

Connaught Engineering was at this time busy with a new all-independent out-and-out racing-car, known as the 'A'-type. The unfinished car was ready for trial at Silverstone in August 1950, when it suffered an unfortunate accident. After repair the car was entered at Castle Coombe, and this highly effective Formula II machine finished second in its first race, in the hands of McAlpine. The engine used an aluminium cylinder block, ran with four amals and was fitted with a preselector gearbox. The chassis was built entirely by Connaught although Lea-Francis i.f.s-type stub axles and king pins were used. The great success for this model came in later years in the hands of Alan Cottam, who has campaigned an example in VSCC races and hill climbs for some eight years, seldom failing to achieve an award in what has proved to be a totally reliable and fast racing car.

Lea-Francis entered two cars in the BRDC Silverstone production-car race, August 1950. The maker's demonstration 2½-litre sports-car (5026) was driven by Ken Rose. A wider grille had been fitted after cooling problems at Goodwood where Rose had finished fourth in a three-lap scratch race. Bob Spikins was commissioned to drive an 'Eighteen' saloon (5022) fitted with an engine built to sports specification. This particular car had been taken to Lindley Aerodrome, now famous as the MIRA test ground, where it achieved 105mph watched by all the Lea-Francis executives and directors. The two cars were, nevertheless, completely outclassed at Silverstone, and finished well down the field.

Sales of competition engines to firms and private owners began to increase in 1948 with deliveries to the racing fraternity already mentioned. A serious effort to influence the American midget racing-car scene was also mounted by Albert Ludgate and Ken Rose who undertook two trips to the USA. There they successfully demonstrated the 'Leaf' but to little effect.

Miss Wilby, who still ran her 1939 coupé, purchased a standard sports 69mm engine which the Lea-Francis service department fitted into her chain-driven Frazer-Nash. The whole operation cost £424, which must have seemed a considerable sum in 1948! The 75mm bore dry-sump engine supplied to Sir Clive Edmonds for use in the HRG, together with Mark IV gearbox totalled £513. Douglas Hull installed this unit in the chassis. The Albatross Marine concern ordered a 1½-litre engine in 1950 specifying an iron cylinder block, 15:1 compression and twin H4 carburettors, angled at 12°, to suit the downward cant of the engine when fitted in the racing Hydroplane for which it was intended. This interesting craft still survives. D A Knudsen of Lisbon purchased a special sports 2½-litre engine and gearbox running on a compression of 7·63:1, the power output coaxed up to 125bhp, while Siata in Italy also ordered a 2½-litre engine for development, later to lose interest and cancel. In May 1951, Connaught took a 2½-litre sports engine and gearbox, presumably for use in one of their sports-cars, as did Geoffrey Crossley in 1953. Iota racing cars of Bristol also took a sports 14hp engine and gearbox for use by Dick Caesar in one of his specials, and R G Shattock bought one of the engines which Ludgate had used in America for installation in one of his special Atalantas, later to appear at Blandford and other circuits.

Lea-Francis owners took part in several

TOP
Rose and Croft-Pearson with the Monte Carlo estate car, Chassis 4148, in 1950

ABOVE
Ken Rose demonstrates the DWS jacks of a Mark IIIA saloon

rallies, notably Croft-Pearson from the Isle of Man, who entered an unlikely contender in the 1950 Monte Carlo event in the form of a 14hp estate car (Chassis No. 4148). Co-driven by Ken Rose, the car started from Glasgow and after a trouble-free run, albeit through very bad weather, finished in 103rd position out of a total of 135 starters. Two '14 Sports' also contested the 1950 Torquay Rally – one crashed but Davies finished in fourth place.

Three cars took part in the 1951 RAC Rally including Bullock in his '14 Sports' (Chassis No. 7002), and C M B Kite and Charles Follett in $2\frac{1}{2}$-litre sports cars (Chassis Nos. 5142 and 5218 respectively), all finishing without loss of marks. Kite achieved success in the 1952 Isle of Wight Rally winning the 3-litre class while he and R Miller also contested the 1952 RAC Rally.

The 1953 MCC Edinburgh Rally was supported by Thornton in the works '14 Sports' (Chassis No. 3400), but he burnt out the clutch. S W Fox fared better in his car (Chassis No. 3426), which the works had converted from left- to right-hand drive.

Norwich agent Stanley Boshier travelled far from home to compete in the Lisbon Rally in 1950, taking second prize in the Concours D'Elegance. His car was a specially prepared Eighteen saloon (Chassis No. 5088), fitted with twin carburettors, twin fuel pumps, remote-control gear lever and a high-ratio rear axle. G A Riederer purchased a left-hand-drive Eighteen off the 1951 Earls Court stand, and took it to Yugoslavia, competing in the Adriatic Rally in 1952. This resulted in a class win and second fastest time for a gruelling hill climb of $10\frac{1}{2}$ miles in length.

Several other modern Lea-Francis cars acquitted themselves well in rallies and trials of the early fifties, both at home and abroad.

The four light saloon received some alterations in readiness for the 1950 season. The rear-window glass was now curved to follow the roof contours, while the boot lid was attached at the top on external chromium hinges, and was extended in length to include the spare-wheel compartment formerly enclosed by a separate lid. A Lea-Francis red-enamel emblem was positioned in the centre of the lid, while the rear lamps were now located in the rear quarter panels. This model was designated Mk IIIA, and the first car (Chassis No. 4226) was completed in May 1949.

Production figures for 1950 revealed the highest output ever achieved by the Much Park Street concern, with the commendable total of 683 units delivered.

The breakdown of figures indicates that 570 'Fourteens' were built, mostly the Mk IIIA type, although several 1951 models were sold

TOP LEFT
A batch of cars awaiting shipment to Australia, 1950

TOP RIGHT
An experimental $2\frac{1}{2}$-litre sports-car (a one-off) completed by Westland of Hereford

RIGHT
A late type-four light saloon. Chassis No. 9978

125

before the end of the year, the former pattern being only current for the 1950 model year. One hundred and twenty-three estate cars and 67 tax-avoiding vans were built, all by APA, while 17 14/70 six light saloons brought up the total. A mere eight '14 Sports' were despatched, four of which were bare chassis for Connaught. The 2½-litre range comprised 54 sports cars, two special four-seater tourers with six light front-end styling bodied by Westland Motors of Hereford; 'Eighteen' saloons totalled 49. A considerable proportion of 2½-litre production went abroad.

Mechanical changes during 1950 were confined to a few minor details – the 14hp con-rod was stiffened in the area of the small end – but the most significant design change applied to this engine concerned the adoption of detachable thin wall big-end bearings, introduced for production in March 1951. A supplementary Wipac oil filter was fitted for a few months in 1950 at the instigation of Albert Ludgate, but was quickly withdrawn after several of the external feed pipes fractured from vibration.

The four light saloon underwent a major change for the 1951 season. The entire body, including floor and seats was lowered by some 2in, resulting in a much-improved appearance. The boot lid arrangement also reverted to the original pattern, opening from the top and with a separate spare-wheel door, although the latter no longer embodied the ace glass number plate and rear light panel of the original model, the less-tidy separate number plate and illuminating lamp of the 1950 car being retained.

The radiator was also lowered, while the headlamps were recessed into the re-styled front wings. The first prototype was completed in July 1950 (Chassis No. 7864) and after leaving the demonstration fleet passed into the hands of Air Chief Marshall Sir John Baldwin. The steering-box was changed to the 're-circulatory' ball type, with Chassis No. 8520 in December 1950. The 2½-litre changed over at Chassis No. 5276. A new distributor incorporating a vacuum-advance system was adapted at the same time. Claytonrite rubber bushes replaced the previous phosphor bronze type in the wishbone pivots, and brake wheel cylinder diameters were increased.

Production for the 1951 season totalled 579 14hp cars, van versions accounting for a mere two, although 175 estate cars were built. The six light 14/70 showed an increase with 61 completed. Three separate chassis were ordered for bespoke coachwork, and the remainder were all four light saloons. Connaught Cars ordered four final '14 Sports' chassis, and all embodied independent suspension. Sales for the 2½-litre fell off badly, and deliveries were only 11 sports cars and 12 saloons.

The recently introduced Mk VII Jaguar saloon, priced at a mere £1616, together with the XK 120 seriously affected the larger Lea-Francis, which was clearly becoming outmoded, the Big Four now falling out of fashion. The old rivals from Holyhead Road had already taken note, and had presented a new 3-litre 6-cylinder car in time for the 1951 season.

Further experimentation and development nevertheless continued with the existing range, both Girling telescopic and Andrex friction shock absorbers being tried, while a full hydraulic braking system was tested and eventually replaced the hydromechanical layout. The new brakes, embodying two leading shoes at the front with a wide lining area, were extremely powerful and, no doubt aided by the moderate weight of the Lea-Francis car, appeared free from fade. These brakes were adopted for production at Chassis No. 5324 (2½ litres), and 9840 (14hp) in March 1952. The ENV rear axle was now of the Hypoid type, while the axleshafts and hubs were forged in one piece. The Salisbury hypoid axle was also fitted to a few of the final cars.

A new, and more flexible engine mounting system of the Citroen type was also tried and fitted to one or two cars. The 14hp water pump was re-designed during 1951, old ones being converted when returned for overhaul.

Rose and Ludgate both realized that a larger car was needed if Lea-Francis intended to become really competitive in the high-quality market. Jaguar, having abandoned smaller models, had already made an enormous leap forward with the smooth, fast, and well-styled, if bulky, Mk VII Saloon. The rust problem was yet to become apparent, and was of little consequence to the original purchaser who probably changed his car every two years. Armstrong-Siddeley was also testing a 3½-litre engine for use in the Sapphire to be introduced in late 1952. The cross pushrod, hemispherical head layout of this design was of a type which always appealed to Hugh Rose, and in August 1951 Lea-Francis obtained one of these engines, and work began on refining it. This included re-design of the camshaft drive and a new crankshaft was also evolved. Unfortunately this scheme never got further than the drawing board, and George Leek decided, perhaps wisely, that the Much Park Street plant was in no position to mount a serious challenge to Browns Lane, Parkside, or indeed the Radford works, where the design staff of Daimler, like those of Armstrong-Siddeley were about to throw off a dull and stuffy image with a new range of high-performance cars. The 1950 and 1951 Lea-Francis production figures of approximately 12 to 13 cars per week were only just over the break-even point, and it was difficult

A sports engine fitted to a hydroplane by A D Truman of Oulton Broad

to see how these figures could be improved without a costly expansion programme, which would have been beyond the limited resources available.

It seems reasonable to believe, however, that good business could have been done by persevering in the sports car market with gradual development of the existing models allied to re-designed and improved coachwork – a much simpler, and cheaper matter to contemplate than the production of a new range of large saloons – sadly it was not to be!

The drop in sales during 1952 was no doubt partly due to the necessity to increase prices. Figures, including purchase tax, but excluding odd shillings and pence were as follows:

	OLD PRICE	NEW PRICE FROM FEBRUARY 1952
14hp Chassis	£972	£1074
18hp ,,	£1049	£1151
14hp Estate Car	£1573	£1884
14 Four Light Saloon	£1759	£1930
18hp Saloon	£2148	£2366
2½ litre Sports	£1775	£1952

A total of 151 14hp models were delivered in 1952, almost all being four light saloons. A mere four of the over-priced estate cars found buyers, the last one being Chassis No. 9608, which found its way to Tasmania in April. Nine more 2½ litre sports cars were sold, together with five Mark VII Saloons.

One 'Eighteen' chassis was fitted with a four light body (Chassis No. 5310) and was retained for staff use for several years.

A new 2-litre engine was developed and four examples were built in 1952. The basis was the existing 2½-litre unit, but the stroke was reduced from 110mm to 88mm. The dimensions were almost square, the standard 2½ bore size of 85mm being retained. This change resulted in long and unwieldy con-rods, and despite the respectable power output obtained, the engine was an awkward compromise. Also the external dimensions were absurdly large for a capacity of a mere 2 litres. The cylinder block, while following the 2½-litre exactly in appearance, was cast in aluminium, using detachable steel liners sealed by a Wells ring; once again this detail appeared to show Citroen influence. An aluminium cylinder head was also designed, but none were built.

Engine testing commenced on Christmas Eve 1952, and the results obtained were 89bhp at 5100rpm on a compression ratio of 6·84:1, while a rise of 7·6:1 resulted in 98bhp at 5200rpm. All the test engines were fitted with fully machined and polished connecting rods.

One engine was installed in an experimental car (Chassis No. 5334) and much testing was carried out, although the new type was never offered to the public. A clear indication of the increase of fuel consumption with corresponding increases of speed is well borne out by tests carried out on this car, with runs down the London Road near Dunchurch using measures of one-tenth of a gallon per test, with results as follows:

AVERAGE SPEED (mph)	CONSUMPTION (mpg)
20	36
30	32
40	29
50	23
58	19

Rear-axle ratio 4·3:1   March 1953

Albert Ludgate had now left for Australia and F W May was appointed chief engineer.

A valuable contract for the design and manufacture of naval gun trolleys was obtained in 1951 and the build-up of work in this direction used up the spare capacity resulting from a run-down of motor car manufacture. In the event several versions of the gun trolley were made in considerable quantities and this work lasted until approximately 1958.

While the assembly of the final car chassis took place in 1952, coachwork fitting, and final preparation for sale continued in the service department until the last cars were cleared in August 1954.

The final Eighteen saloon (Chassis No. 5342) finished in Jaguar lavender grey, was delivered to Follett in March 1953. This car still exists, although in a derelict condition at the present service works, while a further 2½-litre chassis was given a restyled four light body fitted with elongated front wings running into the front doors. A 2½-litre sports cowl and bonnet were utilized, and the car was known as the '1954 Model' in the works, although it was sketched out by Ludgate as early as 1950. No further examples were built, and this particular car (Chassis No. 5334) may still exist although there is no record in the service history dated later than 1964.

Two final 2½-litre sports-cars were completed in 1953 and both are still in existence. Chassis No. 5340 is in Ceylon, where it resides in the ownership of Mervyn Fernando. Chassis No. 5330 was retained as a new car by the works until 1959, when it was hastily despatched to

The final Earls Court appearance. In the foreground is a Papworth estate car, Chassis 10064

Measham auction sales by the new directors to bring in much-needed cash.

Twenty-five standard 14hp four light saloons were sold in 1953, while two chassis (Nos. 10064 and 10066) were fitted with very smart and well-built estate car bodies by Papworth Industries. Production of this new type was seriously considered, but orders for duplicates were not forthcoming. Four more four light cars were sold in 1954, while the final 14/70 six light saloon (Chassis No. 9986) was converted to 2½-litre specification for the use of the chairman. This car is still running in the hands of an owner in Derby. Prices were reduced in 1953 to aid the clearance of these final cars, the four light being offered at £1262 and the Eighteen saloon at £1956 including purchase tax.

Horace Everitt from Knowle complained to George Leek in 1956 about not being able to buy a new 'Leaf'. GHL promised that he should not be disappointed, and built up one of the experimental overslung chassis (No. 5336) fitted with 14hp engine, with enlarged valves and ports. A Laycock overdrive was fitted which made a great improvement to high-speed cruising, and the clutch was hydraulically operated. They had to make do with a second-hand four light saloon body, suitably refurbished, but the car was duly delivered to its owner who was delighted. Everitt was later to play a part in trying to salvage the dying business.

The sale of a small number of engines continued with the despatch of two 75mm units, one with 12:1 compression pistons to Ludgate in Australia. This was used in a special racing car and proved highly effective, winning many races in the Antipodes in the hands of Alfred Beasley.

J C Walwork ran through the RAC Rally in 1953 using 2½-litre sports (Chassis No. 5052) but finished dismally in 98th position out of a total of 100, but M F Mackie won the Novices' Prize in the 1000-mile tour of Ireland using a '14 Sports' (Chassis No. 7074). Thornton entered the Edinburgh Rally of 1953 in his similar car (Chassis No. 3420).

The SSCC Boness hill climb in September 1954 resulted in a second place by N Bean in the 1500cc class with a time of 45·46 in a postwar 12hp car, while D Pearson achieved 46·07 in his old Hyper (14).

Lea-Francis engines continued to win races in 1954 with Leslie Marr finishing third in an Oulton Park formula Libre event in his 2-litre Connaught 'A'-type, while A Brown won the 1500cc sports-car championship at Brands Hatch at 69·53mph in a Connaught. J Riseley-Pritchard was in third place using a Lea-Francis-engined Cooper. Don Beauman won the 2-litre event in his 'A'-type Connaught with two other Connaughts second and third. Tony Rolt won two races at the Crystal Palace with a Connaught, while Jack Fairman took a third place in a Turner similarly engined.

Financial results were still reasonably healthy, with a net profit of £16,541 for the year ending 31 January 1956. This result took account of a drastic write-down of obsolete car manufacturing stocks to the tune of £25,000. A dividend of 10 per cent was paid. In addition to the government contracts a great deal of sub-contract jig-and-tool design and manufacture was undertaken for the aircraft and general engineering industries. Lea-Francis were well placed to carry out work of this type for the company maintained one of the best tool rooms in Coventry.

The following year saw the beginning of the slide to bankruptcy. Results for the 12 months to 31 January 1957 resulted in a trading profit of £23,968, but it was thought prudent to reduce car spares value again. A net loss of £2441 was recorded, and the dividend was passed. Leslie Barnes had now retired, the new secretary was M J Parsons, while W H Tyneham also retired from the board.

The following year saw a small net profit of £1919 and a dividend of 6 per cent. Works manager C A Sherlock was appointed to the board. Shortly afterwards George Leek became ill, and was forced to retire. C A Rookes became chairman, the service department was closed and No. 3 Works was sub-let. Hugh McCall was appointed managing director, and George Leek's nephew Victor became acting secretary.

Hugh Rose had retired some years earlier but continued to serve as a consultant, and he designed and built a range of small engines. These single-cylinder units were of 127cc with overhead valves and were beautifully made with much use of aluminium castings. Various applications were tried, including stationary generating units, outboard motorboat engines, and a 'Mo-Ped'. They ran smoothly and quietly, but were far too expensive to manufacture and clearly no market existed for a sophisticated unit of this size.

Considerable trade in second-hand and reconditioned Lea-Francis cars was carried out until the closure of the service department.

Results for the year ending 31 January 1959 revealed a shattering loss of £56,121, due largely to the ending of several valuable Ministry contracts, which appeared to leave a vacuum in the works. No prospects of any further sizeable contracts could be discerned, and this fact, together with the closure of the service department, caused rumblings among a body of local shareholders. To make matters worse, the bank overdraft which stood at £51,000 in January was said to be increasing week by week and valuable plant was being sold off to provide cash for day-to-day running expenses.

Horace Everitt formed a shareholders' 'ginger group' whose members consisted of Squadron Leader Winfield-Smith – who had achieved fame by becoming the first test pilot appointed by the RAE in 1912 – Fred Brown, a former member of Coventry City Police, Hugh Rose, Captain B L Brady, an engaging character from the City, Miss Vera Braithwaite who held a considerable block of shares, and the author.

Several meetings were held, and a plan was formed which included the removal of the chairman and managing director. They were to be replaced by those members of the Shareholders' Committee who had an engineering background. Winfield-Smith, known to many in industry, was to busy himself with the task of finding sub-contract work, while serious thought was to be given to the business of finding a suitable branded product which could be marketed under the Lea-Francis name. The manufacture of motor cars was not contemplated, at least until fortunes were restored, but the name was to be kept alive in this connection by re-opening the service department.

An Extra-Ordinary General Meeting was called for 14 January 1960, at which it was revealed that the overdraft now stood at £74,000. Henry McCall insisted that the break-even point had been reached, and the order book was full. He remarked rather facetiously that they had 'never had it so good'. The Shareholders' Committee were unconvinced, but decided to adjourn for six weeks pending further information, and the next set of financial results. The new provisional figures issued by the board indicated a further loss of £24,109 although the actual amount revealed when the accounts were finalized to include depreciation, and other expenses, totalled £34,196.

The next meeting held on 29 February was even stormier than the first, and the Masonic Hall in Little Park Street echoed with noise. A mysterious attendee spoke for a firm said to be awarding a £500,000 contract to Lea-Francis. This gentleman strongly suggested that the contract might be withheld if the constitution of the board of directors were to be changed, an utterance which brought forth a bellow of disgust from 'Bones' Brady, who quite rightly thought it an unwarranted interference in the affairs of the firm. No further information was forthcoming about the proposed contract, although it became known later, and proved to be another 'total loss'.

A resolution to sack the chairman and managing director was defeated on a show of hands, but a full poll of shareholders was demanded, and the meeting was adjourned for another week. The poll resulted in the resolution being passed, and the proceedings after this was announced are shrouded in mystery.

Horace Everitt was struck down with influenza and could not attend this final meeting with the result that the Shareholders' Committee was without a chairman at this crucial point. Directly after the poll result was read out, both Rookes and McCall resigned, and declared the meeting closed. The Shareholders' Committee, now speaking for a majority of the shares, was never consulted or approached. One week later the Press announced that Kenneth Benfield, and Alderman Harry Weston had been appointed chairman and managing director respectively, together with Charles W Payne as deputy chairman and R Bowden, FCA, as financial advisors. George Andrews and C A Sherlock remained on the board, together with C H Ward as secretary.

Immediately after the installation of the new management work began on the design of a new car. Kenneth Benfield aspired to become a captain of the motor industry and instructed

A 127cc overhead-valve engine unit, 1958

the drawing office to see to it that cars were completed in time for the following Earls Court Show in October 1960, since it was then March; the task was clearly enormous, but with sterling efforts by Messrs Nottingham, Dakin and Jack Gannon, who rejoined the firm after a term with Jaguar, the deadline was achieved, and the first completed car was revealed at the AGM held at the Chesford Grange, Kenilworth, four days before the opening of the London show. The new car was christened Leaf-Lynx.

Albert Ludgate's original drawings for a tubular chassis for the '14 Sports' in 1948 were dusted down and adapted to take a Ford Zephyr engine. The firm had it in mind to resuscitate the old 4-cylinder 2½-litre engine, but discovered that most of the main patterns and jigs had been destroyed in the McCall era, and with no time to spare, not to mention money, the well-tried Ford Zephyr unit appeared to be the only quick alternative.

The ladder-type chassis was made from 3½in diameter tubes of 10-gauge wall thickness; three tubular cross members were provided behind the engine and gearbox, while a stiff boxed-in front cross member carried the suspension pivots. The side members were bent upwards to the strange angle of 2° 42' forward of the rear axle. Standard Lea-Francis torsion bar i.f.s. was used, but with telescopic shock absorbers, which had also been tried some eight years before; 14hp rear shackles were pressed into service to carry the conventional semi-elliptic rear suspension. Dunlop disc brakes were fitted, and the same firm supplied the ventilated disc centre-lock wheels.

Proprietary parts also included the gearbox, which was a Triumph TR3 unit (to which a Lea-Francis designed remote control was fitted), together with a Laycock overdrive. The rear axle, of Salisbury type, used a 4·1:1 crown wheel and pinion. Steering was by a rack and pinion of Lea-Francis design, and the double-jointed steering column was adjustable for height and rake.

The 2553cc engine was tuned to provide 107bhp at 4500rpm by an increase of compression rise to 8:1, special dual exhaust system and three 1¼in SU carburettors. Small ram pipes were fitted without air filters, while the humble origin of the engine was concealed somewhat by a cast-aluminium valve cover bearing the Lea-Francis name.

One experimental engine was fitted with a supercharger, but this idea was shelved. Thirty Zephyr engines were ordered in August, but only three were actually purchased at £95 each, together with one loan unit later returned.

Abbey Panels were commissioned to manufacture a steel 2/4-seater roadster body, to Benfield's outline sketch. The wooden patterns cost some £1100 while the only three bodies built were miraculously completed, including upholstery in Connolly's mushroom hide, by October and charged at £2,744-14s each. Abbey Panels also did some initial preparation work on a four-door saloon, utilizing roof panels from a Jaguar Mk II saloon. This was to have been fitted on an extended 9ft 3in wheelbase chassis, the standard Lynx measuring 8ft 3in.

The first car was finished in mauve, and with gold-plated fittings was unveiled at the Annual General Meeting held at the Chesford Grange Hotel on 17 October 1960, following which it travelled on to Earls Court. This car was incomplete mechanically (Chassis No. 30000). A second car was completed at the same time (Chassis No. 30012) and was used for demonstration purposes at Earls Court, followed by a period in Follett's showroom. One of the cars also travelled to the Amsterdam Show in March 1961.

The third car built (Chassis No. 30010) was used for development work, and was eventually sold in June 1961 to York Noble for £1000. All three cars are now in the ownership of Keith Tricker of Sudbury. No positive orders for cars were received and the project was abandoned, although one additional chassis was completed (Chassis No. 30002) and despatched to Moretti Coachworks of Turin in March 1962, for bodywork to the design of Fiore. Shortage of funds caused the cancellation of this project and the chassis may still be there. Parts for two further chassis were made, but were never assembled.

A Lea-Francis Go-Kart, using the 65cc engine, together with a 'Nobel 200' three-wheeler were despatched to the New York Show in April 1960, but nothing positive emerged.

The 12-month period up to 31 January 1961 resulted in the worst figure of all time with a loss of £76,692 (admittedly arrived at after the write-off of £9000 in the value of obsolete parts). Nevertheless, the company was effectively bankrupt and trading should have ceased there and then, if not before.

C W Payne and George Andrews both resigned, and the day-to-day running of the business was in the hands of a greatly over-worked C H 'Bill' Ward, whose efforts with the general sub-contract engineering work kept the firm alive, while the new directors squandered the remaining resources, together with personal investments of their own on the abortive car project.

A few York Nobel glass-fibre-bodied three-wheelers began to arrive in February 1962 but the project died after 31 vehicles had been delivered. The arrangements for this transaction called for Lea-Francis to purchase the knocked-down vehicles from Shorts of Belfast for £250 each and presumably they were re-invoiced to York Nobel Industries when completed and despatched. A four-wheeler was also planned, but did not materialize and the whole project was a failure. Shorts also suffered considerable losses.

The year 1961 at last saw the development and manufacture of the most promising project

Lynx roadster, 1960

ABOVE AND RIGHT
The Crusader, August 1962

undertaken for some years. It was a small garden tractor to be known as the 'Unihorse'. Powered by a BSA side-valve engine of 420cc and equipped with a three-speed gearbox, this well-built and versatile machine was well received. It was priced at £245 with a rope start or £295 with 12-volt electric starter, while a large variety of optional equipment, including bulldozer, power take-off, high-pressure water pump, etc. was available. Only a small number were built before the appointment of a receiver, but Quinton Hazel Ltd sold off this part of the business to Williams Ltd, chain-wheel manufacturers of Smethwick, who took over manufacture. 'Lea-Francis' was of course removed from the badge to be replaced with 'Unihorse'.

Unbelievable as it may now seem, Kenneth Benfield instigated the design and manufacture of yet another car early in 1962. He engaged Arthur Ramsay, a former employee of Armstrong-Siddeley Motors, and gave him responsibility for the project. The chassis of this new car was also built from 3½in diameter tubes, but the shape was complex; it followed the Lynx closely as far as the rear of the gearbox, then split into four to a point adjacent to the forward end of the rear-wheel arch. Here it was 'waisted'-in to join a fabricated structure which carried the Salisbury differential and inboard disc brake unit of the independent rear suspension.

Traditional Lea-Francis front wishbones and torsion bars were adopted for the rear suspension medium. From this point further tubes extended, splayed outwards to terminate in a very heavy rear cross member, embodying an aperture through which the spare wheel was inserted. Front suspension and rack-and-pinion steering were similar to the 'Lynx'. A strange feature concerned the exhaust system, which, at one point amidships, passed through a pipe welded into the chassis; quite how the problem of noise and servicing were to be overcome, is not clear. The engine and gearbox unit fitted into the experimental car, on loan from the British Motor Corporation, was of a type used in the Austin-Healey 3000 model, although a V8 Chrysler unit was intended for production versions.

Four-door saloon coachwork not unlike the contemporary Ford Zephyr was fitted, indeed the windscreen and back light glasses were from this model, while Rover 3-litre bumpers were used. This comparatively large saloon was

2½-litre sports (chassis 5280) leaving the present service works after re-building in 1970

LEA FRANCIS CARS LTD. COVENTRY.
STANDARD 14 H.P. ENGINE. 6 LIGHT. MK. VI SALOON BODY. (HRW 883) TYRES 6×16
ACCELERATION. FROM STEADY M.P.H. OF :- I.F.S. AXLE 4.875

	10 to 30	20 to 40	30 to 50
TOP.	11 SECS.	11 3/5 SECS.	11 SECS.
THIRD.	7 4/5 SECS.	8 4/5 SECS.	10 2/5 SECS.
SECOND.	5 4/5 SECS.		
FIRST.			

FROM REST THROUGH GEARS TO :-

	SECS.
30 M.P.H.	7 4/5
50 M.P.H.	17 4/5
60 M.P.H.	27 2/5
70 M.P.H.	37 4/5
80 M.P.H.	

[SPE]EDS ATTAINABLE ON GEARS.   M.P.H.

1ST.
2ND.
3RD.
TOP.

21.2.49

SPORTS 2 SEATER   2½ LITRE 85×110.4 CYL   3½ TO 1 AXLE 5·25″×17
ACCELERATION   FROM STEADY MPH OF :- (SECS)   (GKV 904)

	10-30	20-40	30-50	40-60	50-70
TOP =	8·5	8·7	8·8	8·8	9·9
~op					

1ST

FROM REST THROUGH GEARS TO
   50 MPH IN 8·4 SECS
STANDING ¼ MILE " 19
MAX SPEED 9·9 SECS =⎫
           9·7 "   ⎬ 91·3 MPH

PETROL CONSUMPTION AT 20 MPH   40 MPG
                       30   40·3
                       40   38·5
                       50   34·5
                       60   31·5
                       70   26
                       80   22

ONE 1¾ SU H6 CARB JET 100 SPEC^L NEEDLE
BARO = 30″·0 AIR 7·2°C BRIGHT & DRY
TEST MADE BY SU CARB Co 17·2·49   DATA SHEET № 84.   21·8·'49

Works performance data sheets, 1949

14 H.P.

LEA FRANCIS CARS LTD. COVENTRY.

STANDARD ENGINE: SALOON BODY. A.P.A

ACCELERATION. FROM STEADY M.P.H. OF :-

	10 to 30	20 to 40	30 to 50
TOP.	13 1/5 SECS.	12 3/5 SECS.	14 SECS.
THIRD.	9 1/5 SECS.	9 2/5 SECS.	11 3/5 SECS.
SECOND.	6 4/5 SECS.		
FIRST.			

FROM REST THROUGH GEARS TO :-

	SECS.
30 M.P.H.	8 2/5
50 M.P.H.	19 2/5
60 M.P.H.	35
70 M.P.H.	57
80 M.P.H.	

SPEEDS ATTAINABLE ON GEARS :-

	M.P.H.
1ST.	22
2ND.	38
3RD.	56
TOP.	72

SPORTS ENGINE: SALOON BODY.

ACCELERATION. FROM STEADY M.P.H. OF :-

	10 to 30	20 to 40	30 to 50
TOP.	11 4/5 SECS.	11 4/5 SECS.	12 3/5 SECS.
THIRD.	8 SECS.	8 1/5 SECS.	9 SECS.
SECOND.	5 3/5 SECS.	6 SECS.	
FIRST.			

FROM REST THROUGH GEARS TO :-

	SECS.
30 M.P.H.	6 2/3
50 M.P.H.	14 4/5
60 M.P.H.	24
70 M.P.H.	37
80 M.P.H.	

SPEEDS ATTAINABLE ON GEARS :-

	M.P.H.
1ST.	26
2ND.	44
3RD.	65
TOP.	79

NOTE: SPORTS ENGINE PEAKS AT 5,500 R.P.M. APPROX. AS AGAINST 4,600 ON STANDARD.

DATA SHEET No. 83

to be known as the Mk II Crusader, while a short-chassis GT coupé of futuristic appearance was intended to complement the larger model. This last model was to be known as the Mk II Corsair – incidentally, design staff from the Ford Motor Co. inspected these drawings, and later borrowed the name for one of their own models. The 'Crusader' was mechanically completed and the body was partly panelled when, in September, the company's bankers appointed the firm's auditor, Col. R B Leech, as receiver. All further development work ceased and the staff concerned were paid off.

Up to 180 people had been employed during the early part of the Benfield era, but the number dropped to a mere 40 under receivership. Sub-contract machining continued under the guidance of Bill Ward until Col. Leech concluded a deal with Eric Quinton Hazel, who purchased the assets in November 1962 for the sum of £55,000. The Quinton Hazel business was one of the most amazing success stories of the post-war era. Starting as a one-man business in Colwyn Bay, this spare-part factoring concern grew by virtue of many acquisitions, until it became the largest manufacturer of replacement parts in Britain. Sometimes referred to a little unkindly as a 'pirate parts maker', the quality of its wares has always been first class and an exact replica of the original.

The tractor business was immediately sold off, while the assets of the motor-car division were purchased by the author, although the business continued at Much Park Street until June 1963, in order that the tax loss situation was not invalidated.

Chassis 14062 with new replica body, awaiting despatch at Studley, August 1976

The spares and service organization was then transferred to Studley, near Redditch, where it remains to this day. George Andrews joined the new service works in 1963, and stayed until his death in October 1968.

A steady flow of repair work continues, while spare parts orders are handled by F A Deans, from a stores which boasts of holding an enormous range of parts for all models. This situation places the Lea-Francis in a better position than any other make of obsolete car. The Quinton-Hazell group formed a subsidiary, titled Lea-Francis Engineering Ltd, and uses this name as a brand for certain of the replacement parts manufactured by them, notably water pumps and clutches.

A factory was initially occupied at Balsall Common, but later transferred to Redditch.

The group was taken over by the Burmah-Castrol organization in 1972, and Quinton-Hazell, the indefatigable entrepreneur, later resigned, only to build a second empire, using the Supra Chemical Concern as a basis.

At the time of writing, a final new '14 Sports' chassis is being assembled from parts in stock (Chassis No. 7124) and is to be fitted with a f/h coupé body of traditional appearance. Nor will this be the final Lea-Francis, for plans are afoot to resurrect the old name yet again.

A new company was formed in February 1977 for the purpose of building a limited-production high-grade sporting car of $3\frac{1}{2}$ litre capacity. The directors of the Company are C P Englebach and A B Price. Road testing on the first chassis will commence in January 1978.

The dashboard of 14062

Keith Poynter in 14051 at Prescott, 1976

L.F.O.C.

A Lea-Francis Club was contemplated during the war years, but it petered out in infancy, while the same applied to a Register which the author began in 1949.

In 1953 a handful of enthusiasts formed the Lea-Francis Owners' Club. The club gradually gained strength, George Andrews became president and various events have been held, while the official journal, *The Leaflet*, has appeared regularly. For the last 14 years the main club event has been a driving test and concours d'état, held in the delightful grounds of Stanford Hall, near Rugby.

The current president is Tom Delaney. Peter Pringle held the post of chairman for many years, a position now relinquished. Roger Harle is the new incumbent, while Keith Poynter, one of the founders of the club, regularly competes in LFOC and VSCC events in his Hyper with great success. The club is now stronger than at any time in its 23-year life.

The present secretary is W G Adams, Amberway, Oxhill, Warwickshire.

Index

ABC 36
Abbey Panels 118, 122, 132
AC 41
AC-Delco 89
ACU (Auto Cycle Union) 26
Adams, WG 140
Admiralty 28
Agabeg, AP 94
Ainscough, WS 89
Aitken, Hon. Max 78
Albatross Marine 123
Alderson, Arthur 21, 29, 32-5, 37
Aldington, HJ 79, 80, 95
Alfa-Romeo 74, 75-6, 78, 80, 82, 94, 98-9, 104
Alford and Alder 108
Allnatt, Major AE 112-13
Alvis 54, 57, 62, 64, 69, 70-1, 73, 75-6, 82, 97, 100-1, 104, 108, 111
Amac 23, 27, 29
Amilcar 69, 70
André 69
Andrews, George 16, 40, 49, 116, 131, 133, 139, 140
Anzani 41, 44-5, 55-7, 68
A P Aircraft Ltd 113, 120, 126
Appleyard, J 26
Ariès 64
Armstrong, AG 57
Armstrong, JAW 29
Armstrong-Siddeley 92, 98, 114, 116, 126, 135
Arnold, Allan 77-9, 94, 99, 102
ASC (Auxiliary Service Corps) 27
Ashby 78
Aston-Martin 62-3, 76-8, 95, 101
Atalanta 123
Attwood, Harry 101
Austin 69, 77-8, 82, 94, 96, 99, 100
Austin-Healey 135
Austin, Herbert 32
Austro-Daimler 68, 69, 71
Autocar 90, 100, 111, 119
Auto Machinery Company 10
Autopulse 61
Autovia 102-4
Avebury, Lord 102
Avon Bodies Ltd 32, 37-40, 44, 48-9, 79, 84-5, 87, 90, 104, 109, 111, 114
Avon Standard 83
Avon Tyres 69

Bacon, HJ 64
Baer 65, 85
Bagshaw, KGR 58
Baird, GR 116, 121
Baker 94

Baker, FP 100
Baldwin, Sir J 124
Balls, Vernon 70
Ballybannon 82
BARC (Brooklands Automobile Racing Club) 55, 74-5, 79, 98-101
Barnes, Leslie 130
Barnett 29
Bass 27
Bayliss & Forbes 84
Bayliss-Thomas 12, 29
BBA 69
Bean 41
Bean, N 130
Beatenson 87
Beauchamp, Lord 79
Beauman, Don 130
Becker, Gerry 87
Beeston-Humber 10
Benetfink & Company 12
Benfield, KB 131-2, 135, 138
Bentley 62, 69-71, 74, 76, 78, 86, 101
Bent Wood Company 41
Berk 55-6
Berkhamsted Motor Club 104
Bertelli 76, 78
Bertram, Oliver 78
Best & Lloyd 61
Beverley-Barnes 92
BHB 55
Bicknell, CB 94
Birkin, Sir HRS 69, 71
Birmingham MCC 47
Black, Sir John 29
Blandford 121, 123
Bliss, REP 78, 83
Blooman, PA 68, 73
Blundell, Alfred 33
BMC 135
BMCRC (Brooklands Motor Cycle Racing Club) 29
BMW 105
BNC 102
BOAC 104
BOC (Bugatti Owners Club) 121
Bohnalite 88
Boillot, Georges, Cup 64, 68
Bolton, H 100
Boness 121
Borg & Beck 89, 109
Bosch 32
Boshier, S 124
Boswell 85
Bott, EB 105-6
Bowden Cable 15
Bowden, R 131
Boyd-Harvey 58

B P Spirit 69
Bradford & District MC 57
Bradshaw, Belsize 33-5, 105
Brady, Capt. 131
Braithwaite, Miss V 131
Bramptons Limited 17, 30
Brands Hatch 130
BRDC (British Racing Drivers Club) 77, 82, 122
Brighton & Hove MC 95
Bristol 105
British Goodrich 69, 92
British Motor Trading Co. 33, 36
Briton Cars 36
Brooklands 29, 38, 42-3, 49, 55-6, 58, 62-4, 67-8, 73, 77-9, 83, 93-5, 98-100, 102, 113
Brooks 17
Broomfield, F 68, 73, 77
Brown, A 130
Brown, F 131
Brown & Sharpe 10
Browning Gun 112
Brunell, WJ 42
BSA 16, 26, 112, 135
Bugatti 15, 41, 55, 62-5, 68-71, 78-80, 97, 99, 100-1, 103
Bullock 124
Burgess 86
Burghley 44
Burleigh, Lord 12
Burmah-Castrol 139
Burman Company 31, 108
Burman, Humphrey 77, 83, 99-101, 104, 111, 121
Burney, Sir D 92
Burney, Gordon 75, 76

Caesar, Dick 123
Calcott 32, 44
Calthorpe 44, 105
Campari 76, 83
Campbell, Malcolm 62-3, 65, 68, 70, 78-80
Carbodies Limited 92, 97-8, 100, 104, 109
Carless Cup 42
Carlton Carriage Co. 111
Carr 75
Carraciola 76
Castle Coombe 122
Castrol 38, 61, 69
CAV 47
Central Garage 84
Chandler, EJ 122
Charles, HN 54
Charlesworth Bodies 106, 111, 113, 115, 119
Chetwynd, Hon. AD 75, 78-9, 83, 94, 99, 116
Chetwynd, The Hon. Mrs 94, 99
Childe, R 75, 76

141

Chrysler   135
Citroen   116, 126-7
Clarke, RE   121
Clarke, TG   94, 98
Clayton   40
Claytonrite   113
Cleaver, FCE   58
Clement-Garrard   23
Clyno   26, 36
Coatalen, L   105
Cobb, John   82
Cobbold, GC   66
Colmore Cup   26, 38, 41, 47, 101, 104
Components Limited   16
Compton   106
Connaught   115, 119, 121-3, 126, 130
Connell, F   101
Continental Cars   119
Conville, A   30
Cook, Humphrey   69, 70
Cooper   130
Cooper Car Co.   62
Cooper, R   104
Cooper-Stewart   47
Cooper, W   29
Corsica   111-2
Cosmic Car Accessories   116
Cottam, Alan   122
Coventry-Climax   34, 86
Coventry Corporation   17
Coventry Holdings Limited   106
Coventry Simplex   28, 34
Coventry Supply Garage   36
Coventry-Victor   33
Coventry & Warwickshire MC   47
Cowell & Whittet   115, 122
Cox Street   12
Cozens, Leo   78
Cozette   55, 58, 61, 65, 93
Craig, Alexander   15, 18, 21-2, 32, 34
Craig, WY   79
Craigantlet   82, 99
Creak-Davies, W   104
Croft-Pearson   124
Cromard Special   122
Cross & Ellis   39-41, 45, 48-9, 53-6, 58, 61, 65, 70, 73, 78, 84-7, 90-2, 96-7, 104, 113
Crossley, Geoffrey   123
Crossley Motors   105
Crump, RS   38
Crystal Palace   130
Crystal Palace Show   12, 15, 21
Curzon, Viscount   71
Cushman, Leon   71
Cycle Engineers Institute   18
Cycling   12, 15

Daily Mail   71
Daimler   33, 36, 98, 126
Dakin, P   132
Dallason   41
Davenport, WR   26-7
Davies   124
Davis, SCH   70, 74-6, 79, 80, 82, 94
Dawson, Col.   15, 28
Delage   65, 68, 83
Delaney, Doris   61, 94
Delaney-Gallay   91
Delaney, LT   33, 42, 47, 58, 61, 67, 80, 82, 85, 90-1, 94
Delaney, LT & Sons Ltd   58, 92
Delaney, Tom   80, 83, 86, 93-4, 98-9, 100-2, 140
Dennys of Dumbarton   18
Denyer, ALS   101, 104, 116, 121
Dewandre   45, 47

Dingle, JP   43, 47
Don, Kaye   63-5, 68-71, 73, 76-78, 80, 82, 100, 105
Don, Rita   102
Donington Park   95, 100-1, 104
Double-12   78-9
Douglas   27
Downie, NW   26
Downing, KH   121
Drayton, TW   83
Drewett, JW   98
Driscoll, LK   78-9, 82-3, 93-4, 98
Driskell   102
Du-Faux   55
Dugdale, GC   79, 94, 98
Dunfee, Clive   80, 82
Dunham, CGH   100
Dunlop   17, 39, 40, 42, 54, 132
Dursley-Pedersen   10
Dutilleux   71
DWS   113
Dykes, Urquhart   70, 73

Earls Court   120, 124, 132
Eason-Gibson, J   100
Eccles, Lindsay   79
Edwards, Sir Clive   119, 121, 123
EHP   55
Elce & Co. Ltd., WH   31
Electrical & General Trust   112
Eldridge, Ernest   56, 66
Eley & Son   36
Elliott-Pyle, Dr R   50
Ellison, JW   76, 78
Elwes, JC   94
Englebach, CP   139
England, Gordon   45, 47-8, 85
ENV   54, 108, 126
ERA   104
Esplen, W   83
Essex, MC   47, 55-6, 62, 67, 73, 75
Evans, R   98
Everest   23
Everitt, H   130, 131
Ewbank, Robert   33
Excelsior   29
Eyston, Basil   68
Eyston, George   62-3, 65, 69, 70-1, 73, 75, 76, 82

Fagan   15
Fairman, Jack   130
Fairrie, J   62
Fane, AFP   94
Fawcett, Miss Enid   98
Featherstonehaugh   98
Ferodo   27, 77
Fernando, Mervyn   129
Ferrari   122
Field, JF   80, 82-3
Findon, Eric   85
Fiore   133
Fitch, AS   40, 47, 85
FN   69
Follett, Charles   106, 111, 114, 116, 119, 124, 132
Ford   69, 102, 132, 135, 138
Fowler Bros   116
Fox, SW   124
Francis-Barnett   26, 29
Francis, Graham Inglesby   10, 12, 15, 16, 27-8, 40
Francis, Gordon (Don)   25-7, 29, 32
Francis, GT   38
Francis, WH   15

Frazer-Nash   41, 42, 69, 76, 78, 79, 80, 99, 101, 123
Frazer-Nash, Archie   82

Gainsborough   53
Gamble, GT   58, 64, 73, 77, 83
Gannon, FA   99
Gannon, J   116, 132
Gardiner & Towers   104
GEC (General Electric Co.)   104
Gillow, Victor   80, 82, 94
Girling   103, 108, 126
GKN   74
Gloria   27
Gold Vase Race   63
Goodrich   74, 85, 91
Goodwin, Harold   41
Goodwood   121-2
Gordon, N   67
Graden, W   100
Gray, CA   99
Green, CN   38, 42
Green, Wilf   69, 70, 73-7, 80, 82, 95, 100
Gregg, W   82, 94
Griffin, FA   12, 15
Griffin & Stone   15, 25
Gulson Eng   54
Gunter, Sir Ronald   77
Guy, Sidney   105
GWK   28
Gwynne   38, 69

Hall, ER   101
Hallam, Frank   47, 67, 73, 77, 82, 101
Hampson, HJ   12, 33
Hancock, HR   30
Hardy-Spicer   54-5
Harle, R   140
Hartford   45
Harvey, AL   57
Harvey, CM   57, 64, 70
Hayes   47
Hayward, CW   112, 120
Helliwells Aircraft   114
Hendy, Gordon   62-3, 74-6, 78-80, 83, 94, 104
Hepworth, HC   104
Hewitson, Jack   57, 84
Hewitt, Helen   28
Heyn, Major RG   80, 82
Heynes, W   54, 89
Higgin, Dan   76, 80, 82-3
Hillman   10, 29, 65, 105
Hindle, JE   45, 87
HMV (His Masters Voice)   114
Hodder, TO   74, 75, 78-9
Holland, WE   83, 100
Horton, RT   40-1
Howe, Earl   77-9
Hoyal Body Corp   62
HRG   116, 119, 121, 123
Hull, Douglas   123
Humber Limited   18, 37, 65, 104
Humphrey-Sandberg   47, 50
Hutchings, HC   83, 94

IAE (Institute of Automobile Engineers)   18, 89
Ingall, CH   21, 23, 25-9, 34
Invicta   94, 99, 101
Iota   123
Iraq, King of   49
Irish Grand Prix   75, 80, 94
Italian Government   28
Ivanowsky, B   75-6, 80, 82
Ivins, F   94

Jackson, GL 74-5
Jaeger 47
Jaguar 126, 129, 132
James, JM 104
Jameson, ANC 78
JAP 23, 26, 29, 94
Jay 10
Jenkinson, Denis 115
Jensen Motors 118
Joel Limited 116
Johnson, Dr 85
Junior Car Club 42-3, 56-7, 63, 68, 77, 79, 94, 98-9, 101

Keene, Arthur 114
Kelvin Hall 53, 54, 120
Kendrick, WE 58
KI-Gass 49
Kirkstone 45, 49
Kite, CMB 124
KLG 69
Knudsen, DA 123

Lacy, CWG 78
Lagonda 69
Lamb, JF 99
Lammas-Graham 102
Lanchester 18, 23, 98
Lawrence, H 66, 83
Laycock-de-Normanville 113, 130, 132
Lea, Alan 21, 25, 27-9, 33-4
Leafabric 48, 53, 73
Lea, J 84
Lea, Norman 15, 22-3, 25-7, 29
Lea, Richard Henry 10, 12, 15-7, 21, 23, 27-8, 31-5, 92
Lea, ST 33
Leaf Engineering Co. 104, 106
Leatham, EJJ 94
Lee, H Pelham 34
Leech, Col. RB 138
Leek, GH 87, 104-6, 113, 120, 126, 130
Leek, V 130
Lees, JM 99
Leigh, Lord 11
Le Mans 74-5, 79, 83, 93-4
Lewes Hill Climb 68, 83
Lewis, Hon. Brian 80
LFOC (Lea-Francis Owners Club) 40, 80, 140
Light Car Club 79, 94, 102
Linfield, HS 100
Livesey, JV 63
Llewelyn, AS 78-9
Lloyd-Jones, Ted 116
Lloyd-Lord 45
Lobster 55-6, 58, 63, 65, 67
Loftus-Tottenham, T 111
Lones, Clive 80
Lord, AO 45
Lord-Six 45
Lorraine-Dietrich 64
Lucas 32, 47, 69
Ludw Loewe & Co, Berlin 10
Ludgate, A 116, 123, 126, 129, 130, 132
Luvax-Bijur 108, 113, 116

Macdonald, W 85, 87
Machlachlan, A 75, 83, 93-5, 99, 101
Mackie, MF 130
Madresfield 79, 95
MAG 26-7, 29
Mangoletsi, G 101, 104
Mansell, DK 78
Manville Trophy 47
Marandaz 76
Marconi 29

Margetts 77
Marr, LD 42, 130
Martlett 93
Marshall, Gordon 102
Martin, Charles 104
Mason 71
Masons College 18
Matthews, FS 12, 15
Maudslay 18, 19, 21-3, 27
Mauleverer, AA 42-3, 83
Maxwell, GE 68
Maxwell, L 68, 73, 77, 83
May, FW 129
Mayes, HH 121
Mays, Raymond 99
Mazengarb, AS 101
McAlpine, Kenneth 121-2
MCC (Motor Cycling Club) 26, 29, 31, 42-3, 47, 58, 62, 64, 68, 73, 77, 83, 95, 101, 122, 124
McCall, H 130-2
McFarren, Hugh 82
McVeigh, J 67
Meadows, Henry 34, 36-8, 40, 42, 44-6, 49, 54-6, 58, 61, 64, 68, 74, 86-7, 97, 111,
Meeson, EL 74, 76
Mellor, R 77
Mercedes-Benz 49, 69, 71, 76, 78-9, 101
MG 40, 54, 94, 101, 119
Midland CC 41
Midland Light Body Co. 106
Midland Motor Cycling 111
Millar, Cameron 83
Miller 66
Miller, Capt. 68
Miller, R 124
Mills, L 101, 104
Minerva 94
Minnion & Keene 118
MIRA (Motor Industry Research Association) 123
MMEC (Midland Motoring Enthusiasts Club) 121
Monte Carlo Rally 78
Montgomery 98
Moretti 133
Morgan 41, 80
Morgan Hastings 87
Morgan, R 101
Morris-Goodall 95
Morris Motors 29, 65, 85, 96, 122
Moss Eng. 113-4
Motor 33, 44
Motor Bodies Limited 36
Motor Cycle 27, 30
Motor Cycle Show 26
Motor Sport 101
Mulliner 21, 103
Munro, Donald 94
Myers, RA 76

Nall 106
Napier 18
Nash, Marcus 15, 16, 23, 27, 29
National Cycle Show 15
Newall, J 29
Newcastle MCC 38
Newman, George 62
Newsome, SH 62-4, 67-70, 73-6, 79, 80, 82-3, 94, 99
New York Show 133
Nivex 96
Norris, Norman 41-3, 47, 55-7
Nottingham, P 116, 132
Nuvolari 82
NW London MC 66

Oats, RF 55-6
Observer 100
Oetzmann, EN 94
Olympia 17, 29, 34-5, 37, 39, 43, 46, 53-4, 79, 83, 87, 111
OM 55-6, 69
Osborne, CT 98
Oulton Park 130

Palladium 38
Palmer 27
Papworth Industries 130
Parkes, DW 67
Parsons, MJ 130
Patent Office 22
Paul, CA 71, 80, 82, 99
Payne, CW 131, 133
Peacock, Sir Kenneth 63-4, 74-6, 79, 82-3, 94-5, 99, 100
Pearson, D 130
Pearson, F 102
Pellew, H 75, 77
Penn-Hughes 78
Percival, GH 85, 90-2
Perkins, AH 112-3
Perkins, M 111
Perkins, WS 99
Phoenix Park 75, 80, 99
Piccadilly 12
Podmore 58
Pollack 78-9
Polson, Sir Thomas 33
Pool, EG 116
Popplewell, DW 26
Poynter, K 140
Pratts 38
Pratt & Witney 10
Premier Cycle Co. 10, 12
Prescott 121
Pressure-Vac 56
Price, AB 139
Price Limited, AB 40
Pringle, PW 140
Prioleau, John 100
Purdy, Harold 66, 70

Quinton Hazel, Eric 138
Quinton Hazel Ltd. 135, 139

R34 29
RAC (Royal Automobile Club) 34, 38, 49, 69, 71, 98, 101, 130
RAE (Royal Aero Establishment) 131
RAF (Royal Air Force) 50
Ramponi 74-6
Ramsay, A 135
RASC (Royal Army Service Corps) 27
Rayson, EK 100
RBL 121
Read, HL 106, 112-3
Redditch, MC 47
Reflex Road Light Co. 16
Renold, Hans 17, 21
Rex, AM 26
Richardson, J 30
Ridley, CV 109
Riederer, GA 124
Riley 41, 69-71, 76, 78, 80, 82, 87, 94, 100, 102-6, 108-9, 111, 113, 115-6
Riley, Ken 101
Rimmer, T 40
Rimmer, WG 54, 87
Riseley-Pritchard, J 130
Riverlee Bodies 114
RNAS (Royal Naval Air Service) 27, 29
Robinsons 36, 39-41

143

Roe, AV 112
Roe, Mrs KN 101
Rolls-Royce 101
Rolt, APR 130
Roman Co. 17
Rommel 85
Rookes, CA 130, 131
Roots 56
Rose, Hugh 9, 105, 113, 115-6, 120, 122, 126, 130-1
Rose, K 116, 121-4
Rosenfields 87
Rossleigh 114, 118
Roth, Dr 98
Rover Co. 22, 29, 135
Royal Irish Automobile Club 75
Royal Ruby 36
Rubery 44
Rudd, John 12
Rudge 28, 45-6, 54-5
Ruston-Hornsby 33, 40
Rutland, Duke of 62

Salisbury Axle Co. 126, 132, 135
Salmson 55, 62, 69, 94
Saltmarsh 43
SCAP 58, 87
Scintilla 93
Scotland Yard 38, 49
Scott, EWD 106
Scott, John 106
Scott, Mrs WB 63
Scott, WB 78, 83
Scottish Show 36, 44
Seldon, GH 83
Shardlow, Ambrose 65
Shattock, RG 123
Shaw, George Bernard 23
Shaw, James W 74-6
Shelsley Walsh 38, 64, 67, 77, 79, 83, 94-5, 99, 104, 121
Sheppard, MW 104
Sherlock, CA 130-1
Shorts of Belfast 112, 133
Shuttleworth 99
Siata 123
Silentbloc 95, 103
Silverstone 121-2
Simplex, Amsterdam 36
Sinclair, Sir W 76, 83, 85, 91-2
Singer & Co. 10, 12, 21, 32, 101
Singer, George 10
Singh, Prince Jaideep 119
Skefco 40
Skelly, WJ 121
Sloane 98
Smith, CE 41-2
Smith, FR 89
Smith, Geoffrey 27
Smith, Geoffrey 104
Smithson 101
SMMT (Society of Motor Manufacturers & Traders) 47, 55, 58
Solex 40, 46, 56, 101
Sopwith Cup 42
Southern Caravans 114, 118
Sparkbrook Manufacturing Co. 12, 15
Spero, HC 79, 80, 83, 94
Spikins, Bob 121, 123
Sproston, AJ 26, 29, 30-1
Sproston & Grace 27

SSCC (Scottish Sporting Car Club) 130
SS Jaguar 54, 62, 108, 114
Standard Motor Co. 18, 62, 65, 106, 109
Stanley Cycle Show 11
Stevens, AS 122
Stevens, GP 47, 58
Stevens, HS 42-3, 47, 58, 66, 68
Stone, James 12, 15
Stromberg 89, 93
Sturgess, FG 99
Sturmey-Archer 15, 16, 33
Stutz 69
SU 101-2, 111, 116, 132
Sullivan, W 80, 82-3, 99
Sumner 10
SUNBAC (Sutton Coldfield & North Birmingham Automobile Club) 26, 42
Sunbeam 10, 18, 68, 77-8, 97, 104-5
Sunbeam MCC 66
Supra Chemicals 139
Surbiton, MC 42-3, 63-4, 68
Sutton, RMV 62-4, 67-9, 73, 80, 82, 98-9
Swift Co. 36
Sykes, AA 33
Symons, Col. 113

Tait, CJN 83
Talbot 80, 97-9
Tatlow, HE 33, 38, 40-3, 47, 56-7, 61-2, 67, 74, 76, 87
Taylor, AC 94
Taylor, Alec 84, 90
Taylor, H 42
Taylor, J 55, 68, 69
Temple Press 44
Tennant, TB 42
Terrys Springs 69
Thistlethwayte, 'Scrap' 69, 71
Thomas, EW 67, 75, 77
Thomas, Sir Miles 104
Thompson-Bennett 29
Thompson, RCA 98
Thornton, H 122, 124, 130
Tickford 97
Tile Hill 12
Timberlake, HH 76, 82, 85
Timms & Co. 36
Tongue 104
Took, GE 68, 78-9, 83, 95
Tracta 69
Tresilian, SS 101
Tricker, K 133
Triumph 27, 33, 106, 108, 132
TT (Tourist Trophy) 65, 69, 73-4, 76-7, 82-3, 94, 98-9
Turner, CE 41
Turner, Charles 87, 90-1, 96-8, 104
Turner, Jack 122, 130
Turner, LW 58
Turner, Philip 68, 74, 79
Twyneham 106, 130

Ulster Automobile Club 57, 67, 69, 99

Van Eugen, CM 36-8, 41, 49, 53-5, 58, 68, 84, 86-7, 89, 91-2, 96, 102-4, 120
Van Horn, FG 80
Varzi 82
Vauxhall 41, 74
Velocette 98
Vesey Cup 42

Vickers, RC 83, 100-1
Victory Cup 41, 47
Vidler, HJ 83, 99-101
VSCC (Vintage Sports Car Club) 79, 116, 122, 140
Vulcan Motors 12, 33-4, 36-40, 42-51, 53-4, 66, 85-7, 90

Wagstaffe, CH 99-101
Waite, Col. ACR 82
Walker, PD 58
Wall Street 54
Walwork, JC 130
War Office 27
Ward & Co. 36
Ward, CH 106, 131, 133, 138
Ward, EN 79, 83
Wardman, CB 33, 40, 45, 49, 51, 65-6, 69, 71, 84, 86
Wardman Limited, CB 31, 84
Wardman, RB 50
Ware, Bert 90
Warner, 'Plumb' 84
'Warwick' 48
Watkins, Eustace 84
Watson, GW 34
Watson, MB 94
Watson, W 45
Weaver, HW 33
Wellstead, HR 75
Westland Motor Company 114, 118, 120, 126
Weston, Harry 131
Weymann 48, 78, 83, 85, 90
Wharton, Ken 122
Whitaker, JW 83, 94, 98, 100
Whitcroft, CR 82
Whitehead 104
Whittendale, JH 63
Whitmore, HR 26
Widengren, HJ 77
Wilby, Miss 123
Wilkin, GW 36, 38, 40, 43
Wilks, Maurice 29
Williams Deacons Bank 83, 87, 100
Williams Limited 135
Williamson, JE 101
Wilson 99
Wilson Gearbox 108, 111
Wilson, WH 68
Wilsons Motors 44
Windrum, JWF 98
Windsor 80
Winfield-Smith 131
Wipac 126
Wisdon, TH 79, 99
Woking Motor Club 66
Wolff, WG 95
Wolseley 84, 94, 99, 104
Wood, CH 101
Wood, GE 31
Woodhouse, JH 37
Woods, Stanley 74, 76
Woollen, H 40

York Nobel Industries 133

Zenith 32, 34, 45
ZF 103
Zoller 53, 55

DOMINIC WOOD
simply MAGIC

THE BODLEY HEAD

LONDON

Dedicated to my mum and dad and my three big brothers, who have given me the most amazing amount of support over the years!

Thanks to Michelle Worthington, Nigel Pope, Mark Leveridge, Neil Roberts, George Blake, Angelo Carbone, Roger Barrons, Ron Heaver, Garry Jones, Brian Doderidge, Philip Hitchcock, Richard McCourt, Duncan Trillo, Anthony Owen, Chris Pilkington, Paul Smith, Exonian Magical Society, The Magic Circle, but most of all to Sam Anstis-Brown for getting me started.

1 3 5 7 9 0 9 8 6 4 2

Copyright © Dominic Wood 2000

Dominic Wood has asserted his right under the Copyright, Designs and Patents Act, 1988 to be identified as the author of this work.

First published in the United Kingdom 2000
By The Bodley Head Children's Books
Random House, 20 Vauxhall Bridge Road, London SW1V 2SA

Random House Australia (Pty) Limited
20 Alfred Street, Milsons Point, Sydney
New South Wales 2061, Australia

Random House New Zealand Limited
18 Poland Road, Glenfield
Auckland 10, New Zealand

Random House South Africa (Pty) Limited
Endulin, 5A Jubilee Road,
Parktown 2193, South Africa

The Random House Group Limited Reg. No. 954009
www.randomhouse.co.uk

A CIP catalogue record for this book is available from the British Library.

ISBN 0 370 32554 0

Printed in Singapore

Check out the star rating to see how difficult the trick is to learn or perform:

★☆☆☆ easy

★★☆☆ moderate

★★★☆ difficult

★★★★ very difficult

CONTENTS

Introduction	4		Vanishing Pencil	25
The Rules of Magic	5		Flash Cash	26
Getting Started	6		Where's the Watch?	28
Ice Cool Magic	8		Magnetic Wand	30
Runaway Straws	9		Invisible Catch	32
Anti-gravity Cups	10		Glass Go	33
Smarty Pants	12		Pick 'n' Predict	34
Wonderful Wand	14		Linking Mints	36
X-Ray Eyes	16		The Key to Magic	38
Snappy Match	17		Double Your Money	40
No Bang Balloon	18		Indestructible String	42
Penny Puzzle	19		Crafty Card	44
Is This Your Card?	20		Putting on a Magic Show	46
Jack Attack!	22		Further Magic	48
It's Knot a Problem	24			

INTRODUCTION

Hello! Welcome to the weird and wonderful world of magic, one of the oldest and most popular forms of entertainment.

I first got hooked on magic when my drumming teacher, Sam Anstis-Brown, made one of his drumsticks vanish. I remember seeing it simply disappear into thin air and I didn't have a clue where it had gone. I tried looking on the floor, up his sleeves, everywhere, but I couldn't find it! It wasn't until about three days later that he told me how he'd done it.

After I learnt that trick I bought some magic books and put on shows for my mum and dad and their friends. I would always practise my new tricks on my three big brothers. I think it used to drive them round the twist so, to get me back, they would take my books and learn my secrets, so make sure you find somewhere to keep this book safe from prying eyes.

Now I perform magic on TV. You may have seen me perform some of the tricks in this book. They look really amazing, but you'll be surprised how simple they are to learn and how easy they are to perform. Very soon you'll have your audience scratching their heads and wondering how the tricks were done. Who knows, one day you might even be performing magic on TV!

Anyway, enough yapping from me, let's get going. Good luck with your journey into magic, but most important of all – enjoy it!

Dominic Wood

THE RULES OF MAGIC

If you want to become a successful magician, the first thing you must do is spend some time learning the tricks of the trade. Pay attention to these five rules, and you will be off to a great start!

1 Ssh! Keep it a secret…
This is the most important rule of all, which is why it is the first rule. If you tell people how a trick is done, then you will not only spoil it for yourself, but also for your audience. They may tell you that they want to know the secret, but this is because people love the unexplained. So let's leave magic… unexplained!

2 Practise, practise, practise…
Remember, never perform a trick straight after you have learned it. I know you may be very excited and want to show off your hard work, but it is important to practise as much as possible. You will do your tricks without any hiccups and your audience will find it much more difficult to work out how it's done.

3 Do not repeat it….
Never repeat the same trick to the same audience at the same time or the same place. A trick that is performed a second time is never quite so impressive, and your audience will watch you more closely and may work out the secret to how it is done.

4 The right moment…
Magic is great when it is done at the right time and in the right place. If you perform magic tricks to your family and friends all the time, they will end up hating it.

5 Short and sweet…
It is far better to do a short magic show and leave your audience wanting more rather than doing a two-hour show and making your audience bored.

GETTING STARTED

Every magician needs a magic wand to cast spells and perform their tricks successfully, so the next step to becoming a proper magician is to get hold of one of these. You can buy a wand from a toy store, but it is much more fun to make one yourself. Here are a couple of ways how:

PAPER WAND

WHAT YOU NEED
- A piece of black paper
- A piece of white paper
- A long pencil
- Glue

1. Cut the black paper so it is slightly longer than the pencil, and about 5 cm wide.

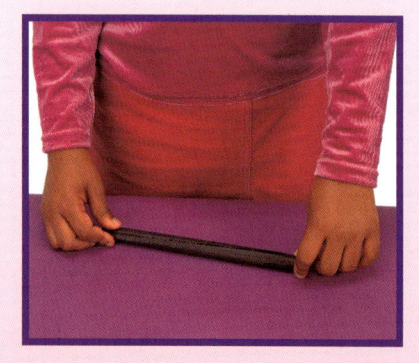

2. Wrap the black paper around the pencil. Spread glue evenly along the edge of the paper and stick it down to form a tube.

3. Leave the tube to dry and then glue a short piece of white paper around each end.

4. Finally, slide out the pencil and, as if by magic, you now have a magic wand!

WOODEN WAND

WHAT YOU NEED
- A wooden cane (approx 30 cm long)
- Black paint
- White paint

1. Take the piece of wood and paint it black.

2. When it is dry, paint a white band roughly 3 cm long at each end and let it dry again. This wand is much more solid and will last a lot longer than the paper one.

★ STAR TIPS ★

When you are painting or gluing, make sure that you lay down lots of old newspaper, just in case you spill any glue or paint on your best table.

A chopstick makes a good magic wand, especially if your magic has an oriental style or look. You can paint it black and white, or just leave it plain!

MAGIC WORDS

Real magicians use special magic words while they cast their spells. Although there are lots of famous magic words, you can say anything you like. It can be great fun inventing words and rhymes that will fit in with your show, but in case you can't think of any good ones right now, here are a few to get you started:

ABRACADABRA!

SIM SALA BIM!

HOCUS POCUS!

HEY, PRESTO!

GIBBLEDY, GOBBLEDY, GOOP!

IZZY WIZZY, LET'S GET BUSY!

SMELLY PYJAMAS!

ICE COOL MAGIC

A small amount of water is poured into a cup, a magic word is spoken and amazingly when the cup is tipped over all that falls out is an ice cube.

WHAT YOU NEED
- Toilet paper
- A large cup
- A real or plastic ice cube
- A small bottle of water

PREPARATION

Put some toilet paper in the bottom of the cup. Place the ice cube on top of the toilet paper.

PERFORMANCE

1. Show the cup to your audience, making sure they cannot see inside it.

2. Pour a small trickle of water from the bottle into the cup.

3. Now breathe into the cup and explain to your audience that your breath will freeze the water. The reason for doing this is to allow time for the water to soak into the toilet paper.

4. Tip the mouth of the cup towards you until it is upside down, and catch the ice cube as it falls out.

RUNAWAY STRAWS

This is a fun trick to perform when you are in a fast-food restaurant, or it can be done on your magic table. Two straws are placed parallel to each other on a table. A magic spell is cast over your finger and when it is placed between the two straws, they roll apart from each other. Spooky!

PERFORMANCE

WHAT YOU NEED
- Two drinking straws

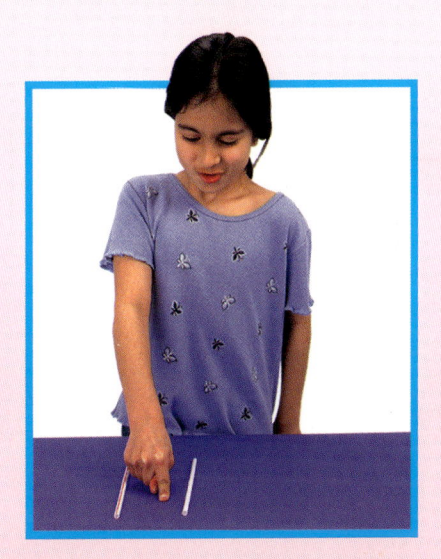

1. Place the two straws parallel to each other on a smooth, flat table so that they are at least 5 cm apart.

2. Cast a magic spell over your first finger and tell your audience to watch the straws very closely. (If they are watching the straws, they will not notice what you are doing.)

3. Place your finger on the table in between the straws and secretly, quietly and softly, blow on your fingernail. Your breath will pass over your nail and off to the sides, pushing the straws apart at great speed.

ANTI-GRAVITY CUPS

★★☆☆

This is a trick with no strings attached! Your magic powers make it look as if you can defy the laws of gravity. Two cups are placed upside down on a book. When the book is turned upside down, the cup stick to it. **WOW!**

WHAT YOU NEED
- Two drawing pins
- A notebook with a hard cover
- Two plastic cups

PREPARATION

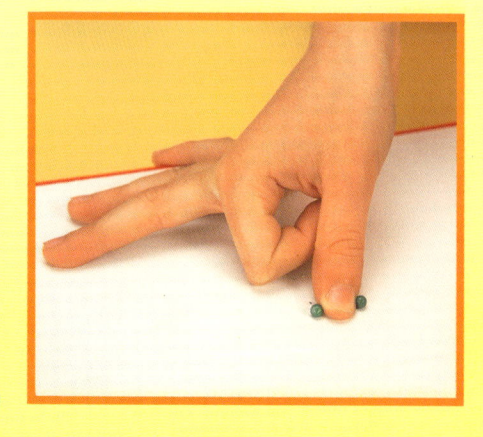

Open the notebook and push the two drawing pins through the cover so that the pins are sticking out the front. Make the distance between the pins the same width as your thumb.

PERFORMANCE

HEY PRESTO!

1. Hold the book face up with your thumb on top between the pins and your fingers on the bottom.

2. Now take one of the cups and place it mouth down on the cover of the book so that the rim of the cup is sandwiched between one of the pins and your thumb. Do the same with the other cup on the other side of your thumb.

3. Cast a magic spell, then slowly turn the book upside down. The cups will stick to the book.

4. Wave your hand above and below the book to prove there are no strings.

5. Ask a member of your audience to say 'Now' whenever they want. When they do, remove your thumb and let the plastic cups fall to the floor, but keep hold of the book.

★ STAR TIPS ★
Take extra care when using drawing pins to make sure you don't pierce your thumb on the pins.

SMARTY PANTS

Three tubes of Smarties are shaken in turn to show that two are empty and one is full. The tubes are mixed around and a member of your audience is asked to guess which tube has the Smarties in. But no matter which one they choose, they will always be wrong!

WHAT YOU NEED
- Four tubes of Smarties
- An elastic band
- A jacket or long-sleeved jumper

PREPARATION

1. Put on a jacket or a long-sleeved jumper.

2. Empty three tubes of all their Smarties and put them aside to share with your friends later.

3. Attach the fourth tube (still full of Smarties) to the inside of your right wrist with the elastic band and cover up the tube with the sleeve of your jacket or jumper. Make sure the end of this tube cannot be seen up your sleeve.

PERFORMANCE

1 Put the three empty tubes in a row on the table in front of you. Tell your audience that one of them is full.

2 Pick up two of the tubes with your left hand – when you shake them, they will sound empty (because they are!).

3 Now pick up the third tube with your right hand and shake it. The tube hidden up your sleeve will rattle and everyone will think that the tube you are shaking is full.

4 Ask a member of your audience to keep an eye on the full tube, while you mix the tubes around. Make sure that each time you pick up the tube that is meant to be full you do it with your right hand, so it rattles.

5 When you have mixed them around, ask your helper to point to the full tube. Whichever one is chosen, shake it with your left hand – it will sound empty!

6 Now shake one of the other tubes with your right hand. This time it will rattle. You can repeat this trick – but don't do it too often or someone might work it out.

★ STAR TIPS ★

You don't have to use tubes of Smarties. The trick works equally well if you fill a matchbox with beans or lentils, and have empty matchboxes on the table.

WONDERFUL WAND

Magicians usually use magic wands to make magic happen, but in this trick the magic happens to the wand itself! A magic wand is placed inside a clear plastic bottle, whereupon it takes on a life of its own and starts to float inside the bottle with no visible means of support.

WHAT YOU NEED
- Blu-tack
- Very thin, black cotton
- A safety pin
- A magic wand
- A clear plastic bottle

PREPARATION

1. Cut off a 50 cm length of cotton. Attach a small amount of Blu-tack to one end and tie the other end to the safety pin.

2. Attach the safety pin to the inside of your jacket and stick the small piece of Blu-tack to one end of the wand.

PERFORMANCE

1 Turn the plastic bottle upside down to prove that it is empty. You could even sound a note by blowing across the top of it.

2 Now place the wand inside the bottle (Blu-tack side first).

3 Move the bottle away from your body. The wand will start to move up and down inside – it will look like it is floating. Make sure you do this at some distance from your audience, or in a dimly lit room, to make sure they don't see the cotton.

4 Once you have made the wand go up and down a few times, take it out and hand the bottle to your audience for examination. While they are looking at the bottle, secretly remove the Blu-tack from the wand. Then you can hand them the wand. If you wanted to be mean, you could ask them to try the trick out for themselves.

★ STAR TIPS ★
Once you have made the wand rise from the bottle, why not try the same trick, but have the wand rise from your hand instead. Try it, it really works!

X-RAY EYES

Demonstrate your powerful X-Ray vision in this clever coin trick. Five coins are placed in a row on the table, and then you turn around. A member of your audience is asked to turn the coins over two at a time and then cover one with their hand. When you turn around, you immediately tell them whether the hidden coin is showing heads or tails.

WHAT YOU NEED
- Five coins

PERFORMANCE

1. Lay out the coins in front of you, making sure that they are all facing heads up.

2. Now ask a member of your audience to turn the coins over two at a time while your back is turned and to slide one coin forward and cover it with their hand.

3. When you turn back, look at the other coins. If there are an even number of heads showing, then the covered coin is heads. If there are an odd number of heads showing, then the covered coin is tails.

4. Once you have worked out what side the coin is, pretend you have X-Ray vision and that you will use your powers to look through their hand to see what the coin is. Tell them and watch their faces…

SNAPPY MATCH

A match is wrapped up in an empty handkerchief and a member of your audience is invited up to snap the match in half. A spell is cast... and the match is magically restored.

WHAT YOU NEED
- Two matches
- A clean handkerchief

PREPARATION

Most cotton handkerchiefs have small openings in the seams at the corners. Find one in your handkerchief and push a match inside the seam so it is hidden.

PERFORMANCE

1. Lay the handkerchief flat on the table and place a match in the middle. Fold the four corners of the handkerchief into the middle, so that the match hidden in the seam lies next to the one you have just put there.

2. Invite a member of your audience to come up and snap the match. Hand them the handkerchief in such a way that you make sure they snap the hidden match, but of course they will think they are snapping the match they just saw you put in the handkerchief.

3. Now put the handkerchief back on the table. Say a few magic words and wave your wand. Everyone will be astonished when you open the handkerchief and reveal that the match is still in one piece.

NO BANG BALLOON

This trick will make your audience put their fingers in their ears, but they don't have to... well, unless it goes wrong! A fully inflated balloon appears to be normal, but once you cast a spell, it becomes indestructible. To prove this, you push a needle in one side and out the other, but the balloon doesn't pop.

WHAT YOU NEED
- A balloon
- Sticky tape
- A long needle
- Vaseline

PREPARATION

1. Blow up a balloon and put a small piece of sticky tape at the very top and the very bottom.

2. Rub some Vaseline on the needle to make it slide through the balloon more easily.

PERFORMANCE

1. Tell your audience that you will pop the balloon and it will make a very loud bang.

2. Now, with a steady hand, push the needle through the sticky tape at the top of the balloon. Because the tape is holding the balloon together, it won't pop! Keep pushing the needle until you reach the bottom, then push the needle out, through the other piece of sticky tape.

3. Finish the trick with a flourish. Pull out the needle and pop the balloon!

PENNY PUZZLE

This clever puzzle will offer a tricky challenge. A coin is balanced on a match over the opening of a bottle, and a helper is asked to make it fall in without touching the match, the bottle or the coin. When they have given up trying, you drip a few drops of water on the match, and the coin falls into the bottle. Easy!

WHAT YOU NEED
- A match
- An empty bottle
- A coin
- A glass of water

PERFORMANCE

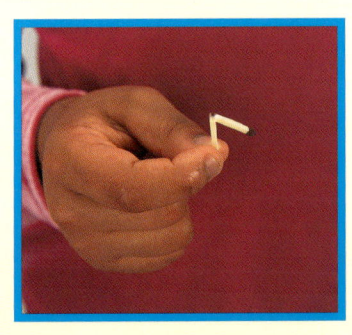

1 Take the match and snap it in half so that it forms a V shape, but make sure it is not completely broken.

2 Place the V-shaped match on top of the bottle. Carefully place the coin on top of the match so that it can fall straight down without hitting the edge of the opening.

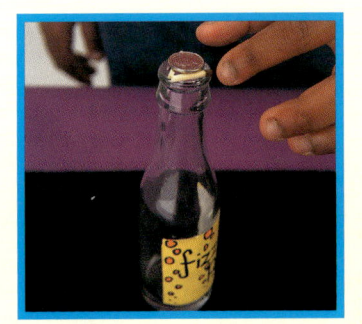

3 Ask a member of your audience if they can think of a way to make the coin fall into the bottle without touching the coin, the match or the bottle, and without blowing. Unless they know the secret, they will not be able to.

4 When they have given up, simply dip your finger into the glass of water and allow a few drops of water to drip onto the broken part of the match. The match will begin to straighten, allowing the coin to fall into the bottle.

IS THIS YOUR CARD?

This easy card trick will make it look as if you have special mind-reading skills. A member of your audience is asked to choose a card from a pack of cards, remember it and then put it back. The pack is shuffled and then you look through the cards. Amazingly, you find the card that they chose.

WHAT YOU NEED
- A pack of cards

PREPARATION

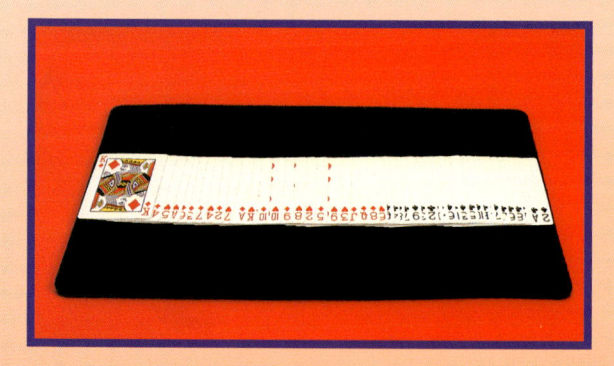

1. You do not have to make anything special for this trick. Simply arrange the pack of cards so that all the black cards (Clubs and Spades) are at the bottom, and all the red cards (Hearts and Diamonds) are at the top.

PERFORMANCE

1 Ask a member of your audience to pick a card and remember what it is.

2 Ask your helper to put their card back, but to keep thinking about it so that their thought waves pass across to you. Offer them the pack so that they replace the card in the opposite half of the pack from where they picked it.

3 Square up the cards and put them on the table. Take a batch of cards from the top of the pack and put them beside the pack. Put the cards from the bottom of the pack on top of the cards on the table. This is called a cut.

4 Square up the cards and cut them again. Do this several times, and while you are cutting the cards, tell your audience that you are mixing them up. In fact, it doesn't matter how many times you do this, you will still be able to find the card they chose.

5 After you have cut the pack enough times to make your audience believe it is properly mixed up, look through the cards (making sure no one else sees the faces). There will be a card that is a different colour to all the other ones around it. This will be the card they chose. Whip it out with a flourish, and leave your audience amazed!

JACK ATTACK!

Here's another card trick that's simple, but very effective. Three Jacks are taken out of a pack and shown to the audience. One is placed on top of the pack, one on the bottom and one in the middle. A helper is asked to cut the pack once to mix it around, the audience shouts 'Jack Attack!' and when your helper looks through the pack, they find all three Jacks in one place.

WHAT YOU NEED
- A pack of cards

PREPARATION

1. There is little to do for this trick, just make sure that one Jack is at the top of the pack.

PERFORMANCE

1. Look through the pack of cards and take out three Jacks, leaving the Jack you prepared earlier on the top. Show the Jacks quickly to your audience, so they don't get a chance to see what suits they are.

2. Now put one Jack on top of the pack, another Jack on the bottom and, finally, put the last Jack anywhere in the middle.

3. Place the cards on the table and invite a member of your audience to come up and cut the pack so that the bottom section of cards now lies on top. Even though cutting the pack gives the illusion of mixing the cards up, actually it is doing the opposite and bringing the Jacks together!

JACK ATTACK!

4. Ask your audience to shout 'Jack Attack!' and then ask your helper to look through the pack. They will find all three Jacks are now in the same place!

★ STAR TIPS ★

If you can find an identical pack of cards, you can do the same trick but with four Jacks, which is much better! Prepare the pack by putting the two spare Jacks on top. After you have found the four Jacks, put one Jack on the top and one on the bottom, but this time put two in the middle. And you know what to do next!

IT'S KNOT A PROBLEM

This knotty puzzle will amaze your friends, and when you show them how it's done, they'll all want to have a go. You take a piece of string and tie a knot in it without letting go of the ends, seemingly performing the impossible.

WHAT YOU NEED
- A piece of rope or string approx 1 metre long

PERFORMANCE

1 Challenge a member of your audience to tie a knot in the piece of string without letting go of the ends. No matter how hard they try, they won't be able to.

2 Once your helper has tried for some time and finally given up, lay the string in front of you.

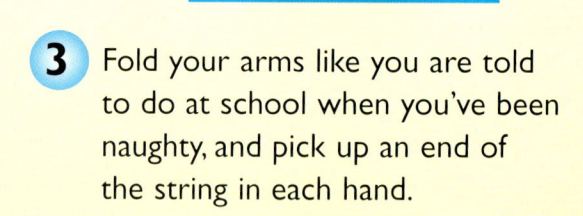

3 Fold your arms like you are told to do at school when you've been naughty, and pick up an end of the string in each hand.

4 Now, without letting go of the ends of the string, uncross your arms. You will find that you have formed a knot. No problem!

VANISHING PENCIL

This was the first trick that I ever learned, and it made me want to start learning magic. A pencil is thrown as if it were a dart, but it vanishes into thin air. AMAZING!

PERFORMANCE

WHAT YOU NEED
- All you need (surprise, surprise) is a short pencil

1 To start, you must be standing with your left side towards your audience. Hold the pencil by the writing end in front of you and level with your right ear.

2 Move the pencil backwards and forwards as if you were aiming a dart at a dartboard. On the third backward movement, slide the pencil behind your right ear and leave it there.

3 Immediately bring your hand forward and pretend to throw the 'pencil', whereupon it vanishes.

★ STAR TIPS ★

You must practise this very slowly, because the slower you do it, the easier it will be. Once you can do this trick confidently at a slow pace, you can start to speed up a little bit.

Make sure that you don't pause for too long while you are putting the pencil behind your ear.

FLASH CASH

This trick won't make you rich, but your friends will be handing you pieces of paper for the rest of your life. Four blank pieces of paper are shown on both sides and then folded into a small package. Amazingly, when the package is opened, the paper has changed into real money!

WHAT YOU NEED
- Four £5 notes
- Four pieces of paper (the same size as the £5 notes)
- Glue

PREPARATION

1. Holding all the paper together, fold the top third down and the bottom third up. Then fold the left and right thirds in, so that you end up with a small package. Now do the same with the £5 notes, and then stick the two packages together.

2. Once the glue has dried, keep the notes folded, but open the paper.

PERFORMANCE

1 Start by showing your audience the pieces of paper. Show both sides of three of the pieces, but when you show them the piece with the package on the back, cover it with your fingers.

2 Square the pieces of paper (keeping the package on the bottom), and fold them up. As you make the final fold, secretly turn the whole lot over and, without stopping, start to unfold the £5 notes.

3 When all the £5 notes are unfolded, show them to your audience in the same way you did the paper. There you go, money from nowhere. Imagine if you could do it for real. Wow!

★ STAR TIPS ★

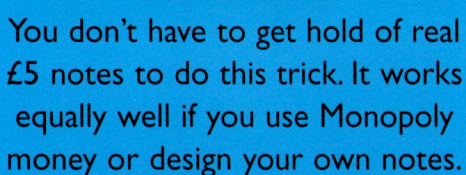

You don't have to get hold of real £5 notes to do this trick. It works equally well if you use Monopoly money or design your own notes.

Use thin paper, otherwise it is difficult to make a neat bundle.

As a little joke, you could write "I.O.U. £5" on each of the blank pieces of paper and pretend that a friend of yours owes you £20 and has given you these I.O.U.'s instead.

WHERE'S THE WATCH?

After you've performed this trick, everyone will think that time really can fly! A watch is borrowed from someone in your audience and covered with a handkerchief. Three people in the audience check that it is still under there, but when you shake out the handkerchief, the watch has vanished!

WHAT YOU NEED
- A clean handkerchief
- A secret helper

PREPARATION

1 You do not need to make anything for this trick, but you do need to brief a stooge (a friend who is pretending to be a member of your audience, but is actually in on the trick). You will need to practise secretly passing the watch to them and discuss where you are going to make it appear from at the end of the trick.

PERFORMANCE

1 Ask someone in your audience if you can borrow their watch, and then cover it with your handkerchief.

2 Hold the watch through the handkerchief and ask another member of the audience to feel the watch by putting their hand underneath the handkerchief to check that it is still there.

3 Repeat step two with a second member of your audience.

★ **STAR TIPS** ★
Make sure your stooge looks surprised when you find the watch is on their wrist

4 Now ask the stooge to feel the watch, and while they are saying, 'Yes, it is still there,' secretly pass them the watch.

HEY PRESTO!

5 Pretend that you are still holding the watch and go back to the stage. Say some magic words and cast your magic wand, then throw the handkerchief into the air. The watch will have disappeared!

6 When the owner of the watch eventually asks for it back, go over to your stooge and point out that it is now on their wrist.

Magnetic Wand

This great trick will make your audience think that your magic wand really is magical! A wand is held in your hand, but when you open your fingers, instead of falling to the ground, it sticks to you as if you are magnetic.

WHAT YOU NEED
- A watch
- A pencil
- A magic wand

PREPARATION

1 Put on the watch and push one end of the pencil under the watch strap, so that it lies along the inside of your wrist. Position most of the pencil against the palm of your hand and make sure you keep it hidden from your audience. It is very important that they never see the pencil.

PERFORMANCE

1 Keeping the palm of the hand wearing the watch turned towards your body, place the centre of the magic wand in between the hidden pencil and the palm of your hand, so that the wand sticks out either side of your hand.

2 Close your fingers around the wand, so it looks as if you are holding it. Now pretend to sprinkle some invisible magic dust over your hand and wand, and say a magic word.

3 Slowly open the fingers of the hand holding the wand. The pressure of the pencil will keep the wand against your palm and from the front it will look like it's sticking to your hand.

4 After you have explained about your magnetic powers, close your fingers around the wand and remove it with your other hand. You can now let your audience examine the wand for any signs of 'stickiness'.

ABRACADABRA!

★ STAR TIPS ★

While your audience is examining the wand, casually place your hand in your pocket and leave the pencil behind.

Do not practise the trick too much or your wrist will get sore.

INVISIBLE CATCH

A stretch of the imagination is needed for this trick, but your audience will be amazed at the result. A helper is told to throw an imaginary object towards an empty bag you are holding. Even though the object is invisible, it lands in the bag with a definite thud.

WHAT YOU NEED
- A paper bag

PERFORMANCE

1 Hold the paper bag in between your second finger and thumb so that your thumb is on the outside of the bag.

2 Ask a member of your audience to imagine that they are holding an object in their hand and to throw it into the paper bag.

3 As they throw the 'object' towards the bag, snap your finger and thumb together as if you were clicking your fingers. If you do it correctly, this will 'jolt' the bag and it will look and sound as if something has landed inside.

★ STAR TIPS ★
Even though this is more of a joke, you can turn it into a trick by placing a boiled sweet in the bag at the beginning. After you have made the bag jolt, look inside with amazement and take out the sweet, which you then give to your helper.

GLASS GO

Your audience is told that you are going to make a coin disappear by covering it with a tumbler and wrapping the tumbler in paper. However, the tumbler vanishes instead of the coin. Much more impressive!

PERFORMANCE

WHAT YOU NEED
- A coin
- A plastic tumbler
- A sheet of newspaper

1. Sit behind a table that is covered with a cloth and place the coin on the table. Tell your audience that you are going to make the coin disappear but to do so you will need to cover it up.

2. Place the tumbler, mouth down, over the coin. Then wrap the sheet of newspaper around it.

3. Mutter a few magic words and lift the covered glass towards your lap. At this point, your audience will see that the coin is still there, so you should look disappointed.

4. While you pretend to be upset that the coin hasn't vanished, secretly let the glass fall into your lap. This should be done below the level of the table. Even though there is nothing there, the paper will still hold the shape of the glass.

5. Tell your audience that you have failed to make the coin disappear, so you will do another trick instead. At this point, open up the paper and amaze everyone!

Pick 'n' Predict

In this card trick you cunningly make a member of your audience choose the card that you want them to. After they have selected a card from the pack, you take out a piece of paper from a sealed envelope to reveal the name of the card printed on it. Impossible, but true!

WHAT YOU NEED
- Paper
- A pen
- A pack of cards
- An envelope

PREPARATION

1. Write YOU WILL PICK THE FIVE OF CLUBS on a piece of paper and seal it inside the envelope.

2. Before you start the trick, place the Five of Clubs face down on top of the pack of cards.

PERFORMANCE

1 Ask a member of your audience to come up and help you. Tell them that inside the envelope is the name of the playing card that you think they will choose.

2 Pick up the pack of cards and ask your helper to lift off a quarter of the cards, turn them face up and place them back on top of the remainder of the pack.

3 Now ask them to lift off half the cards (including the reversed ones on top), turn them over and again place them back on top of the remainder of the pack.

4 Now fan out the cards from left to right from the top and ask your helper to remove the first face-down card they see. They will not know it yet but they have taken the Five of Clubs, which you secretly placed on top of the pack before you started the trick.

5 Ask your helper to show the card to the rest of your audience and then open the envelope to read the prediction. Of course, it will be correct!

★ STAR TIPS ★

You could make the envelope look like a unopened letter that you received that morning by writing your name and address on the front and sticking on a stamp

Linking Mints

This simple trick can be done with props you could pull out of your pocket. Two Polo mints are put into an empty matchbox. A magic spell is cast, and when they are tipped out, they have magically become linked together. WOW!

PREPARATION

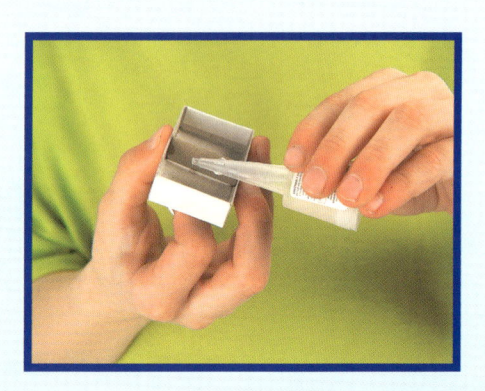

WHAT YOU NEED
- A small piece of card (approx 1 cm by 3 cm)
- An empty matchbox
- Glue
- A packet of Polo mints

1. Stick the small piece of card in the middle of the empty matchbox, so that the tray is divided into two equal-sized compartments.

2. Snap a Polo mint in half and place one of the halves through the hole of another mint. Lick the broken end of one half and join it to its other half. Press quite hard and wait for it to dry. When it is dry, you should end up with what looks like two linked Polo mints.

3. Put the linked mints into one side of the matchbox tray and slide the matchbox sleeve back on.

PERFORMANCE

1. Take two mints from the packet and place them in the empty half of the matchbox. Close the box and place it on the table.

2. Cast a spell with some magic words and wave your wand over the matchbox.

3. Pick up the matchbox and carefully slide it halfway open to reveal the half with the linked mints in. Then, Hey Presto, carefully tip out the two linked mints!

HEY PRESTO!

★ STAR TIPS ★

If there are any matches in the matchbox, ask an adult to take them out and keep them safe for you.

Cover the matchbox in bright paper or foil to make it look more special.

THE KEY TO MAGIC

A lot of people ask me what the key to magic is, well when you've done this trick you'll see! A key is shown to the audience, covered with a handkerchief and, in a flash, completely disappears!

PREPARATION

WHAT YOU NEED
- A key
- A piece of elastic (approx 30 cm long)
- A safety pin
- A handkerchief
- You also need to be wearing a jacket

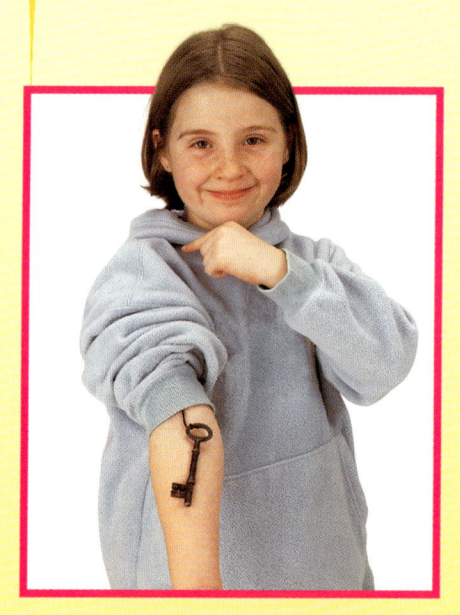

1 Thread one end of the elastic through the hole in the key and tie it on. Tie the other end to the safety pin.

2 Attach the safety pin to the inside of your jacket sleeve at the top, so the elastic runs down your sleeve.

3 The key should hang just below your elbow. Just before you perform the trick, pull the key down your sleeve and secretly hold it in your hand.

PERFORMANCE

1 Tell your audience that you have found the key to magic and open your hand to show them the key. This should get a little laugh!

2 Now cover the key with the handkerchief. When the key is hidden, let go of it and the elastic will make it fly up your sleeve.

3 Once it is safely up your sleeve, remove the handkerchief – the key will have vanished!

DOUBLE YOUR MONEY

If you don't think you get enough pocket money, then try this trick. A 20 pence coin is dropped into an empty matchbox, which is then closed. When the matchbox is opened again, the coin has become a 50 pence piece.

WHAT YOU NEED
- An empty matchbox
- A small knife
- 50 pence coin
- 20 pence coin

PREPARATION

1 Take the knife and carefully cut a small slot in the end of the tray. It should be just big enough for the 20 pence coin to slide out but small enough to keep the 50 pence coin in. Ask an adult to help you do this.

2 Now position the tray so it is halfway inside the matchbox sleeve, and sandwich the 50 pence coin in between the tray and the top of the sleeve.

PERFORMANCE

1. Take out the matchbox that you prepared earlier. Explain to your audience that coins can grow just like humans and drop the 20 pence coin into the tray. Then tip the matchbox back to let the coin secretly slide out of the slot into your hand.

2. Now close the box. As you do this, the 50 pence coin will fall into the tray. Shake the box so that the coin can be heard rattling inside.

ABRACADABRA!

3. Say a magic word, then open the box to reveal the 50 pence coin!

★ STAR TIPS ★

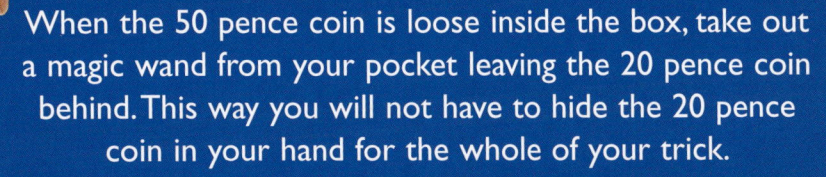

When the 50 pence coin is loose inside the box, take out a magic wand from your pocket leaving the 20 pence coin behind. This way you will not have to hide the 20 pence coin in your hand for the whole of your trick.

You can do this trick with other combinations of coins. Just make sure that the one left in the box is bigger than the one that you are going to tip out.

Indestructible String

★★★★

A piece of string is threaded through a drinking straw and the straw is cut in half. Mysteriously, even though the straw is now in two halves, the string remains in one piece.

WHAT YOU NEED
- A drinking straw
- A piece of string which is at least 10 cm longer than the straw
- Scissors

PREPARATION

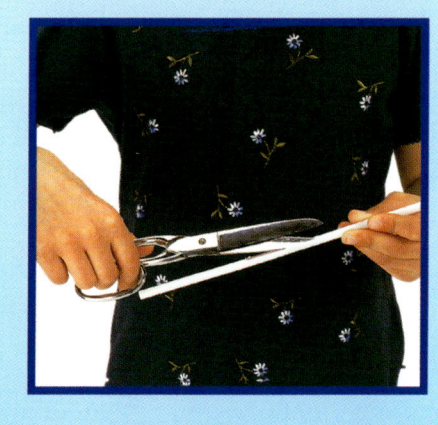

1. Prepare your straw by making a 5 cm long slit down its middle.

PERFORMANCE

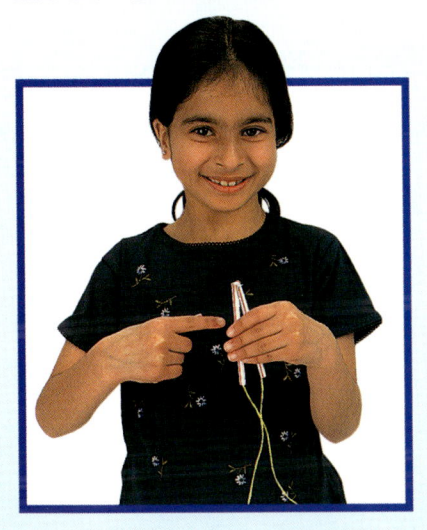

1 Thread the string through the straw and fold the straw in half.

2 Hold the straw roughly 3 cm from the folded point between the fingers of one hand.

3 With your other hand, secretly pull the ends of the string downwards. This will bring the centre of the string down the slit and away from the folded point.

4 Now, very carefully, cut the straw in half where it has been folded. Your audience will believe that you have cut the string as well as the straw.

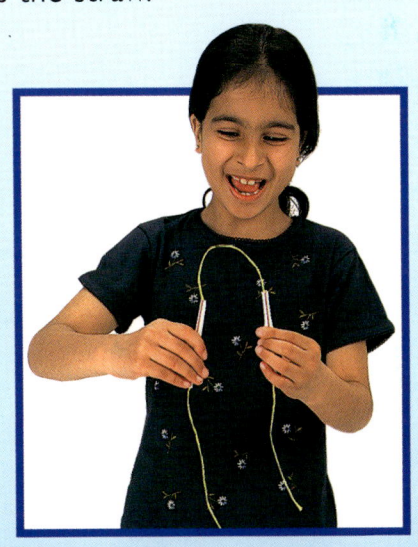

5 Take one half of the straw in each hand and pull your hands apart. The straw is clearly in two halves, but magically the string is still intact.

★ **STAR TIPS** ★

To make it more of a mystery, you could get a helper to cut the straw in half, but you must tell them to be careful, otherwise they could cut you.

43

CRAFTY CARD

You need to have nimble fingers to perform this trick successfully, but once you have mastered the movement, it will look very impressive. The Jack of Hearts is produced and covered with a handkerchief. A magic spell is cast over the card and when the handkerchief is removed, the card has changed into the Queen of Clubs.

WHAT YOU NEED
- The Jack of Hearts
- The Queen of Clubs
- Glue
- Another playing card
- A clean handkerchief

PREPARATION

1. Take the Jack and fold it exactly in half (face inwards). Fold the Queen in the same way.

2. Now put some glue on the back of one half of both cards. Stick the glued halves of the Jack and the Queen together, so they are back to back.

3. Put some glue on the face of the extra card and stick it to the back of the remaining halves of the Jack and the Queen.

4. Once the glue has dried, you will end up with a special card, which has a flap in the centre. When it is folded one way, it will show the Jack. When it is folded the other way, it will show the Queen.

PERFORMANCE

1 Take the special flap card and hold the flap down so it looks like an ordinary Jack of Hearts. Show both sides of the card to your audience.

2 Now cover the card with a handkerchief. As you do so, flip the flap the other way to change the card into the Queen of Clubs, and hold it closed.

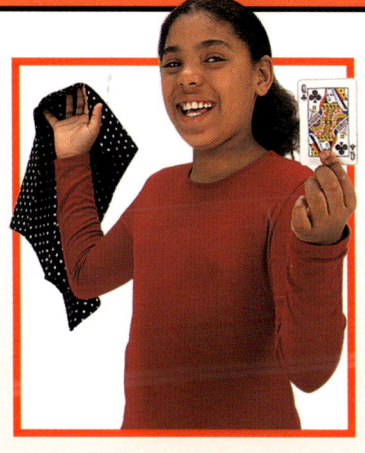

3 Cast a spell with your wand and say a magic word. Remove the handkerchief and show both sides of the card to your audience. They will be astonished to see you are now holding the Queen of Clubs.

★ STAR TIPS ★
Once you have perfected the 'flap' move under the handkerchief, try and change the Jack to a Queen by just moving your hand over the card. If you practise hard, it will look very impressive!

PUTTING ON A MAGIC SHOW

After lots of practice and preparation you will be ready to put on a magic show. But making sure you do all the tricks successfully isn't the only thing you have to think about. It's also important to be wearing the right clothes, saying the right things and making sure the stage is right. Here are a few handy hints to make sure your show's a spectacular success!

Practising for a Show
You can practise for a magic show in several ways. If you stand in front of a full-length mirror, you will see the trick as your audience will see it. You can also practise in front of a video camera, if you have one. The good thing about doing this is that you can play back the video and watch what areas need improvement and also what looked good. However, the best kind of practice is actually performing in front of an audience. The more you perform, the more you will learn and the better you will get.

Looking the Part
It has been traditional for magicians to wear a top hat and tails for the last two hundred years. However, things have changed and not all magicians look like this any more. It's quite useful to wear a jacket – the pockets are handy to put props in and you can hide tricks up the sleeves – but wearing items that make you look unique will make sure you and your act stand out.

Setting the Stage

An imaginative and dramatic stage will create a great impression, but there are some things that all sets should have. If you are using lots of different props, it is useful to have a table to put them on, and there are lots of tricks that need to be performed on a table. You can make a normal table look magical by covering it with a cloth, and then decorating it with a crystal ball or some candles.

How to Handle Your Audience

You need to think about where to position your audience. Most of the audience should be directly in front of you, but some may sit slightly to one side. This is OK, but be careful – if they sit too far round to the side, they might see how some tricks are done.

When you invite a member of the audience to help you with a trick, always choose your helper carefully! Don't choose anyone who likes to be centre of attention – they might upstage you and ruin your show.

When someone is helping you with a trick, always treat them with respect. There's a difference between having fun and making fun!

A Star Performance

Start your show by introducing yourself and then kick off with a trick that is quick and to the point to establish that you are a magician. Never include a member of your audience in the first or last trick.

Patter, or what you say, is very important. It acts as a distraction when you want your audience to look away from your hands, and a trick is more interesting if you have a story to go with it.

Tommy Cooper used to tell jokes while doing his magic. You can do the same – look in a joke book and put some jokes into your act. However, if you are not a confident speaker, you can perform your magic to music. I used to do this a lot when I started performing. When you pick your music, you should choose something that helps create a magical atmosphere – not heavy metal!

FURTHER MAGIC

When you can do all the tricks in this book, you will be off to a great start in becoming a magician. But what should you do next? Firstly, you must practise as much as you can. You also need to learn new magic tricks, to keep your shows full of surprises. If you are really serious, you could join a magical society, to learn their secrets and meet more young magicians.

New Magic Tricks

As well as learning tricks from magic books, you can also buy tricks from special magic shops. Lots of shops have catalogues, so you can have a good look before you choose the tricks you want. When you are starting out, it is a good idea to ask them to recommend some simple tricks. Here are just some of the places you could try:

International Magic
89 Clerkenwell Road
London EC1R 5BX
Tel: 020 7405 7324

Mark Leveridge Magic
13A Lyndhurst Road
Exeter
Devon
EX2 4PA
Tel: 01392 252000
Or check out their web site:
www.markleveridge.co.uk

Davenports Magic
7 Charing Cross
Underground Shopping Arcade
The Strand
London WC2N 4HZ
Tel: 020 7836 0408

Magical Societies

There are many magical societies around Britain, but the leading society for young magicians is The Young Magicians Club. They have regular meetings and a regular newsletter is also sent out. You can visit their web site at: www.youngmagiciansclub.co.uk but if you don't have access to a computer, you can write for more information to:
The Young Magicians Club
The Magic Circle HQ
12 Stephenson Way
London NW1 2HD